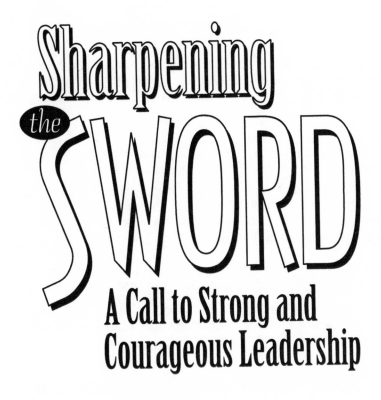

Sharpening the SWORD

A Call to Strong and Courageous Leadership

STEPHEN D. HOWER

CPH.
SAINT LOUIS

Copyright © 1996 Concordia Publishing House
3558 S. Jefferson Avenue, St. Louis, MO 63118-3968
Manufactured in the United States of America

Library of Congress Cataloging-in-Publication Data

Hower, Stephen D., 1952–
    Sharpening the Sword: Fifty true stories of well-known people with Christian application / Stephen D. Hower.
      p.   cm.
    ISBN 0-570-04872-9
    1. Christian leadership. 2. Christian leadership—Case studies. I. Title.
BV652.1.H68 1996
253—dc20
                                      96-14011

2 3 4 5 6 7 8 9 10   05 04 03 02 01 00 99 98 97 96

Foreword

Of all the biographies and autobiographies that I have read, Booker T. Washington's *Up from Slavery* stands out as the most thought-provoking reflection on the great principles of leadership. Although his book overflows with passages worthy of quoting, one stands out with particular reference to this work.

> The older I grow, the more I am convinced that there is no education which one can get from books and costly apparatus that is equal to that which can be gotten from the contact with great men and women. Instead of studying books so constantly, how I wish that our schools and colleges might learn to study men and things!

Some might think it a strange quotation as an introduction to a book—the very thing it devalues! But the great truth of Washington's advice is central to this study.

This is not a book offering new formulas for success. No one should read it thinking they will find the illusive key to effective leadership. Effective leadership, like Christian values, is more often caught than taught. It is my hope that, through the example of these famous men and women, readers will gain inspiration and motivation that will better equip them for their role as a Christian influence in the kingdom of the Lord. Not all the character sketches are about well-known Christians. Some of the men and women, it might be argued, were not Christian at all. Each character study does, however, provide insight into a godly character trait substantiated in Scripture and useful for Christian study. There is value in the lessons successful leaders have learned if only through the observation of God's natural principles at work. There is eternal value when those principles are applied by Christians to promote the saving Gospel of the one Savior, Jesus Christ. Lastly, this study is not offered to encourage self-promotion nor enhance personal recognition. The very effort to achieve such a goal would guarantee its failure. As Ralph Waldo Emerson said, "See how the masses of men worry themselves into nameless graves, when here and there a great unselfish soul forgets himself into immortality."

Stephen D. Hower

Dedicated to
Joshua and Jacob
and other Christians
with leadership potential

Contents

CHAPTER ONE

BOOKER T. WASHINGTON
Focus

The ability to maintain the clarity of your goal and concentrate so completely on it that all other distractions do not impede or interfere with its accomplishment is a powerful leadership quality. The athletes call it "focus," or "being in the zone." Those who admire the quality call it poise. How important is it?

> *"My concentration level blocks out everything. Concentration is why some athletes are better than others."* Edwin Moses (Hurdles—Two-time Olympic Gold Medalist)

> *"You must have the ability to block everything out. Forget that the second baseman just muffed a double-play ball or that the umpire is missing a lot of calls or that your wife just charged $700 at Bloomingdale's."* Tom Seaver (Baseball—Hall of Fame)

> *"Concentration is when you're completely unaware of the crowd, the field, the score. The real secret to success as an athlete is control of yourself and concentration. ... It comes down to the ability to control yourself in stress situations."* Tom Landry (Football Coach and Super Bowl Champion)

11

"Hitting is concentration. Free your mind of everything. Study the flight of the baseball from the pitcher." Reggie Jackson (Baseball—Hall of Fame)

"Ninety percent of my game is mental. It's my concentration that has gotten me this far." Chris Evert (Tennis Professional Champion)

"I had to learn to concentrate, to ignore the gallery and the other golfers and shut my mind against everything but my own game." Ben Hogan (Golfing Legend)

"When I'm trying to solve a problem or learn something, I do tend to get obsessed with it. But I find I can only accomplish what I want to accomplish by a process of total absorption." Alan Alda (Actor, Producer, Director)

"Concentration is my motto—first honesty, then industry, then concentration." Andrew Carnegie (American Industrial Giant.) [1]

The importance of concentration and focus is not ignored by Scripture. God, who made all things, including man, understands exactly how things get accomplished. By inspiration the apostle Paul wrote:

> Endure hardship with us like a good soldier of Christ Jesus. No one serving as a soldier gets involved in civilian affairs—he wants to please his commanding officer. Similarly, if anyone competes as an athlete, he does not receive the victor's crown unless he competes according to the rules. The hardworking farmer should be the first to receive a share of the crops. (2 Timothy 2:3–6)

In every case, the soldier, the athlete, the farmer understand exactly what is expected and commit themselves to achieving the goal, enduring the hardship because of the outcome. The ability to concentrate on the mission is an essential ingredient to its achievement.

Booker T. Washington understood the value of dedication

and focus. Born a slave on a Southern plantation, he rose to become one of the most highly respected men of his day, and one of the most highly regarded educators of all time. As founder, first teacher, and president of Tuskegee Institute in Alabama, he did more than any person of his time to help his race overcome the devastating effects of slavery.

Washington's attitude about slavery helped him rise above its debilitating effects. He believed that the hardship actually increased his ability to concentrate on his goal and improved his chances of success.

> In later years, I confess that I do not envy the white boy as I once did. I have learned that success is to be measured not so much by the position that one has reached in life as by the obstacles which he has overcome while trying to succeed. Looked at from this standpoint, I almost reach the conclusion that often the Negro boy's birth and connection with an unpopular race is an advantage, so far as real life is concerned. With few exceptions, the Negro youth must work harder and must perform his tasks even better than a white youth in order to secure recognition. But out of the hard and unusual struggle through which he is compelled to pass, he gets a strength, a confidence, that one misses whose pathway is comparatively smooth by reason of birth and race."[2]

Washington learned through experience and observation that the key to achievement was focused concentration on your goal. Complaining about the difficulty of a situation, the unfairness of society, or the lack of opportunity was a sure way to remain miserable and poor. He is remembered for many wonderful accomplishments, but perhaps the greatest is the benefit so many have derived from his attitude about life. He believed the future was most promising for the determined, and the prospect of success not limited to only the best and the brightest.

> I am constantly trying to impress upon our students at Tuskegee—and on our people throughout the country, as far as I can reach them with my voice—that any man, regardless of colour, will be recognized and rewarded just in proportion as he learns to do something well—learns to do it better than some one else—however humble the thing may be. As I have said, I believe that my race will succeed in proportion as it learns to do a common thing in an uncommon manner; learns to do a thing so thoroughly that no one can improve upon what it has done; learns to make it service of indispensable value."[3]

Notice Washington didn't say it was the new thing, or the new idea, or the extraordinary talent which brings success. He suggested that those who do common things in an uncommon manner will find success. As Solomon said, "What has been will be again, what has been done will be done again; there is nothing new under the sun" (Ecclesiastes 1:9).

People's basic needs are the same no matter what their circumstance or station in life. The rich and the poor alike need to love and be loved. Both the corporate executive and the worker in his factory need shelter, clothing, and food. The migrant worker and the college professor each want an opportunity to succeed. The farmer in Iowa and the sailor in Louisiana both need a good weather report. The athlete and the computer expert want recognition for their achievements and a worthy challenge. The immigrant from Cuba and the chairwoman of the Daughters of the American Revolution both want a quality education for their grandchildren. And everyone needs the slate wiped clean and a fresh start in life. Everyone needs the hope that comes through Jesus. There is nothing new under the sun. "No man," Washington believed, "who continues to add something to the material, intellectual, and moral well-being of the place in which he lives is long left without proper reward. This is a great human law which cannot be permanently nullified."[4]

How does an average person accomplish such a lofty goal? How does one become essential to the society in which he lives? Washington's answer was demonstrated in the events of his life. "In order to be successful in any kind of undertaking," he advised, "I think the main thing is for one to grow to the point where he completely forgets himself; that is, to lose himself in a great cause. In proportion as one loses himself in this way, in the same degree does he get the highest happiness out of his work."[5]

How closely his counsel parallels the counsel of Christ. When speaking to His disciples, Jesus didn't ask them to "give it their best shot." He did not require the best of their efforts or quality time for the kingdom. No, Jesus wanted it all. He wants every breath we take to be life lived for Him. Read Matthew 10 and listen closely to the instructions He gives to those who would follow Him.

> Anyone who loves his father or mother more than Me is not worthy of Me; anyone who loves his son or daughter more than Me is not worthy of Me; and anyone who does not take his cross and follow Me is not worthy of Me. Whoever finds his life will lose it, and whoever loses his life for My sake will find it." (Matthew 10:37–39)

There is one essential difference between the counsel of Booker T. Washington and the Savior. If you "lose yourself" in business, education, or athletics, you may enjoy success in this life, but have little hope in the next. To lose yourself completely for Christ is to know success both now and in eternal life. It is not an insignificant difference, as Jesus so clearly taught. "What good is it for a man to gain the whole world, and yet lose or forfeit his self?" (Luke 9:25).

Even in Old Testament times the faithful knew the difference between having it all here and now, or looking forward to heaven's reward. King David asked God to save him from earth-bound attitudes. "O LORD, by Your hand save me from such men, from men of this world whose reward is in this life. You still the hunger of those You cherish; their sons have plenty, and they store up wealth for their children. And I—in righteousness I will see Your face; when I awake, I will be satisfied with seeing your likeness" (Psalm 17:14).

Concentration, dedication, and focus in life are elements of leadership that people admire and reward. The focused individual will be noticed by his superiors, be able to acquire financial stability for his family, and enjoy the respect and admiration of his friends. The focused Christian leader can have more. In addition to the blessings which the world can provide, the Christian leader will enjoy a peace which the world cannot give, the certain hope of God's help in this world and the assurance of God's acceptance in the life to come. All the glory of earthly achievement will pale by comparison to the joy we will know at the greeting of the Lord in heaven. "Well done, good and faithful servant! You have been faithful with a few things; I will put you in charge of many things. Come and share your Master's happiness!" (Matthew 25:21, 23).

More Scriptural Insight

1 Samuel 15:17–23	In what way had king Saul lost his focus?
Romans 12:1–8	What does Paul's advice say about the subject of distraction and focus?
Luke 10:38–42	Using this story for reference, how do Christians today become distracted?

A Leader's Prayer

Gracious Lord, I am often distracted from the work You have equipped me to accomplish. As my Savior, You came with eyes focused clearly on Calvary. In faithfulness You accomplished my salvation despite the cost. By the power of the Holy Spirit drive away all doubts and distractions. Enable me to do what I could never do apart from Your blessing—serve You with all my heart, soul, and mind. I am often tempted by my flesh to "major in minors." Help me to remember that my life is not my own. Help me to see that greater satisfaction and fulfillment come through focused concentration on spiritual things. Like Peter, once distracted by wind and waves, I begin with courage but end up floundering in weakness and fear. You alone were able to keep the will of our heavenly Father perfectly. Now You stand before His throne able to intercede for me as the One who experienced temptation but never succumbed to its power. Forgive my failures and strengthen me through Your Word to meet the challenge. Give me freedom from my guilt and power over the weakness of my resolve. Help me to recall that when I am weak You are strong. Maintain my focus on those things of eternal value. You have not called me to success, but faithfulness. All glory, honor, and praise be to You and You alone. Hear my prayer and accept my requests through the merit of the empty cross, for in Your grace I stand redeemed, renewed, and enabled. Amen.

Notes

1. Howard Ferguson, *The Edge*, (Cleveland: Getting The Edge Company, 1990), 5-37–5-43.

2. Booker T. Washington, *Up from Slavery*, (New York: Penguin Books, 1986), 39–40.

3. Ibid., 280.

4. Ibid., 282.

5. Ibid., 181.

CHAPTER TWO

LEE IACOCCA
Diversity

Everything that is true has tension.

Sin and grace.
Faith and works.
Law and Gospel.
Life and death.
Mercy and justice.
Confession and absolution.
World mission and Christian nurture.
Justification and sanctification.

Emphasize any one aspect more than its counterpart and truth becomes error. Truth needs context like a spring needs compression. Without tension, a good thing is worse than useless, it is dangerous.

The need for tension is especially understood by Christian leaders. Wisdom and balance come through diversity. Show me a leader who duplicates himself in staffing and I'll show you an ineffective staff. Show me a leader who surrounds himself with tacit, passive, and blindly obedient loyalists, and I'll show you a "rollercoaster organization" that rises and falls without the stability necessary to make lasting, consistent progress toward a predetermined goal.

The body of Christ is compared in Scripture to the human body. Paul wrote,

> Now the body is not made up of one part but of many. If the foot should say, "Because I am not a hand, I do not belong to the body," it would not for that reason cease to be part of the body. And if the ear should say, "Because I am not an eye, I do not belong to the body," it would not for that reason cease to be part of the body. If the whole body were an eye, where would the sense of hearing be? If the whole body were an ear, where would the sense of smell be? But in fact God has arranged the parts in the body, every one of them, just as He wanted them to be. If they were all one part, where would the body be? As it is, there are many parts, but one body. (1 Corinthians 12:14–20)

A healthy organization will have tension in its staff, its mission, and its financial position. No one knows this better than a successful businessman. No one knows this better than Lee Iacocca.

Iacocca's name is synonymous with business success and salesmanship. Who else ever talked the United States Congress into a $1.2 billion loan for private industry—and then repaid it so quickly that Washington didn't even know how to cash the check! Lee Iacocca knows the value of diversity and tension in a successful organization.

The son of Italian immigrants, Iacocca rose like a rocket through the Ford Motor Company. He introduced the three-year payment plan as assistant sales manager in the lackluster Philadelphia district, taking them from last to first place in national sales in only three months![1] He designed and built the now classic Mustang in the mid-60s, breaking all the sales and profit records of that day. When ousted from Ford in a devastating power play, he returned as Ford's worst nightmare, reestablishing Chrysler as a major player through innovation, quality, and the sheer popularity of his tough-talking, straight-shooting advertisement campaigns. When he looked America in the eye and told us, "If you can find a better car— buy it," he won the hearts of millions, determined to reclaim lost pride in an American product.

Iacocca would be the first to acknowledge the value of balance in a successful organization. In his autobiography he writes:

> By their very nature, financial analysts tend to be defensive, conservative, and pessimistic. On the other side of the fence are the guys in sales and marketing—aggressive, speculative, and optimistic. They're always saying, "Let's do it!" while the bean counters are always cautioning you on why you shouldn't do it. In any company you need both sides of the equation, because the natural tension between the two groups creates its own system of checks and balances. If the bean counters are too weak, the company will spend itself into bankruptcy. But if they're too strong, the company won't meet the market to stay competitive.[2]

These are lessons best learned from books and not from experience! I wonder how many ministries have been destroyed for the reasons Iacocca mentions?

Every Christian leader should examine any tendency to "stack the committee" in his favor. I would venture a guess that most Christian leaders are not bean counters. We are, for the most part, visionaries that can destroy our churches and organizations with our wild optimism and unrestrained confidence.

The associate director of business and finance in our ministry was hired only after a long and careful search. We almost didn't hire her, thinking no 24-year-old, inexperienced young woman would be "tough enough" to stand up to the egos and aggressive personalities of our ministry directors. She proved us all wrong. I don't know how they train top-notch accountant types, but it must require crawling under barbed wire while live ammunition flies overhead. It is also no coincidence that our chairman is comptroller for a multi-million dollar corporation, our vice-chairman a contract lawyer, and our treasurer a CPA for Price Waterhouse! Instinctively, the congregation recognized the need for balance.

Obviously, Iacocca was not from "bean-counter" lineage! He was the hard-charging salesman, district manager, creative-type that bean counters attempt to wrestle to the ground and pin.

He talks openly about the great benefit he experienced from working closely with Robert McNamara, a man he calls the "quintessential bean counter." McNamara, of course, became secretary of defense during the Kennedy years and also served as president of Ford Motor Company.

McNamara once told Iacocca, "You could sell anybody anything. But we're about to spend one hundred million dollars here. Go home tonight and put your great idea on paper. If you can't do that, then you haven't really thought it out."

"It was a valuable lesson," Iacocca comments, "and I've followed his lead ever since. Whenever one of my people has an idea, I ask him to lay it out in writing. I don't want anybody to sell me on a plan just by the melodiousness of his voice or force personality (sic). You really can't afford that."[3]

Christian leaders should take special note. We pride ourselves on being people of faith, even chiding our brothers and sisters who "walk by sight." Faith is necessary, even essential for our work. We must believe in a God of miracles and unmeasured power—*but* the Lord never discouraged prudence and planning.

In the gospel of Luke, chapter 14, we read those "sometimes disturbing" illustrations of a man who began a tower and was not able to finish it, and how the wise king seeks peace through negotiation before engaging in battle.

The work of seeking and saving the lost is too important to flounder for lack of balance. Take a hard look at your organization and ask yourself, "Who dominates, the bean counters or the hard-charging optimists?" Maybe it's time to restore the balance. Maybe it's past time.

More Scriptural Insight

James 4:13–17	Summarize the counsel given to "movers and shakers."
Luke 16:1–15	Is it wrong to be wise in the ways of the world?
Matthew 25:14–30	How do faithful servants distinguish themselves?

A Leader's Prayer

Lord, Christian leaders are rarely bean counters, neither do we often see the value of such in Your kingdom. Help us to understand the importance of diversity in our work. Give us the confidence to empower people who may disagree with us. Give me a more humble spirit, more willing to listen and less quick to speak. It is hard to lead, Lord. Hard especially when so few lack mature faith. Help me to be more patient and to understand the value of allowing faith to take hold before demanding immediate action. I certainly don't want to be less courageous, or hesitant to follow your leading, but grant that I may always do it wisely. Make me more thankful for obstacles and tough questions. Help me to understand that You often use my opponents to sharpen my thinking and clarify my plans. Thank You, Lord, for bean counters. In Jesus' name. Amen.

Notes

1. Lee Iacocca, *Iacocca, An Autobiography,* (New York: Bantam Books, 1984), 39.
2. Ibid., 43.
3. Ibid.

CHAPTER THREE

ZIG ZIGLAR
Keeping the Home Fires Burning

Surprise! Those who know Zig Ziglar, author of *See You at the Top* (which sold more than 1.5 million copies!), would expect him to be featured under the heading of "Enthusiasm" or "Salesmanship." By any standard, Zig is still one of America's premier motivational speakers and knows what it takes to succeed. He was all those things before declaring complete dependence on Christ, but since "D-Day," July 4, 1972, (his *D*eclaration of complete *D*ependence on Christ) he is even more clear and able to guide others down a path of godly success—success which begins at the cross and is best nurtured in a godly home.

Jesus once said, "What good will it be for a man if he gains the whole world, yet forfeits his soul? Or what can a man give in exchange for his soul? For the Son of Man is going to come in His Father's glory with His angels, and then He will reward each person according to what He has done" (Matthew 16:26–27).

Zig would certainly agree, success without eternal assurance is empty and worthless. Likewise, success in the kingdom of God at the expense of our families is unnecessary, empty and void of the joy intended for the faithful.

In a moment of humble self-disclosure, Dr. James Dobson recalls the tender but firm way his father called him to accountability when his career was flourishing and his head was swimming with the intoxication of success.

> "I have observed," his father wrote, "that the greatest delusion is to suppose that our children will be devout Christians simply because their parents have been or that any of them will enter into the Christian faith in any other way than through their parents' deep travail of prayer and faith. But this prayer demands time, time that cannot be given if it is all signed and conscripted and laid on the altar of career ambition. Failure for you at this point would make mere success in your occupation a very pale and washed-out affair indeed."[1]

Christian leaders can be caught in the same trap disguised as success. Recently, the congregation I serve called an extremely talented young husband and father of two to assume the position of director of youth ministry for our church. Kevin had all the qualifications: a sincere and humble faith, a heart for youth; he was creative, a motivator of people, a natural leader, able to multiply his talent through delegation; and he was a truly gifted musician as well. I knew it would be a difficult decision for Kevin since he was already serving in a dynamic and Christ-centered church, but there seemed to be something else yet unresolved.

One night, when my meeting ended unexpectedly early, I called to see how the decision was progressing and to pray for their family. Kevin was at a meeting, but I was able to talk at length with his young wife. Thankful for my call, she revealed her deep concern that Kevin might give himself so completely to the dynamic challenges of our church that he could destroy the boundaries they had established to protect and nurture their family. Her fears were well-founded.

A scan of Scripture will quickly reveal Christian leader after Christian leader who, in complete and unrestrained service to the Lord and their own egos, failed their families. Jacob's home was torn by schism, the prophet Eli's sons stole from the offerings, Samuel's sons took bribes and perverted justice, David's family fought and murdered for the throne, and Solomon's son destroyed the kingdom.

As Christian leaders we must offer more than dynamic professional opportunities to families like Kevin's. We must model faith that has personal as well as professional implications. Can God really bless and prosper a Christian leader whose family is unraveling behind him or her? Remember, one of the prominent biblical qualities of a Christian leader is a stable home. "He must manage his own family well, and see that his children obey him with proper respect. (If anyone does not know how to manage his own family, how can he take care of God's church?)" (1 Timothy 3:4–5).

Zig Ziglar reminds us of our obligation to our spouse and children. In his book *Raising Positive Kids in a Negative World,* he shares a conversation he had with his son, Tom.

> "Son," Zig asked, "if anybody should ask you what you like best about your dad, what would you say?" He pondered for just a moment and said, "I'd say the thing I like best about my dad is that he loves my mom." I naturally asked why he would say that, and he responded, "Well, Dad, I know as long as you love Mom, you're going to treat her right; and as long as you treat her right, we'll always be a family, because she sure does love you. As long as you love each other, Dad, and treat each other right, I'll never have to make a choice of living with you

or living with Mom." "Of course, I had no way of know-ing," Zig reflects, "but that very day one of his closest friends had been given that choice. The need for parents to demonstrate their love for each other before their chil-dren is so important. If they truly do love each other, they'll be thoughtful and considerate of each other. Not only will they benefit, but the children will benefit enor-mously."[2]

Zig Ziglar's writings have much to say about maintaining the Christian family and being alert to threats against the home. His newest book, *Courtship after Marriage*[3] provides some practical suggestions for maintaining true love and affection for your God-given spouse. He contends it is the "lit-tle things" that will make the difference, much like a diet he began 17 years ago. "I lost 37 pounds in 10 months by losing 1.9 ounces per day. People who are successful at whatever they do reach their objectives by a series of little things they do every day. If you do the little things I am suggesting (on a daily basis), they will make a big difference in your relation-ship with your mate."[4]

His new book was featured in a recent article in *Focus on the Family* magazine in which he revealed seven keys to a vital ongoing courtship:

1. Start Today
2. Spoil Each Other: "Look for things that can ease your mate's path and make your own life and marriage happier."
3. Express Appreciation: "For what it's worth, as I've dealt with leaders in business, industry and government, I've noted that almost without exception the higher in the organization, the more courteous and polite these men and women are. The 16th century French writer De Sales was right: 'Nothing is so strong as gentleness; nothing so gentle as real strength.'"

4. Know When to Apologize: "Remember, when disagreements take place, who makes the move to make up isn't important. The one who makes the move demonstrates the greater maturity and love, as well as the greater concern that the marriage not only will survive, but thrive in an atmosphere of love and understanding."

5. Take Time Out: "The time for each other is the important issue, not where you spend the time. You can set aside, on a regular basis, time for a casual walk, just so you can be in a together situation. Even an unhurried stroll will open the door of thoughtful conversation, and you'll be amazed at how much a regular 30-minute walk will do for the marriage."

6. Develop a Sense of Humor: "I encourage you as husbands and wives to do things together that will help you laugh. Interestingly enough, people tell me they enjoy humor, that they like to laugh and that truly funny things are enjoyable to see. Yet very few of them spend any time developing and using their own sense of humor."

7. Know That Gifts Matter: "We all like to be remembered and feel important on our birthdays, anniversaries, Valentine's Day, Christmas, and other special holidays. But we should also remember those occasions when there are no occasions. Drop your mate a note in the mail, 'just because.' Pick up a single flower and take it home, 'just because.' "[5]

There are two strong passages that serve as constant reminders of God's absolute commitment to marriage. He is so committed to marriage that He often frustrates our relationship with Him when we violate our vows, or take unfair advantage of our wives' vulnerable natures. How Christian

leaders can compromise this vital relationship and still anticipate God's favor in their professional life is beyond my ability
to understand!

In the first passage, through the prophet Malachi He
unloads His divine frustration on unfaithfulness by saying,
"Another thing you do: You flood the LORD's altar with tears.
You weep and wail because He no longer pays attention to
your offerings or accepts them with pleasure from your hands.
You ask, 'Why?' It is because the LORD is acting as the witness
between you and the wife of your youth, because you have
broken faith with her, though she is your partner, the wife of
your marriage covenant. Has not the LORD made them one? In
flesh and spirit they are His. ... So guard yourself in your spirit, and do not break faith" (Malachi 2:13–15).

Try as we might, it is not possible to rationalize God's
expression in Malachi as some Old Testament "ceremonial
law" no longer applicable to New Testament Christians. In the
letter of 1 Peter 3, the Lord reiterates His counsel, this time to
both husbands and wives, but especially reminding husbands, "Be considerate as you live with your wives, and treat
them with respect as the weaker [more vulnerable] partner
and as heirs with you of the gracious gift of life, so that nothing will hinder your prayers" (1 Peter 3:7).

When both Testaments warn men that the Lord frustrates
the prayers of those who break faith and take undue advantage of their wives' vulnerability, it should ring some bells. We
cannot long succeed in the exercise of Christian leadership if
the Lord Himself is opposed to us! It's amazing that some
Christian leaders publicly declare their primary commitment to
ministry and secondly to their family. The Lord never asks us
to make such a choice. His Word reminds us that we can't
effectively serve the Lord without loving our wives! If you
asked Zig, he would contend the opposite is also true—you

can't fully love your wife until you enter the service of the Lord.

> Had you asked me if I really loved my wife prior to knowing Jesus Christ, I emphatically would have assured you I did, because to the best of my ability I did love my wife. But once Christ entered the picture and I understood that each of us lives forever, then I entered a new and far greater dimension of love. I loved her before in my own way; I love her today in the way that our Lord would have me love her. The relationship is so much more beautiful, so much more complete, so much more exciting.[6]

More Scriptural Insight

Philippians 2:1–11   Why have some called this the ultimate wedding text?
Colossians 3:9–23   List the various aspects of a sound relationship.
1 Corinthians 13:4–8   Which is your strength? Which is your weakness?

A Leader's Prayer

Lord, marriage and family was of Your creation. It is a good and wonderful gift that can enhance and prosper individuals well beyond what they could be or accomplish alone. Hear my confession of failure. Often I have not completely fathomed the value of my spouse or understood Your deep commitment to my marriage. Forgive, renew, and restore me to a more complete and mature relationship with my partner in life. Thank You for the counsel of Your Word and for the teaching of men such as Zig Ziglar. Help me to discover the value of that counsel and to model Your standards in my life for the benefit of those I lead. Thank You for the blessings of marriage and family. Thank You for the blessings of my family. Help me to be a richer and more complete blessing in the life of those I love. Let love always dwell in our home, the kind of love that keeps no record of wrong and where husband, wife, and children all consider it their primary mission to forgive, encourage, and support each other in Christlike love. Grant it for Jesus' sake. Amen.

Notes

1. Gloria Gaither, *What My Parents Did Right,* (Nashville: Star Song Publishing Group, 1991), 72. Used by permission.

2. Zig Ziglar, *Raising Positive Kids in a Negative World,* (Nashville: Oliver Nelson, A Division of Thomas Nelson Publishers, 1985), 235. Used by permission.

3. Zig Ziglar, *Courtship after Marriage,* (Nashville: Thomas Nelson Publishers, 1990). Used by permission.

4. Zig Ziglar, "It's Always Courting Time," *Focus on the Family* (February 1991): 6.

5. Ibid., 6–7.

6. Zig Ziglar, *Confessions of a Happy Christian,* (Gretna, LA: Pelican Publishing Company, 1985), 25.

CHAPTER FOUR

SAM WALTON
Innovation

Innovator, business analyst, author, and creative thinker Tom Peters once said, "With the possible exception of Henry Ford, Sam Walton is the entrepreneur of the century!"[1] It's a high compliment and well-founded. John Huey's book *Sam Walton—Made in America* is a firsthand account of an American phenomenon. It should be required reading in every business school, university, military academy, and seminary—wherever future leaders are trained.

I especially urge the study of Sam's life by every Christian leader. His humble spirit, sense of fairness, and off-the-wall kind of innovation could transform many a stale and stalled ministry. In one of the final chapters Sam reveals "Ten Rules That Worked for Me." Truth can be learned in a number of ways: through the study of God's Word, through the wisdom of others, or by the old "trial and error" method of discovery. Sam believed in all three methods and Christian application could be easily made to each of his 10 rules:

1. Commit to your business.
2. Share your profits with your associates.
3. Motivate your partners.
4. Communicate everything you possibly can to your partners.
5. Appreciate everything your associates do for the business.
6. Celebrate your successes.
7. Listen to everyone in your company.
8. Exceed your customers' expectations.
9. Control your expenses better than your competition.
10. Swim upstream.[2]

It will surprise no one on our staff that I like rule number 10 the best. Sam confesses:

> This is a big contradiction in my makeup that I don't understand to this day. In many of my core values—things like church and family and civic leadership and even politics—I'm a pretty conservative guy. But for some reason in business, I have always been driven to buck the system, to innovate, to take things beyond where they've been. On the one hand, in the community, I really am an establishment kind of guy; on the other hand, in the marketplace, I have always been a maverick who enjoys shaking things up and creating a little anarchy.[3]

Christian leaders by definition must be strong swimmers for all the "against-the-current" kind of things they must be about. The work of the Lord is about change—changing sinners into saints, changing human nature into godly nature, changing maintenance ministries into missions. Like Sam said, there appears to be a contradiction at work here. We serve a changeless Christ, who is the same yesterday, today, and even forever,[4] but the way we proclaim that Gospel is in constant change. A good friend and Christian leader likes to say we must distinguish between the "means of grace" and the "means of growth." The former does not change, but the latter must. Effective leadership does not occur by defense of the status quo.

The Lord Himself is a God of innovation. Think even briefly about all the means and methods He used to reveal Himself to His people: a burning bush, a pillar of fire and cloud, a ladder stretching into heaven, a man's donkey, a fiery chariot, strange visions, graffiti on a king's wall, angels, and a baby born in Bethlehem.

When the Lord came to Moses on Mount Horeb, God gave him validating signs to confirm his divine mission to both Pharaoh and the enslaved Israelites.[5] The miracles weren't essential to Moses' mission, but they were essential to his courage. Perceiving Moses' reticence, the Lord innovated, providing miraculous signs; a hand would alternately become diseased or whole, a staff that could transform from staff to snake and then to staff again.

Jesus once told His disciples, "I tell you the truth, anyone who has faith in Me will do what I have been doing. He will do even greater things than these, because I am going to the Father" (John 14:12). I don't think the Savior meant we would walk on water rougher than He had transversed, or feed 6,000 with only one loaf and half a fish. He meant that His Father would accomplish incredible miracles through very ordinary people with very ordinary skills, abilities, and resources. Christian leaders have seen this promise fulfilled almost daily in the way God blesses their lives and activities.

It is our privilege to walk by faith, not by sight as Paul commands.[6] The high school where my boys attend has as their motto "A Workshop in Christian Living." I have always liked that description of a Christian high school, or any Christian endeavor. We know who we serve, we know what we proclaim, but we are always discovering how God wants that message shared. It is human nature to want it nailed down, concreted in place, and welded fast, but the Word of God will not be bound. Describing this activity to a defender of the old ways, Jesus told Nicodemus, "The wind blows wherever it pleases. You hear its sound, but you cannot tell where it comes from or where it is going. So it is with everyone born of the Spirit" (John 3:8). The Spirit of God is a dynamic that can be observed, like wind driving a leaf across a freshly mown lawn, but we cannot always anticipate, predict, or determine how, when, or where that leaf will move.

Jim Walton, Sam and Helen's youngest boy, commented on his father's love of innovation. "Dad always said you've got to stay flexible. We never went on a family trip nor have we ever heard of a business trip in which the schedule wasn't changed at least once after the trip was underway. Later, we all snickered at some writers who viewed Dad as a grand strategist who intuitively developed complex plans and implemented them with precision. Dad thrived on change, and no decision was ever sacred."[7]

Most successful Christian leaders understand the need for flexibility and innovation and spend a great deal of their time observing their culture. If Christians accept Paul's model and are to be all things to all people so that we might by all means save some,[8] we must first know the people we will save. Different settings require different approaches, and growth or transition in any ministry will require constant adjustment and innovation to keep the mission alive and effective. God save us from ministries that expect others to adjust and adapt to their rigid way of conducting the Lord's dynamic ministry. Those unable or unwilling to change will go the way of Sam's unyielding competition.

In commenting on the accusation that he was the ruination of the small town merchant, Sam fixes the blame where it belongs. "When we arrived in these little towns offering low prices every day, satisfaction guaranteed, and hours that were realistic for the way people wanted to shop, we passed right by that old variety store competition, with its 45% markups, limited selection, and limited hours. ... His customers were the ones that shut him down, they voted with their feet."[9]

If the local merchant fails to appreciate the dynamic of innovation, he loses a few sales, maybe even his livelihood. If Christian ministry fails to adjust and adapt to the needs and lifestyle of the people, everyone loses, for time and eternity.

More Scriptural Insight

2 Corinthians 3:4–18   What gives life and what kills?
John 12:20–26   What must happen for Christians to bear much fruit?
1 Corinthians 9:16–23   List the points Paul makes about ministry.

A Leader's Prayer

Gracious Lord, we are not all creative people. Help us to see creativity in those around us, to learn from those who are gifted innovators so that we can understand better how to use the means of growth to more effectively proclaim the "means of grace." Give me patience also, Lord. There are many people like Sam Walton who want innovation and dynamic approaches in almost every aspect of life except in the church. Lord, grant us a gentle and understanding spirit. As you enable us to open other's eyes to the overriding importance of mission, mission, mission, help us not to forget the needs and concerns of the saved. We thank You, Lord, for all the advancements we have experienced that have changed our lives and increased our ability to minister. Thank You for the computer, fax machines, cellular phones, sound systems, satellite transmissions, Christian television and radio programs. Thank You for ease of transportation and the relatively inexpensive and inexhaustible supply of Christian literature, magazines, and newsletters. Thank You for the innovations that we have enjoyed. Help us to help others through any and every God-pleasing means available for Christ's sake. Amen.

Notes

1. John Huey, *Sam Walton—Made in America; My Story,* (New York: Doubleday Publishers, 1992), 250.

2. Ibid., 246–249.

3. Ibid., 47–48.

4. See Hebrews 13:8.

5. See Exodus 3–4.

6. See 2 Corinthians 5:7

7. John Huey, 70.

8. See 1 Corinthians 9:22.

9. John Huey, 177.

CHAPTER FIVE

HARVEY MACKAY
Keep the Main Thing
the Main Thing

Distractions will kill you. When my boys were younger and just beginning little league baseball, I remember spending as much time teaching concentration as the development of any other skill. Conversely, I showed them how deliberate, off-paced pitching, or stepping in and out of the box when batting, could distract and destroy the concentration of their opponent. The ability to concentrate on the task at hand is essential to success. Little things helped, such as quietly repeating the word "contact" or "stitches" when waiting for a pitch. A single word helped them shut out the banter, parental screaming, and reminded them of the one thing important— making contact with the ball. Instead of just trying to hit the ball, they were looking for the ball's stitches, requiring more precise focus, which increased their concentration and likelihood of success. Both became good batters.

Harvey Mackay knows the importance of keeping the main thing the main thing. Author of the number one best-seller

Swim with the Sharks without Being Eaten Alive and its sequel *Sharkproof,* Mackay knows what it takes to succeed. He devised the six million dollar ticket buyout to keep the Minnesota Twins in Minnesota, and led the charge to build the "noise box," A.K.A. Metrodome stadium. A nationally renown speaker, motivator, regionally ranked tennis star, avid runner and marathoner, Mackay was also instrumental in bringing the Super Bowl to Minneapolis in 1992. When he speaks about squeezing value from your day and prioritizing a hectic schedule, others would do well to listen.[1]

In his book *Sharkproof,* Mackay offers practical advice and examples for people struggling in the extremely competitive job market of the 90s. He writes, "Stay focused, do not let yourself become distracted from your goals." As an example, he offers up an account of Harmen Killebrew's induction in the Baseball Hall of Fame.

> "He talked about his childhood," Mackay relates, "the small western town where he'd grown up, the warm and loving family that had nurtured him. Every summer evening he and his brother and his dad would play catch in the backyard until they could no longer see the ball. His mother would grow hoarse trying to call her men into the house for dinner."

> "One evening, slightly exasperated, she tried a new tack. "Now get in here. You're tearing up the grass," she called from the back door. "We're not raising grass," her husband responded quietly, "we're raising boys."[2]

In commenting on the story, Mackay reminds his reader, "A job is only a job. It is just the grass under your feet. The nurturing and the growth and the preservation of you as you is what matters."[3] Don't let the tail swing the dog. Keep the main thing the main thing, maintain your perspective or you'll be lost in a whirlwind of detail.

Successful leaders live in the eye of a storm. Details, questions, and conflicts fly like torrential rain beating against an opened umbrella. Successful leaders have the ability to stay dry, sort out the distractions, focus their energies on critical issues, while delegating the rest away. There are plenty of good people who will attempt to confuse the process, calling attention to less important details by declaring them essential.

One of the shortest, and yet favorite, Bible stories of many is the account of Jesus' visit to the home of His friends in Bethany, just outside of Jerusalem. He often stayed there and "commuted" the distance back and forth to the temple during special observances commanded in the law of Moses. For Lazarus, Mary, and Martha, it must have been like living in Florida, observing the annual migration of geese, butterflies, relatives, and friends.

Luke tells us that while Mary sat at the feet of Jesus, feasting on the conversation and wisdom of His comments, Martha "was distracted by all the preparations that had to be made. ... 'Martha, Martha,' the Lord answered, 'You are worried and upset about many things, but only one thing is needed. Mary has chosen what is better, and it will not be taken away from her'" (Luke 10:38–42).

In the exercise of Christian leadership, sorting out distractions from vital ministry is crucial. We must be able to recognize the difference between the essential mission and other nonessential, distracting demands upon our time.

My good friend and newly elected young congregational chairman once embarrassed us both by repeating an old joke I had told to a small group to illustrate the importance of keeping the main thing in focus. At a meeting to discuss congregational restructuring, he asked a rather large group of traditional members if they knew how many Lutherans it took to change a light bulb. "The answer," he said with a smile and chuckle, "is at least three! One to change the bulb and at least two others to talk about how wonderful the old bulb had been." The point was well made, but the audience identified too closely with the "discussion group"!

Christian leaders can't afford to be taken captive by the way things used to be done unless those ways can be shown effective in the pursuit of the changeless mission of Christ. New places and new challenges call for new strategies. The mission of salvation transcends all cultures, ages, and settings. Undaunted by change and unflinching in purpose, the faithful leader will chart a course based on a clear and stated mission. The distractions and constant challenge of well-meaning diversionaries will receive little attention. It is Christ we serve, as Paul advised young Timothy, "Preach the Word; be prepared in season and out of season." He reminded him, "the time will come when men will not put up with sound doctrine. Instead, to suit their own desires, they will gather around them a great number of teachers to say what their itching ears want to hear" (2 Timothy 4:2–3). To be a populist preacher of the Word is an oxymoron.

More Scriptural Insight

Ecclesiastes 12:9–14	What did Solomon say was the main thing?
1 Timothy 1:5	What was the goal of Paul's teaching? (Explain)
John 21:24–25	Why did John choose to report only certain accounts about the life of Jesus?

A Leader's Prayer

The world isn't getting any less complex, Lord. All around me swirl the details and demands of life. Help me sort out all the personal and professional demands made upon my time. Lord, I want to give the best of my limited time, talent, and resources to those things of eternal significance. Help me to see and understand Your will for my service that I might best use my office and my allotted time of life to the best of my ability for the greatest good. When the details strangle me and the demands of so many pull me down, come quickly to my rescue. Surround me with good counsel and strong support and give me a receptive heart, O Lord. Help me in this struggle to maintain my Christ-centered focus. Amen.

Notes

1. Harvey Mackay, *Sharkproof,* (New York: Harper Business, 1993), postlog.

2. Ibid., 290–91.

3. Ibid., 291.

CHAPTER SIX

GARTH BROOKS
Taking the Heat

E xercising leadership is a wonderful thing! Everybody admires the fellow out front. Every wife wishes it were her husband, every young executive dreams of the day. Yes, it seems everybody aspires to the responsible position of leader—except those that God has tapped to serve in that capacity!

Effective leadership comes at a price, and one of the costs that makes the job so "pricey" is the absolute certainty of opposition. I know of no one who has exercised effective leadership without facing committed, often unrelenting opposition.

> Martin Luther was denounced as a heretic and had a price put on his head.
>
> Abraham Lincoln was not even allowed on the ballot of 10 states in the election of 1860. Then, between the time of his election and his inauguration, more than half a dozen states seceded from the Union!
>
> Booker T. Washington was criticized for advocating edu-

cation as the key to overcoming prejudice without speaking strongly against it.

Thomas Edison was ridiculed for his lack of formal education, obstructed by the gas companies, and often unable to gain funding for his projects.

Henry Ford was burned in effigy for refusing to produce instruments of war for England at the outbreak of World War I.

W. Edwards Deming led the management revolution of Japan because he found little support for his management philosophies in America.

Sam Walton was laughed at by fellow retailers, and had trouble financing his stores in the "backwaters" of America.

Lee Iacocca was thrown out by the Fords.

Norman Vincent Peale was widely criticized by other Christian pastors.

James Dobson has been called narrow-minded and homophobic.

Charles Swindoll is accused of having too much fun for a pastor!

Leadership has its price! Tom Peters, the oft quoted business analyst, has even suggested success is impossible without opposition. "Not just people who disagree with you," he says, "but absolute corporate traitors who hate everything you stand for!"

The popular country western singer Garth Brooks seems to understand Mr. Peters' point of view. His song, "Going against the Grain" is a call for courage in the face of opposition!

Folks call me a maverick,
Guess, I ain't too diplomatic,
I just never been the kind to go along;

Just avoiding confrontation,
For the sake of confirmation,
And I'll admit I tend to sing a different song.
Sometimes you just can't be afraid to wear a different hat.
If Columbus had been bothered, this ol' world might still
    be flat.
Nothing ventured, nothing gained.
Sometimes you gotta go against the grain!

Well, I have been accused of making my own rules,
There must be Rebel blood just running through my veins,
Well, I'm no hypocrite,
What you see is what you get,
And that's the only way I know to play the game.
Ol' Noah took much ridicule for building his great ark.
But after forty days and forty nights,
He was looking pretty smart.
Sometimes it's best to brave the wind and rain.
By having strength to go against the grain.

Well there's more folks, than a few;
Who share my point of view,
But they're worried if they're gonna sink or swim.
They'd like to buck the system,
But the deck is stacked against them,
And they're a little scared to go out on a limb.
But if you're going to make a difference,
If you're going to make your mark,
You can't follow like a bunch of sheep,
You gotta listen to your heart.
Go bustin' in like ole John Wayne!
Sometimes you gotta go against the grain!

Nothing ventured, nothing gained,
Sometimes you gotta go against the grain![1]

Garth knows all about the price of success. He has done his share of "going against the grain." His onstage appearances resemble rock concerts with dramatic special effects, almost unheard of for a country artist. His video "The Thunder Rolls" was banned from the Nashville Network because it depicted a wife who shot her abusive and unfaithful husband. When challenged to "tone it down," Garth stood his ground, explaining, long before the O. J. Simpson tragedy, that domestic violence needed to be brought into the light of day.

More recently, conservative Christians have objected to the lyrics of "We Shall Be Free" wherein Garth sings, "When we're free to love anyone we choose. ... we shall be free," an unconventional reference to gay rights in the midst of a country song! Again, Garth has stood his ground, albeit with a slight twinge of conscience. In an interview with Rolling Stone magazine, he said, "I feel bad any time somebody brings up the Christian aspect against 'We Shall Be Free.' It was meant to be a gospel song. It was meant to be the truth as I saw it. ... I do believe that God exists. I do believe in the Bible. But I can't see that loving somebody is a sin."[2] While faithful Christians can rightfully challenge Garth's theology, there is much to be learned from his example and the lyrics of "Going against the Grain."

Leaders attract their share of critics and second-guessers. Christian leaders are rarely spared the privilege. Not all critics are intentionally troublesome. Some may actually want to help or spare leaders the possible trauma of failure. Christian critics can be divided into four categories: protectors, defectors, correctors, and rejectors.

The protectors are folks who want to spare Christian leaders from the inevitable pain associated with their position. Even Jesus had a protector in the person of Peter. Remember how after He had discussed the various opinions of people about His identity, the gospels tell us, "From that time on Jesus began to explain to His disciples that He must go to Jerusalem and suffer many things at the hands of the elders, chief priests and teachers of the law, and that He must be killed and on the third day be raised to life" (Matthew 16:21). Peter, the one who had just been commended by the Lord for correctly acknowledging that Jesus was "The Christ, the Son of God," quickly took Jesus aside. Matthew tells us Peter began to rebuke the Lord saying, "This shall never happen to You!" (Matthew 16:22). He wanted to spare Jesus the very purpose for which He had come! Sometimes, well-meaning and loving friends may attempt to spare Christian leaders the pain of their God-given mission. If leaders concede to their protectionistic wishes, the mission is lost.

The defectors are Christians who initially like the results of an effective Christian leader, but when success begins to bring change to the familiar, defectors often become critics. They are motivated by fear of success not failure. As progress begins to be made, they quickly assess the situation, realize how such leadership will change the nature of something they love, and begin defecting. Sometimes their defection is motivated out of genuine concern for the loss of heritage or intimacy. Other times it may be as selfish as loss of power, importance, or position within a new and larger organization.

The correctors are critics that fear failure. They are not an optimistic lot. They are identified by the phrases "what if," "it'll never work," "we tried that once," "the church down the street made that mistake," and the favorite and time-tested, "we could never afford to do that here." Not all correctors are mean-spirited. They are accustomed to playing their cards close to the vest. Typically they have walked by sight so long they think "walking by faith"[3] was a Pauline reference to making it to the bathroom late at night without the benefit of a night light. Correctors don't improve with time. Even after observing many miracles, they are modern-day Israelites, willing to return to slavery at the sight of any obstacle. They can pray for miracles, even see fulfillment, but secretly believe blessings are rationed and they have filled their quota. These are not optimistic people.

Last, but certainly not least, are the rejectors. Every Christian leader is blessed to have a number of rejectors "wherever two or more are gathered." I once described these people as folks "raised in cages and poked with sticks." These are ornery people. They don't single out Christian leaders for special treatment, they criticize and oppose almost anything, anywhere, anytime, anyplace. You will read their names in the editorial pages of the paper, they lead the parking-lot discussions outside the school, their groceries aren't bagged properly, and the paperboy ought to be fired. They are inclined to find something wrong with anyone who attempts to lead any endeavor. They are people in special need of our prayers and understanding. In fact, the only people who need our prayers and understanding more than the rejectors are the family members of the rejector. Affirmation and praise are rare in their homes, probably because they were raised by critical parents themselves.

There are three God-pleasing responses to every attack upon Christian leaders. First, you should ask if there is any validity in the accusation. Is any part of the criticism with merit? If so, course correction is called for in a spirit of gratitude and thanksgiving. It is our duty, in love, to offer heartfelt Christian admonition to brothers and sisters in Christ.[4]

Secondly, remember the critic is not your enemy, and Christian leaders who "square off for a fight" only concede victory to Satan and all who want to impede their progress. Paul's advice to Titus is still sound: "Warn a divisive person once, and then warn him a second time. After that, have nothing to do with him. You may be sure that such a man is warped and sinful; he is self-condemned" (Titus 3:10–11).

Lastly, know that the unfounded criticism of protectors, defectors, correctors, and rejectors can do you no harm! Solomon, the wisest man who walked the earth, must have had people second-guess his wisdom too. He wrote sound advice in the proverb, "Like a fluttering sparrow or a darting swallow, an undeserved curse does not come to rest" (Proverbs 26:2).

Most leaders already know this. All successful future leaders will have to learn it. Garth's third verse is an indictment of the many who wish to lead but refuse to pay the price.

As Garth would say, "Nothing ventured, nothing gained. ... Sometimes you gotta go against the grain!"

More Scriptural Insight

Matthew 11:11–19	What is the point of Jesus' comments?
2 Samuel 15:1–12	Why was Absalom successful in undermining his father?
1 Corinthians 4:1–5	What did Paul think about critical people and comments?

A Leader's Prayer

O Lord, when I think of all the criticism and abuse hurled at You while dying on the cross, I realize my complaints are petty, and my hurts minor. Help me to remember it is You and You alone that I serve. When others seek my downfall or undermine my authority, help me to understand that hurting people hurt others. Move me to greater compassion and help me to achieve greater obedience, recalling Your words, "revenge is mine, and I will repay." Lord, I commend my critics to Your care. When those times come and I am tempted to criticize the leadership of a fellow Christian, help me recall the Fourth Commandment and my duty to love, honor, and respect those that You have allowed to assume authority over me. When I am in the midst of others who are inclined to criticize and undermine spiritual authority, help me to be an influence for good. Not only do I ask Your help in overcoming the temptation, I also ask that You would enable me to be an encourager and helper of those in spiritual authority. In this way help me further the cause of the Gospel until that day comes when every knee bows and every tongue confesses Jesus Christ as Lord. Amen.

Notes

1. Written by Bruce Bouton, Larry E. Cordle, Carl Jackson, "Goin' Against the Grain," From the Liberty Records label, "Ropin' the Wind," 1991, Produced by Allen Reynolds. Copyright © 1991 PolyGram International Publishing, Inc. and Slide Bar Music. Used By Permission. All Rights Reserved.

2. Yanthony Decurtis, "Garth Brooks, Ropin' in the 'Whirl'-Wind," *Rolling Stone* (April 1, 1993): 31–35ff.

3. See 2 Corinthians 5:7.

4. Consult 1 Corinthians 5.

CHAPTER SEVEN

H. NORMAN SCHWARZKOPF
Duty

Leadership is established on a social pyramid. We move up from the base to the top only to be replaced. So derive your satisfaction from the exercise of your duty, not the achievement of the pinnacle which is only temporary."[1] Those words help explain the four-star general's philosophy of enjoying the dynamic of leadership more than the honors, rewards, and trappings of successful leadership.

His autobiography, *It Doesn't Take a Hero,* is the story of that philosophy put into action. The title comes from Schwarzkopf's March 15, 1991, interview with Barbara Walters, when he said, "It doesn't take a hero to order men into battle. It takes a hero to be one of those men who goes into battle."

During a speech he made in St. Louis, Schwarzkopf described the time his commanding officer was suddenly called away, putting him in command of a sizable force at a crucial time. His commander, he said, left him with two guiding principles of leadership that have proven true.

1. When in charge, take command.
2. Do what's right.

Simple. But anyone who's borne the onus of leadership knows just how difficult those simple eight words can be to implement. Often what makes the exercise of effective leadership so difficult is the large number of ineffective and self-centered leaders working "with you" for the same cause. General Schwarzkopf credits Major Tom Whelan who helped him through a period of deep disillusion that could have led to resignation. "There are two ways to approach it," Whelan said. "Number one is to get out; number two is to stick around and someday, when you have more rank, fix the problems. But don't forget, if you get out, the bad guys win."[2]

It sounds just like a mission developer I know who was working very hard to start and sustain a number of new congregations in various towns. Everywhere he went other religious leaders were contradicting him and creating confusion. Although it was painful and unpopular, he knew he had to keep right on doing the right thing without worrying too much about the political fallout. His name was Paul and he explained his thinking in the letter he wrote to the church at Galatia:

> Am I trying to win the approval of men, or of God? Or am I trying to please men? If I were trying to please men, I would not be a servant of Christ. (Galatians 1:10)

Schwarzkopf later discovered that you can learn just as much from a bad leader as you can a good one. Some of the lessons he has learned along the way were summarized recently in an interview with a national business magazine.

1. **You must have clear goals.** You must be able to articulate them clearly to others.
2. **Give yourself a clear agenda.** Every morning, write

down the five most important things to accomplish that day, and get those five done.

3. **Let people know where they stand.**
4. **What's broken, fix now.** Don't put it off. Problems that aren't dealt with only lead to more problems.
5. **No repainting the flagpole.** Make sure all the work your people are doing is essential to the organization.
6. **Set high standards.** People won't generally perform above your expectations, so it's important to expect a lot.
7. **Lay the concept out,** but let your people execute it. Tell them in the clearest terms what you want done, but let them suggest the best way to do it.
8. **People come to work to succeed.** So don't operate on the principle that if they aren't watched and supervised, they'll bungle up the job.
9. **Never lie. Ever.**
10. **When in charge, take command.** Some leaders who feel they don't have adequate information put off deciding to do anything at all. The best policy is to decide, monitor the results, and change course if it's necessary.
11. **Do what's right.** The truth of the matter is that you always know the right thing to do. The hard part is doing it.

When asked to summarize his concept of leadership, the general was quick to respond, "Leadership is not the same as competency. There are many competent people in the world who can get a job done, but it is not always achieved through the exercise of leadership." Leadership, in his opinion, "Is the ability to get people to do willingly what they ordinarily would not do."[3] Understandably, he saw military duty as the ultimate test of leadership, getting others to follow commands that required the ultimate risk, the risk of their own lives.

On this, Jesus and the general would agree, "Greater love has no one than this, that he would lay down his life for his friends" (John 15:13). History has shown, however, that duty without principle, and honor without cause, may lead men to commit atrocities that would be unworthy of the ultimate sacrifice. The motto for West Point is "Duty, Honor, Country," for these soldiers are asked to sacrifice their lives. In reflecting on his training, Schwarzkopf recalled,

> We spent days trying to come to terms with the fundamental immorality of war. ... West Point tried to prepare us for the ethical and moral ambiguities we might someday face as officers. The academy wanted to ensure that we would never be like those Nazi generals who stood up after World War II at the Nuremberg trials and shrugged off their participation in atrocities by saying "Dienst ist Dienst"—in effect, "I was only doing my duty."[4]

Before pledging to "suffer all, even death," it is important to know what one would be willing to die for. During the early days of the Christian church it was possible to be arrested, jailed, beaten, and even killed for speaking boldly about faith in Jesus. When Peter and the other disciples were forbidden by government authorities from teaching about Christ, their response was simple, "We must obey God rather than men!" (Acts 5:29). When they continued to speak openly about Christ, they soon found themselves on trial for insurrection. After considerable discussion, the wise Gamaliel, a leader among the pharisees, advised, "Leave these men alone! Let them go! For if their purpose or activity is of human origin, it will fail. But if it is from God, you will not be able to stop these men; you will only find yourselves fighting against God" (Acts 5:38–39). Luke comments, "His speech persuaded them. They called the apostles in and had them flogged. Then they ordered them not to speak in the name of Jesus, and let them go. The apostles left the Sanhedrin, rejoicing because they had been counted worthy of suffering disgrace for the Name!" (Acts 5:40–41).

The question remains, "Are we willing to live for that which we would die for?" Many Christians have boldly stood before their congregations and vowed to suffer all, even death, rather than forsake the Christian faith. With sincere intent they are willing to suffer even death. On the very same Sunday of their vow, they will politely pass the plate without contribution, realizing the Sunday brunch is going to cost $9.95 per person. Next weekend they may not be in worship at all due to late Saturday night commitments. The test of leadership is not discovered in what one will die for, but more importantly, what cause is worthy of life!

No wonder the Scriptures say, "I urge you, brothers, in view of God's mercy, to offer your bodies as living sacrifices, holy and pleasing to God—this is your spiritual act of worship. Do not conform any longer to the pattern of this world, but be transformed by the renewing of your mind. Then you will be able to test and approve what God's will is—His good, pleasing and perfect will" (Romans 12:1–2). Worship is defined as "offering our bodies as living (not dying) sacrifices." The Lord calls this our "test." The proof is in the living, not in the dying only. James certainly understood this when he wrote, "Show me your faith without deeds, and I will show you my faith by what I do. You believe there is a God? Good! Even demons believe that—and shudder" (James 2:18–19).

How do you get people to willingly do what under ordinary circumstance they would not? Schwarzkopf says, "One of the first lessons I learned was that there was no single way for the leader of a small unit to command the soldiers' respect: you had to address each person in terms he could understand.

The college kids were persuaded by logical explanations, the farm boys by common sense, and what the dropouts understood was their leader's size and strength, and the fact that he could be one tough son of a b—."[5]

Schwarzkopf is right to understand the differences in people and to motivate each group by means of understanding their perspective. The apostle Paul recommended a similar approach with the Gospel when he said he dealt with people on their terms and in their culture.

> I make myself a slave to everyone, to win as many as possible. To the Jews I became like a Jew, to win the Jews. To those under the law I became like one under the law (though I myself am not under the law), so as to win those under the law. To those not having the law I became like one not having the law (though I am not free from God's law but am under Christ's law), so as to win those not having the law. To the weak I became weak, to win the weak. I have become all things to all men so that by all possible means I might save some. I do all this for the sake of the gospel, that I may share in its blessings. (1 Corinthians 9:19–23)

The greatest motivation of all is the same for Jew or Gentile, slave or free. Everyone has a great need for the salvation that comes from faith in our Lord Jesus Christ. Just as a West Point plebe finishes his first day by marching out to Trophy Point and takes his vow of allegiance to support the Constitution of the United States, so Christian leaders must keep the cross of Christ as the substance behind all their methods. "If we live, we live to the Lord; and if we die, we die to the Lord. So, whether we live or die, we belong to the Lord" (Romans 14:8).

More Scriptural Insight

2 Corinthians 8:1–9   What is it Paul calls a "test" of the Corinthian Christians?
James 1:22–27   What is true religion?

Matthew 7:24–29   How does Jesus distinguish between wise and foolish people?

A Leader's Prayer

Dear Father in heaven, thank You for all the Scriptures that comfort, encourage, and promise Your help in every time of need. Thank You also for those Scriptures that challenge us to take our faith seriously and to accept our duty as souls bought with the blood of Jesus Christ, our Lord. Help us every day to better understand our duty and to gain insight into the accomplishment of our assigned task. Give power to our words, wisdom to our thinking, and enable us to maintain the highest standards of excellence while acknowledging various levels of spiritual maturity among those we lead. Help us not to become disillusioned and quit such important work. When other leaders mock our zeal and challenge our motives, help us to concentrate even more clearly on Your goals for our life. Enable us to also be encouraged by the example of others, both living and dead, who gave themselves completely to Your service. Bless our efforts and cause others to be encouraged through the exercise of our Christian leadership. This we ask in the name of the only Savior, Jesus, our advocate. Amen.

Notes

1. H. Norman Schwarzkopf, Speech made in St. Louis during the Success '94 conference, November 10, 1994.

2. H. Norman Schwarzkopf, *It Doesn't Take a Hero,* (New York: Bantam Books, 1992), 96.

3. H. Norman Schwarzkopf, St. Louis speech, November 10, 1994.

4. H. Norman Schwarzkopf, *It Doesn't Take a Hero,* 730

5. H. Norman Schwarzkopf, Biography, 88.

CHAPTER EIGHT

W. EDWARDS DEMING
Teamwork

Once upon a time, two aerospace companies—one American and one Japanese—decided to have a boat race on the Tennessee River. Both teams practiced long and hard to reach their peak performance. On the big day, they both felt as ready as they could be.

The Japanese won by a mile.

Afterwards, the American team became very discouraged by the loss and morale sagged. Corporate management decided that the reason for the crushing defeat had to be found. A corporate steering committee was set up to investigate the problem and to recommend appropriate corrective action. Their conclusion:

> The problem was that the Japanese had eight people rowing and one person steering; whereas the American team had one person rowing and eight people steering.

The American corporate steering committee immediately hired a consulting firm to do a study on the management structure. After some time and millions of dollars, the consulting firm concluded that too many people were steering and not enough rowing.

To prevent losing to the Japanese again the next year, the team's management structure was totally reorganized to four steering managers, three area steering managers, one staff steering manager, and a new performance system for the person rowing the boat to encourage him/her to row harder.

The next year the Japanese won by two miles.

Humiliated, the American corporation laid off the rower for poor performance, sold all its paddles, canceled all capital investments for new equipment, halted development of a new canoe, gave high-performance awards to the consulting firm, and distributed the money saved as bonuses to the senior executives—not exactly a stellar example of teamwork, and our nervous smiles betray the fine line between reality and parody.

America's reputation of achievement has faltered, and some think they know why. In his bid for the presidency, H. Ross Perot once noted, "It takes five years to develop a new car in this country. Heck, we won World War II in four years!"

Many now contend, "Success is best conceived through teamwork, and cannot long exist where teamwork does not prevail." No one has demonstrated that understanding more powerfully than W. Edwards Deming, the mastermind of Japan's rise from laughingstock to postwar industrial giant. Committed to optimum cooperation, Deming favored complete elimination of "motivation by competition" in favor of unifying people in the establishment of mutual strategies, goals, and product development.

Deming's commitment to quality was largely spurned by American businesses that were enjoying a postwar boom with no foreign competition. The demand for goods was so great that quantity, not quality, was the byword for American production in the late 1940s. The Japanese were listening, however, and began to reshape their economy on the Deming principles of quality through teamwork. "Japan ... developed a participatory form of management that drew on every employee's knowledge and abilities, at all levels, through teams and suggestions on systems—and always focused on the customer."[1]

American industry was caught flatfooted by Japan's success but has scrambled to quickly regain lost ground. Companies such as Ford Motor Company have taken note. "Team Taurus," observed Tom Peters, "created a product that won kudos for design and quality, sold well from the very start, and came in almost one-half billion dollars under budget."[2] How did they do it? The Taurus was Ford's venture into the world of teamwork, a la W. Edwards Deming. It was developed by the establishment of a multifunctional team drawn from all levels, including design engineers, the assembly line, suppliers, distributors, and customers. They believed, and went on to prove, that the value of working together is greater than the contribution each made working apart from the others.

God created people to work in teams. It is an integral part of His creative plan, so much so that a "first warning sign" of a person in trouble is withdrawal from friends and colleagues.

I have never believed that God made a mistake in the creation of Adam. He made every other animal male and female, but Adam He made alone. Read again carefully the creation account recorded in Genesis 2. "The LORD God said, 'It is not good for man to be alone. I will make a helper suitable for him' " (Genesis 2:18).

Notice God did not immediately set out to make Eve. No, first He brought every animal before Adam "to see what he would name them." After this important "object lesson" the chapter goes on to say, "but for Adam, no suitable helper was found." By means of this approach, Adam was first given opportunity to frolic with the monkeys, enjoy the companionship of a friendly dog, and was the first to feel the special kinship a rider has with his mount ... "but for Adam, no suitable helper was found." It became obvious to Adam that something was missing in all these experiences. Only after this had been discerned did the Lord meet his need and provide just the right companion.

There are other incidents in Scripture that demonstrate the human need for unity, but maybe none so revealing as the Tower of Babel incident recorded in chapter 11 of Genesis. For sinful reasons, all the people had come together to build a high tower on the plain of Shinar. Upon observation of their work and their strength in unity, the Lord observed, "If as one people speaking the same language they have begun to do this, then nothing they plan to do will be impossible for them" (Genesis 11:6). Because their plans were evil, God dispersed them and destroyed their unity, but not before acknowledging the powerful value of teamwork.

In Jesus Christ we find our unity. All Christian differences of abilities, strengths, and talents serve only to strengthen those united in faith. No wonder the apostle wrote, "Be completely humble and gentle; be patient, bearing with one another in love. Make every effort to keep the unity of the Spirit through the bond of peace. There is one body and one Spirit—just as you were called to one hope when you were called—one Lord, one faith, one Baptism; one God and Father of all, who is over all and through all and in all" (Ephesians 4:2–6).

Unity, even unity in Christ, takes effort. Paul talks about "making the effort" to keep the unity. Perhaps the best effort we can put forth is in the area of communication. It is pretty hard to maintain a team spirit if the team members aren't talking to each other, whether by design or by intention.

For Christians to work together as a team, it is necessary that they be in regular communication. Deming's model works well for us. If the least among us is greatest in the sight of God, then we should have no difficulty consulting "across the board." Paul warns against attitudes that cause people to think more highly of themselves than they ought to think.[3]

Many of the best leaders in industry can be seen spending quality time with younger, less experienced, and relatively new employees. The benefit of building such relationships is twofold. The subordinate gains an appreciation for management, while those in leadership gain insights and important feedback from those closest to the customer on the production process. In similar fashion, Christian leaders will build a team approach to ministry that encourages contribution from all participants in the shared work. This is best accomplished in a variety of settings, including large-group meetings and planning sessions, as well as smaller discussion groups and even one-on-one sharing between those who lead and those who sustain the mission.

Deming reminds us, "Groups of people working in teams can have more success than individuals working alone. And the people who know the work best are the ones who are asked to perform it."[4] Even the Lord demonstrates "Divine teamwork" as the Persons of the Trinity interact, share attributes, and through their oneness, bring about our salvation in perfect order.

More Scriptural Insight

Psalm 133   What makes unity so valuable?
Ecclesiastes 4:9–12   What are the benefits of teamwork?

1 Peter 3:8–12   What ways are suggested to maintain unity?

A Leader's Prayer

Lord Jesus, there must have been times when You felt all alone. Even in the midst of Your closest friends You were not always understood, and sometimes even challenged. I come to You as one who understands both the benefits and the frustrations of teamwork. Help me to develop, appreciate, and maintain a team of other Christians who support the mission You have asked me to lead. Give me a humble and willing spirit that is always "slow to speak and quick to hear" what others have to suggest or say. Lord, there are days when I am in need of others to be strong for me, even though I am called to be a Christian leader. Help me see the strength in being weak and the weakness of always being strong. Raise up people around me who are sensitive to my needs and supportive of my efforts to lead this ministry and mission to Your glory, and for the sake of those we serve. Bless us and help us keep "the unity of the Spirit through the bond of peace." Amen.

Notes

1. Mary Walton, *Deming Management at Work,* (New York: Perigree Books, The Putnam Publishing Group, 1990), 13.

2. Tom Peters, *Thriving on Chaos,* (New York: Knopf, 1987), 132.

3. See Romans 12:16.

4. Mary Walton, 22.

CHAPTER NINE

HARRY S. TRUMAN
Honesty

Say what you will about Harry Truman, but all would agree he was forthright, plainspoken, and honest. True, he was often crude, his language was more than a little coarse, and he could be less than kind in his characterization of others. All that being true, his ability to be direct, candid, and transparent led to great trust on the part of the common man.

He was popular despite pollsters who said otherwise. On the 1948 election he commented, "Even if I lost the election, my feeling for the common people of this country wouldn't have changed. You know what Lincoln said, 'The Lord must have loved the common people, He made so many of them!' Well the feeling I got in that campaign was that most people in this country are not only, like I said, decent people. They want to do the right thing, and what you have to do is tell them straight out what the right thing is."[1]

Truman had served as vice president only 83 days when he assumed the presidency at the death of Franklin Roosevelt on April 12, 1945. Less than a month later Germany surrendered, and by August, only one week after Truman made the controversial decision to drop the atom bomb on Hiroshima and Nagasaki, Japan followed suit. Truman was believed vulnerable. Republicans had gained majorities in both Houses in the elections of 1946, which most believed a precursor to the presidential elections of '48. Few believed Truman would win.[2] President Truman seemed to be the only one confident of the eventual outcome and took great delight in embarrassing newspapers whose early editions had declared Thomas Dewey the victor! Truman's perceived rout was an unexpected and easy victory, surprising almost everyone *except the president.*

Truman ran his campaign believing honesty was the best policy. This was not necessarily the advice of his campaign managers. "People said I ought to pussyfoot around, that I shouldn't say anything that would lose the Wallace vote (secretary of commerce who mounted a third party campaign), and nothing that would lose the Southern vote. But I didn't pay any attention to that. I said what I thought had to be said. You can't divide the country up into sections and have one rule for one section and one rule for another, and you can't encourage people's prejudices. You have to appeal to people's best instincts, not their worst ones. You may win an election or so by doing the other, but it does a lot of harm to the country."[3]

The apostle Nathaniel and Harry Truman had this in common, no one had to guess what they were thinking! I have always enjoyed John's description of Nathaniel's first encounter with the Lord. After Philip had joined Peter and Andrew as disciples of the Lord, Philip found Nathaniel and said, "We have found the one Moses wrote about in the Law, and about whom the prophets wrote—Jesus of Nazareth, the son of Joseph" (John 1:45).

Not especially impressed and, perhaps knowing the Scriptures foretold the Messiah to be born in Bethlehem not Nazareth, Nathaniel responded cynically, "Nazareth! Can anything good come from there?" Knowing of the conversation by means of His omniscience, Jesus, when introduced to Nathaniel said, "Here is a true Israelite, in whom there is nothing false" (John 1:46–47).

There is absolutely, positively, unequivocally, no room for falsehood in the life and witness of a Christian leader. People must always know where the Christian leader stands, and they should be able to trust such a person to always speak the truth in love.[4]

I contend this attribute is what pleased God so much about King David. If we examine the life of David, we see a man with as many weaknesses and failures as most other kings and leaders of the Old Testament. What set David apart was his absolute honesty with God. When confronted by the prophet Nathan regarding his sin against Uriah, by the aid of the Holy Spirit David acknowledged the depth of his depravity and opened his heart to God.

The psalms of David are not all neat, clean, and purified for our sensitive Christian ears. Some of them cry out in pain against enemies, often they cry out in confusion to God. Psalm 13, for example, is an open and honest plea for intervention. David's frustration with God comes through loud and clear, almost as though he were shaking his fist toward an unresponsive God. His honest feelings are clearly seen, but so also is his constant and abiding hope in God's eventual rescue. After the death of David, the Lord would compare every subsequent king to the honest and open relationship He had with His servant David.

The Lord much prefers the questioning honesty of David over against the false piety of many religious leaders. Against the Pharisees and scribes Jesus spoke strong words. "You hypocrites!" He said, "Isaiah was right when he prophesied about you: 'These people honor me with their lips, but their hearts are far from Me. They worship Me in vain; their teachings are but rules taught by men' " (Matthew 15:7–9).

A solid relationship must be built on honesty. You cannot build a marriage, a business relationship, or congregational trust on lies. If the Lord will not tolerate dishonest and deceitful hearts, how can we expect His children to tolerate lies? When we lie, or knowingly misrepresent the truth, we destroy the integrity of our witness. How I wish this were only a minor problem among Christian leaders! It is not. Too many practice the false belief that the end justifies the means. Such compromise can only result in a withdrawal of the Lord's favor and the eventual collapse of leadership.

President Truman believed that honesty would translate into votes. He believed in taking his case directly to the people, resulting in his famous "whistle stop" campaign. When asked how he decided there were enough people to merit stopping the train, Harry responded, "Ten to a thousand." When the biographer asked if he had ever really stopped for only ten people, Harry said, "Many a time, many a time. They'd come out to hear me, and I'd talk to them!"[5]

When asked why he preferred the train to TV, Harry was his usual blunt self. "I wanted to talk to them face to face. I knew that they knew that when you got on the television, you're wearing a lot of powder and paint that somebody else has put on your face, and you haven't even combed your own hair! But when you're standing right there in front of them and talking to them and shaking their hands if it's possible, the people can tell when you're telling them the facts or not. ... They don't go for high hats, and they can spot a phony a mile off."[6]

Jesus described Himself as the Way, the Truth, and the Life.[7] By contrast, Jesus once rebuked unbelieving false teachers by saying, "You belong to your father, the devil, and you want to carry out your father's desire. He was a murderer from the beginning, not holding to the truth, for there is no truth in him. When he lies, he speaks his native language, for he is a liar and the father of lies. Yet because I tell the truth, you do not believe me!" (John 8:44–46).

Given the contrast of Christ and the clear implications of His truth, no Christian leader can justify lying to promote even the most noble of causes. To be identified with Christ is to be identified with truth.

More Scriptural Insight

Genesis 27	What do you know about the deception of Jacob's father and the outcome of Jacob's life as a result of his trickery?
Matthew 26:69–75	Why did Peter lie and what was the result?
Ephesians 4:11–16	What is the goal of every Christian? (Note v. 15)

A Leader's Prayer

O Lord, God of heaven and earth, enable me to be always honest in my relationship with You and with all people. Help me to see the senselessness of deception, the difficulties it brings to me, and the great harm it brings to my witness. Lord, whenever I am tempted to exaggerate or misrepresent the truth, let Your gentle Spirit remind me that nothing good or lasting can be built upon the sand. Let me establish my life and my witness upon the sure foundation of truth. Your Word is truth. Forgive my past errors of judgment and lies. Help me to be compassionate and understanding of others who remain within the grasp of the devil, the father of lies. Grant that I might not see them as the enemy, but as victims who need to be freed from Satan's grasp. Let no harm come to me from their lies and enable me to be an influence for good and a means of rescue to the lost. Empower me, O Lord, to do these things, for apart from You I am helpless and can do nothing. In Jesus' holy name. Amen.

Notes

1. Merle Miller, *Plain Speaking, An Oral Biography of Harry S. Truman,* (New York: Berkley Publishing Corporation, 1974), 262.

2. Drake De Kay, "Harry S. Truman," *The Encyclopedia Americana,* (Chicago: Americana Corporation, 1963), vol. 27, 175–76.

3. Merle Miller, 252.

4. See Ephesians 4:15.

5. Merle Miller, 261.

6. Merle Miller, 250, 258.

7. See John 14:6.

CHAPTER TEN

GENERAL SAMUEL CHAPMAN ARMSTRONG
Forgiving by Nature

Everyone knows that forgiveness is not an option for Christian people. Immediately after the Lord's Prayer, Matthew records Jesus' continued commentary on the subject: "For if you forgive men when they sin against you, your heavenly Father will also forgive you. But if you do not forgive men their sins, your Father will not forgive your sins" (Matthew 6:14–15). Although the Lord's intention is clear, I'm almost certain most Christians don't understand the motive for the Lord's imperative.

If asked, many would say that forgiveness is obviously for the benefit of the one forgiven! That answer is only half right, at best. The benefit of forgiveness is chiefly received by the one who offers forgiveness and is able to maintain a forgiving heart. Bitterness and resentment is a cancer that slowly but persistently destroys its host as a parasite slowly infests and destroys the mightiest oak. In the end, no heart that comprehends the extent of God's love shown in the sacrifice and death of Christ can harbor a spirit of hatred. The converse must also be true. No heart that harbors hatred and bitterness has room enough for the mercy and compassion of God! Like sunlight and darkness these can never cohabit.

All truly great men understand the imperative of forgiveness. It is nowhere more evident than in the life of General Samuel Chapman Armstrong. Unlike the others remembered in this book, his life—and even his name—is an enigma to most, even the well-read. I include him as the "patron saint" of the countless great Christian leaders who have served quietly and faithfully, unknown to the world, and without recognition except in heaven's great hall of honor and in the lives of those touched by their greatness!

Samuel Chapman was born January 30, 1839, the son of American missionaries in Hawaii. After his father's death in 1860 he traveled to the United States where he attended Williams College. When the Civil War broke out, he joined the Union army, motivated by the same love and concern for the plight of the black man as he had witnessed in his father's devotion to the Hawaiian people. He was appointed colonel of a Negro regiment. After the war he accepted a position with the Freedman's Bureau, which gave him full responsibility for a large population of Negroes near Hampton, Virginia.[1] As they say, "the rest is history."

His work brought him to the realization that lack of education and opportunity was the greatest enslavement of all. With the assistance and the support of his Northern friends and the American Missionary Association, General Armstrong was able to establish the Hampton Normal and Agricultural Institute, a prototype and the chief inspiration for Booker T. Washington's Tuskegee Institute in Alabama.

Of General Armstrong, Booker T. Washington would later write, "I have been fortunate to meet personally many of what are called great characters, both in Europe and America, but I do not hesitate to say that I never met any man who, in my estimation, was the equal of General Armstrong. ... It was my privilege to know the General personally from the time I entered Hampton till he died, and the more I saw of him the more he grew in my estimation. One might have removed from Hampton all the buildings, classrooms, teachers, and industries, and given the men and women there the opportunity of coming into daily contact with General Armstrong, and that alone would have been a liberal education."[2]

What so impressed Washington was the gentle and forgiving spirit of the general. He described this spirit of the man by saying, "I never believe he had a selfish thought. He was just as happy in trying to assist some other institution in the South as he was when working for Hampton. Although he fought the Southern white man in the Civil War, I never heard him utter a bitter word against him afterward. On the other hand, he was constantly seeking to find ways by which he could be of service to Southern whites."[3]

This quality of General Armstrong so impressed Washington that he was able to survive one of America's darkest hours and rise unscathed against the hatred and insults he endured as an educated black man during Southern reconstruction after the Civil War. Reflecting on the value of this lesson, Washington wrote. "It is now long ago that I learned this lesson from General Armstrong, and resolved that I would permit no man, no matter what his colour might be, to narrow and degrade my soul by making me hate him. With God's help, I believe that I have completely rid myself of any ill feeling toward the Southern white man for any wrong that he may have inflicted upon my race. I am just as happy now when I am rendering service to Southern white men as when the service is rendered to a member of my own race. I pity from the bottom of my heart any individual who is so unfortunate as to get into the habit of holding race prejudice."[4]

Great leaders know instinctively the truth of General Armstrong's advice. There are several Bible truths that help Christians exercise the kind of forgiveness that General Armstrong and Booker T. were able to model. First, we are asked to forgive not because the individual who has caused us harm is worthy or even asking for our forgiveness; the people chiefly in need of our forgiveness may never seek or desire it! We are asked to forgive because God in Christ Jesus has forgiven us.[5] It is a service we offer to God, who is worthy to have us practice it on His behalf.

Secondly, we should remember that those protected by the Lord cannot be harmed by people who seek their demise. During an especially troubling experience in my ministry which required honesty tempered by love, I became the target of an ugly campaign of rumor and innuendo. It was short-lived and ended well, but it was a learning experience aided by a study of Solomon's Proverbs. I especially recall the simple advice of chapter 26: "Like a fluttering sparrow or a darting swallow, an undeserved curse does not come to rest" (Proverbs 26:2). Not only did I learn through the experience, but that proverb has become my common counsel to many Christian friends encountering the same frustration.

Once we acknowledge the personal value of forgiveness and turn our thinking around, Christian leaders find the opportunity to love our enemies in invigorating and faith-building experiences. I like the way Booker T. summarized the forgiving heart of General Armstrong. He wrote, "He was too big to be little, and too good to be mean." It would be hard to write a greater compliment to a leader of leaders.

More Scriptural Insight

Psalm 130	Thank God for His compassionate nature.
Matthew 18:21–35	If sins were debts, how much would you owe?
Romans 12:14–21	Overcome evil with good. It never pays to wallow.

A Leader's Prayer

Gracious Lord, You are rich in Your mercy to all people. Help me as Your servant to better understand the value of forgiveness in life. My human nature and many of my friends advise me to "give as good as I get" and "don't get mad, get even." It's tempting, Lord, and we both know that, as a Christian leader, I am in a position and well-equipped to defend myself and destroy those who seek my harm. Lord, I want to be like You. Move in my heart and enable me to do the impossible. Help me turn the other cheek and allow no bitterness to linger in my heart. Turn my thinking around and help me see the joy and freedom that comes from a compassionate and loving spirit. All this I pray in the name of Jesus, the author and the perfecter of faith. Amen.

Notes

1. *The Encyclopedia Americana—International Edition* (Chicago: Americana Corporation, 1964), vol. 2, 286.

2. Booker T. Washington, *Up from Slavery,* (New York: Viking Penguin Inc., 1986), 54–55.

3. Ibid., 56.

4. Ibid., 165

5. See Colossians 3:13

CHAPTER ELEVEN

GUIDO MERKENS
Act on the Promises of God

E very young Christian leader needs a mentor, someone to look up to and emulate. Many in our congregation are involved with the national Christian men's movement Promise Keepers. Although at this writing I have been unable to attend one of their national gatherings, I understand they urge that every man should have three other significant men in his life. First, one he can look up to and aspire to emulate; secondly, a Christian peer who believes as he does and will hold him accountable to the Lord and His Word; and lastly, a younger man whom he will guide and mentor for future leadership in the body of Christ.

I have been fortunate to have had many mentors, some I have known personally; others, like many of the people in this book, I have studied from a distance. One of those in the "from a distance" category is Dr. Guido Merkens. Guido founded the ministry of Concordia Lutheran Church in San

Antonio, Texas, and directed it for 40 years. Under his direction, it became one of the largest congregations in my denomination. *Decision* magazine, published by the Billy Graham Evangelical Association, chose his church to be included in its series *Great Churches of Today.*

I have heard Guido speak many times at various national gatherings and recently had the privilege of introducing him to a conference I was attending in Denver, Colorado. But it goes without saying he is better known to me than I am to him! Guido is a positive Christian. He believes and acts on the promises of God. Many Christian leaders know the promises of God and preach on them. No doubt most Christian leaders believe the promises of God to be true, but they are unable to see their relevancy to everyday ministry, and rarely if ever act on them, not understanding that the Lord will keep His Word and bring about extraordinary miracles from quite ordinary people. To my knowledge, Guido has never suffered a lack of faith in God's promises.

One of the stories he likes to tell is on this very subject. This is how he told it in his book *Breakthrough—Practical Spiritual Principles to Lift You to a New Level of Living:*

> There was a factory worker who worked from four o'clock in the afternoon till twelve midnight, and in order to go home to his graham crackers, his milk, and his wife, it was necessary to go down a mile one way around the cemetery and then a mile down the other side of the cemetery.
>
> But one night he questioned, "Why should I go all the way around this cemetery when I could get home so much faster to my graham crackers, my milk, and my wife if I just cut right through?"
>
> This he proceeded to do and did successfully for a number of weeks. Then one day a custodian of the cemetery had prepared a grave and had dug it along the same pathway where the fellow went and had not covered it properly, as

he should have, in preparation for a burial the next day.

So that night our factory worker came blithely rolling down his pathway through the cemetery in the darkness and suddenly, he dropped into the grave that had been prepared. It was a cold, dark and windy night and there he was at the bottom of the pit. He screamed and shouted and yelled for help. Of course, there was nobody there so he tried to get out, but as you know, graves have sheer sides and no steps! So he finally decided, "I'll just go over here in the corner, pull up my coat a little bit, make a pillow and sleep here and wait till morning when somebody's bound to come and put a rope or a ladder down to get me out."

Well, he stayed there very quietly. About two hours later, another man who, at two in the morning had just finished up dining at a restaurant, came through the cemetery along the same path. Boom! He fell in. The factory worker was startled and awakened and realized there was someone else in the grave with him. He stayed quiet in the corner and just observed.

Well, the second fellow did the same thing he had done. He shouted and screamed and yelled and tried to climb out. Finally, the first fellow got up, tiptoed over behind him and put a rather cold hand on his shoulder. And he said, "I tried that already. You're not going to make it out that way." But, you know, he did![1]

Guido makes the point that there is no limit to what a man can do when he is properly motivated! He then reminds us that the best motivational tool is the Bible and it is filled with the promises of God. There is virtually no limit to what a very ordinary person can accomplish if it is God's will as revealed and promised in His Word.

Why more Christian leaders don't study and act on the promises of God I cannot understand. I remember conducting a children's message at a Christian school in Port Arthur, Texas, during the early 1980s. That morning I had asked every teacher to have each child write his/her name on a slip of paper and bring it to morning chapel. During the course of the chapel service we drew the name of one "lucky" child who was to receive a gift from me.

I remember her face to this day. She was a shy little girl, no doubt in the third or fourth grade. As I talked with her and the other students about the promises of God, I took out my checkbook and wrote out a check to her for one dollar. The check was my promise to her, but she would have to act on my promise if she was ever going to receive the benefit of that check. You know, for the next six years—until I moved to the midwest and closed that account—I had the hardest time balancing my checkbook! It was always one dollar off, causing me to recall the little girl who didn't believe my check was worth the paper it was written on!

Too many Christian leaders are like that little girl. They have the promises of God right in their hands, but somehow they believe those promises only worked for people with names such as Abraham, Moses, David, Elijah, and Peter. It must frustrate the heart of God, who tries to balance His Divine Books and know that so many promises are still outstanding! He bids us to "test Me in this" (Malachi 3:10) and reminds us that "Elijah was man just like us!" (James 5:17).

I suppose most Christian leaders fail to cash those promises out of a sense of humility and self-denial. Somehow they suppose themselves unworthy of such promises and believe that the best of the Lord's miraculous work is reserved for others who will serve a greater purpose in the kingdom. What a tragedy! Even a casual study of God's Word reveals unequivocally that the Lord raises up the lowly to shame the great. He accomplishes His best work through earthen vessels so that the glory will be in the accomplishment of His power and not in the poor and lowly servant who only acted as His instrument.[2]

As Christian leaders we must always recall the power is in the promise and its ability to be accomplished rests on the one who made it; never, never, never does the outcome rest on the one who simply acts on the promise. For this reason also, the praise and glory for great accomplishment never fall upon the unworthy servant, but always on the Lord God Creator, who has kept His promise and fulfilled His Word.

Our false sense of unworthiness must end if we are to be all that the Lord wants us to be and accomplish all that He wants us to accomplish. I call it a "false sense of unworthiness" because it is nothing less that a denial of the cross. Jesus has set us free from the bondage of sin that condemned us. The Father in heaven accepted His sacrifice and by His wounds we are washed clean and granted not only eternal life, but access to the Father's storehouse of grace!

The promises of God are offered through His Word and Sacraments to all His children. By merit of the cross we should step up to the Divine Storehouse with His promissory note in hand and optimistically in Christ await the outpouring of His blessing.

Dr. Guido Merkens is fond of saying, "I believe in today. This is the day which the Lord has made. Let us rejoice and be glad in it. And I believe in tomorrow. As Joshua said to the people of God's choosing, 'Sanctify yourselves today and God will do wonders with you tomorrow!'[3] And all the people said, 'Amen!' "

More Scriptural Insight

James 1:2–7	God's blessing is impeded by doubting.
James 5:13–18	Much is accomplished through prayer offered in faith.
1 John 5:13–15	Leaders find confidence when they stand in the will of God.

A Leader's Prayer

Gracious Lord, forgive my halfhearted appropriation of Your promises. I confess that I often study the Bible as though it were a history book, not a living, life-giving guide to fullness of life. Open my eyes to see and my heart to accept all that You intend for my life. As the psalmist asks, "teach me to number my days" so that I might more wisely spend my time enjoying the challenges and the blessings. Grant that I might more clearly see the value of modeling authentic Christianity in my daily reliance on You. Enable "this physician to heal himself" and thus freed from doubt, more wisely counsel from an experiential perspective. Thank You, Lord, for all that You have done and all that You have in store for my future. Help me to remember the phrase "Elijah was a man just like you" so that I might enjoy greater expectation in my prayer life. Thank You for all the mentors in my life, both sainted and living. Enable me to become an example and an inspiration to others who desire to serve You with all their heart, soul, and mind. In Jesus' name. Amen.

Notes

1. Guido Merkens, *Breakthrough—Practical Spiritual Principles to Lift You to a New Level of Living*, (San Antonio: Breakthrough Publications, 1982), 38–39. Used by permission.

2. See 2 Corinthians 4:7–9.

3. Guido Merkens, 40, (Joshua 3:5).

CHAPTER TWELVE

WILL ROGERS
Assuming the Best

I was raised in The Lutheran Church—Missouri Synod, even attended St. Peter's Lutheran School through the first eight grades. It is a good memory of friends, small classes, good teachers—a truly spiritual, positive, and nurturing environment.

Every morning at St. Peter's began with devotions and memory work. We used a small brown memory book filled with Bible passages, hymn stanzas, and the writings of Martin Luther, which we memorized and recited much like the times tables in math class. We not only memorized the Ten Commandments and the petitions to the Lord's Prayer, we also memorized Martin Luther's explanations to these important verses of Scripture. The explanation to the Eighth Commandment made a lasting impression on me.

We memorized it this way:

You shalt not bear false witness against thy neighbor.[1]

What Does This Mean? We should fear and love God that we may not deceitfully belie, betray, slander, nor defame our neighbor, but defend him, speak well of him, and put the best construction on everything.[2]

I especially remember our teacher explaining the archaic language in this somewhat dated explanation. "Putting the best construction on everything means always assuming the best about everyone and every situation," she would say. In fact, the newer translation of the same explanation now reads, "and explain everything in the kindest way."[3]

Assuming the best about other people is an important, even essential trait of godly leadership. It does not mean that we should be naive or ignore potential harm that may come from those who mean us harm. It does mean that we should look for the good in every person and work with them to encourage and foster the good that we find.

Will Rogers, arguably America's greatest humorist, understood the value of such an attitude when working with people. He once said, "When I die, my epitaph or whatever you call those signs on gravestones is going to read: 'I joked about every prominent man of my time, but I never met a man I didn't like.' I am so proud of that I can hardly wait to die so it can be carved. And when you come to my grave you will find me sitting there, proudly reading it."[4]

Born in the Indian Territories on November 4, 1879, Will was raised on a working ranch, son of Clem and Mary Rogers, both of whom were of Cherokee Indian descent. Will later employed his cowboy upbringing to good use as he distracted his audience with rope tricks while sharing his humorous views and opinions of world events. Although he spared no one of reputation in his running commentary, he was often most appreciated by those he targeted. His humor was good natured and never intended to hurt. At the start of the Great Depression, for instance, Will ceased all criticism of the president. "Let's stop blaming the president and the Republicans for all of this," he wrote. "Why, they're not smart enough to have thought of all that's been happening to us lately!"[5]

Assuming the "high road" is important if we are to enjoy godly success. A godly and sainted friend once told me not to fight a skunk on his terms. "We aren't equally equipped to fight at that level," he said with a smile. The point is well made; Christians should never sink to the shameful tactics of those who oppose the Lord and His kingdom. King David resisted sinking to the level of Saul, even though it appeared several times that the Lord had placed his enemy in his grasp. The apostle Paul put it this way, "Do not repay anyone evil for evil. Be careful to do what is right in the eyes of everybody. If it is possible, as far as it depends on you, live at peace with everyone" (Romans 12:17–18). Notice, Paul never said it would be possible to be at peace with everyone. Some just won't allow it. He did say we should make sure there is nothing in our behavior that is destructive of peace.

I like the way the apostle concludes his letter to the Christians at Philippi:

> Finally, brothers, whatever is true, whatever is noble, whatever is right, whatever is pure, whatever is lovely, whatever is admirable—if anything is excellent or praise-worthy—think about such things. Whatever you have learned or received or heard from me, or seen in me—put it into practice. And the God of peace will be with you. (Philippians 4:8–9)

This Scripture confirms what we have often heard, "You are what you think!" We can never achieve high and noble goals if our minds are constantly in the gutter. Jesus is the perfect mentor of such behavior. Even from the cross, even regarding those who drove spikes into His hands, in the place of curses and damnation, Jesus offered intercessory prayer.

"Father, forgive them," he said, "for they do not know what they are doing" (Luke 23:34).

A Christian leader will emulate the example of Christ. To be sure, you will receive your share of abuse, criticism, and second-guessing. It all goes with the territory of working with people who are sometimes spiritual and other times subject to the whims of the flesh. As leaders for Christ we are motivated by Him. Our behavior and expectations are based on the model of love and acceptance we find in the Savior, not in the fickle and unpredictable nature of those we lead.

Jesus urged Peter to forgive "seventy times seven"; in essence, as often as necessary! Knowing of God's patience towards us, we can find in Him all the motive we need to be forgiving and accepting of others. Will Rogers once remarked, "All people are ignorant, only on different subjects!"[6] Knowing that we too have weaknesses, and admitting it to ourselves and others, may help us to be more considerate and gracious in the future.

More Scriptural Insight

Romans 12:17–21	We are to leave all "score settling" to the Lord.
Psalm 133	There is power and blessing in unity.
1 John 2:7–11	Only the blind and those living in darkness breed hatred.

A Leader's Prayer

O Lord, our Lord, how excellent are Your ways and how wise is Your counsel. I especially pray for Your help in taking the "high road." Lord, sometimes those I lead have tested my patience to its limits. I know You desire that my example always reflects Your love and belief that all people are precious in Your sight. Lord, help me to achieve such an attitude in my life and in my work. I know, Lord, that those who have been deeply hurt are most likely to inflict the pain on others. Help me see past my hurt, even past those that mean me harm, so that I might pray for them as Christ did for the soldiers who crucified Him. Give me a spirit that expects and anticipates the best in people and in so doing treats them with respect and dignity as Your child. Help me always to "put the best construction" on everything. This I pray in the name of Jesus, who pardons and sanctifies all who call upon Him ... all who call upon Him in truth. Amen.

Notes

1. Lutherans number the commandments according to the historic pattern of the ancient church. The Eighth Commandment "Thou shalt not bear false witness against thy neighbor" is considered the Ninth Commandment by those who use the Protestant numbering system.

2. Theodore Tappert, *The Book of Concord—The Confessions of the Evangelical Lutheran Church,* An English Translation, (St. Louis: Concordia Publishing House, 1959), 343.

3. Luther's Small Catechism—With Explanation. (St. Louis: Concordia Publishing House, 1986), 11.

4. Art Wortman, *Will Rogers—Wise and Witty Sayings of a Great American Humorist,* (Pasadena, CA: The Castle Press, 1969), 43.

5. Ibid., 4.

6. Ibid., 56.

CHAPTER THIRTEEN

DALE CARNEGIE
Conflict Resolution

Before there was Tom Peters, before there was Zig Ziglar, before Steve Covey, John Naisbitt, Lee Iacocca ... even before W. Edwards Deming, there was Dale Carnegie.

When he wrote his first book *How to Win Friends and Influence People* in 1936, he was pioneering a new field of human relations and leadership development. His faithful wife, Dorothy, wrote after his death in 1955, "Neither Dale Carnegie nor the publishers, Simon and Schuster, anticipated more than modest sale. To their amazement, the book became an overnight sensation, and edition after edition rolled off the presses to keep up with the increasing public demand. *How to Win Friends and Influence People* took its place in publishing history as one of the all-time international bestsellers."[1]

Mrs. Dale Carnegie was right. *How to Win Friends ...* has sold more than 10 million copies and has been translated into every major language of the world. His other books, *How to Stop Worrying and Start Living* and *Public Speaking* and

Influencing Men in Business, have been equally precedent-setting and the basis for an entire industry of seminars and leadership training.

What makes his advice so valuable? Dale Carnegie was one of the first men to realize and then teach that interpersonal skill has as much to do with the success or failure of a person or a business as does the quality of their product or service. His advice is simple, direct, well-illustrated, and as honest as a four-year-old at show and tell.

On the subject of disagreement and conflict resolution, he tells it simple and straight: "You can't win an argument. You can't, because if you lose it, you lose it; and if you win it, you lose it. Why? Well, suppose you triumph over the other man and shoot his argument full of holes and prove that he is non compos mentis. Then what? You will feel fine. But what about him? You have made him feel inferior. You have hurt his pride. He will resent your triumph, and a man convinced against his will is of the same opinion."[2]

In the course of explaining his point of view, Carnegie quotes a ditty he once saw in the pages of the Boston Transcript:

> *Here lies the body of William Jay,*
> *Who died maintaining his right of way—*
> *He was right, dead right, as he sped along,*
> *But he's just as dead as if he'd been wrong!*[3]

No one can serve as a Christian leader for long without encountering conflict. From personal experience (and a good deal of failure!) I have come to see the wisdom of Carnegie's advice. The humble and the truly wise men of God avoided arguments.

How many times did Jesus refuse to engage in useless debate? In Matthew's description of one confrontation, Jesus was asked a question intended to discredit His standing among the people. He deftly sidestepped the trap by asking a question of His own. When His detractors refused to answer, Jesus simply stated, "Neither will I tell you by what authority I am doing these things" (Matthew 21:27).

In one of the first leadership training books ever written, the apostle Paul tells the young pastor Titus, "Avoid foolish controversies and genealogies and arguments and quarrels about the law, because these are unprofitable and useless. Warn a divisive person once, and then warn him a second time. After that, have nothing to do with him. You may be sure that such a man is warped and sinful; he is self-condemned" (Titus 3:9–11).

Avoiding arguments is not the same as avoiding controversy. No leader can lead without engaging in conflict resolution. The better leader will avoid argumentation to promote his view, concentrating on the facts and supporting those positions that are best for everyone without thought of winning or losing a fight. The best leaders will allow others the opportunity to consider their position without humiliating their opposition.

In John 6, Jesus shared truth so difficult to accept that many of His followers began to leave. Jesus didn't chase them down the street demanding the respect due His office or His teaching. Having stated the truth, He allowed folks to walk away, trusting the power of the Spirit to crack the initially hardhearted reception His position received.

Carnegie once commented, "When we are wrong, we may admit it to ourselves. And if we are handled gently and tactfully, we may admit it to others and even take pride in our frankness and broad-mindedness. But not if someone else is trying to ram the unpalatable down our esophagus!"[4]

More Scriptural Insight

Proverbs 9:7–12	How one receives advice often depends on spiritual maturity.
Matthew 18:1–3	When you ask, "Who is greatest?" you have already failed.
Phillipians 2:1–11	Have you considered the other person's point of view?

A Leader's Prayer

Lord, it is so easy to argue. Sometimes I don't care what others say so long as I have the last word. Sometimes I don't even care that much about what is right or wrong. I just want to prove my point and enjoy the win! Help me to achieve a more Christlike approach to problem solving. Help me to forget about who's right and to concentrate more on what you want. Help me to understand how to "speak the truth in love," knowing that truth without love can be more hurtful than allowing wrong to stand. Thank You for accepting me when I'm wrong and for all the patience You have with me; in Christ's name. Amen.

Notes

1. Dorothy Carnegie, *How to Win Friends and Influence People*—"Preface to Revised Edition," (New York: Pocket Books, a Simon and Schuster division of Gulf and Western Corporation, 1980), xii.

2. Dale Carnegie, *How to Win Friends and Influence People,* (New York: Pocket Books, a Simon and Schuster division of Gulf and Western Corporation, 1980), 117.

3. Ibid., 118.

4. Ibid., 128.

CHAPTER FOURTEEN

THOMAS ALVA EDISON
Work Ethic

This question is asked of every successful leader more often than they care to answer. It can be a source of great frustration, but typically is answered in cursory fashion so that polite, superficial conversation might be sustained. The question? "What is the key to your success?"

It seems simple enough, but that is precisely the problem. Those who wish to imitate the success of the one addressed suggest by their very question that there is a "simple" key to success, one tidbit of knowledge they have discovered which has been overlooked by the less fortunate.

Such superficial assessments of Thomas Alva Edison's work caused him no end of frustration. One such episode led to the now famous response, "Genius is ninety-nine percent perspiration, and one percent inspiration!"[1] There rarely is a simple answer to the question which expects a simple, one-line answer. Pasteur once said, "Chance favors the mind that is prepared."[2] The mind is prepared through constant effort and hard work!

Edison was known to work incredibly long hours, especially if he felt the solution to an extremely vexing problem was at hand. He was a capable motivator of his investigative crew and would lay bets, offer prizes, or play his phonograph loudly to keep them alert and on the job. When the results of some prolonged struggle were finally achieved, he might declare a holiday, and take the whole shop fishing! His biographer recalls the exhaustive effort exerted to discover the key to a long-burning incandescent lamp:

> In the later stages of this long campaign, Edison drove his co-workers harder than ever; they held watches over current tests round the clock, one man taking a sleep of a few hours while another remained awake. At this stage of his life (age 31–35) Edison worked with minimum rest periods for three or four hours a day, his enormous recuperative powers helping to sustain him. He would doze off for a catnap on a bench, or even under a table, with a resistance box for his pillow, but his assistants had orders to waken him if anything occurred that required his attention.[3]

You can see why the search for a simple "key to success" might have bothered him. Edison was not a man who could work in the abstract. Virtually every discovery (and he was responsible either directly or indirectly for more than 1,000 original patents) was accomplished through the grueling process of trial and error. Once, when asked if he was not discouraged by the more than 1,000 failures he experienced before finding the right combination of a stable filament and a pure enough vacuum for his light bulb, Edison replied, "Discouraged! I have eliminated more than 1,000 possibilities and am now closer than ever."

Edison lived a long life, was honored by presidents, Congress, and most notably by his good friend Henry Ford, who built Greenfield Village in Edison's honor at a cost of more than $10 million. On the day of its dedication, Edison, now an old man, was deeply moved. "Well," he said to Mr. Ford, "You've got this just about ninety-nine and one-half percent perfect."

"What's the matter with the other one-half percent?" Ford asked.

"Well, we never kept it as clean as this!" Edison chuckled.

The depth and degree of his work might surprise you. Edison was certainly best known for perfection and production of a long-burning light bulb, but that was only the beginning. He then had to build, demonstrate, and train the technicians needed to establish complete electrical systems for public and private use, including large power generating stations.

Among other things he also did the following:[4]

- Learned to read despite only three month's formal education. His mother pulled him out of public school after his teacher called him "difficult and addled."
- Sold apples and newspapers on the Grand Trunk Railroad at the age of twelve.
- Realizing that good news about the Civil War sold papers, he once telegraphed the news of the Union victory at Shiloh ahead of the train and sold a record 1,000 papers in one day!
- Became almost completely deaf because of a childhood illness.
- Was issued card 33 at the new Detroit Public Library, where he would spend the day waiting for the train to be reloaded before its return trip. "I didn't read a few books," Edison said, "I read the library."
- During the closing days of the Civil War he worked as a "Lightning Slinger," traveling across the South telegraphing news of the war to papers, politicians, and generals.

- Invented an easy and quick way for Congress to record its votes electrically.
- Made his first "big money" ($40,000) improving the stock ticker tape machine.
- Lost all his money more than a dozen times by risking his profits on the next invention.
- Eventually became one of the wealthiest millionaires in America.
- Hired literally thousands of men to set up factories and produce in mass quantity the items he had just invented.
- Developed the mimeograph process and sold its rights to A. B. Dick of Chicago.
- Established and funded the first full-time research laboratory at Menlo Park, New Jersey.
- Improved Alexander Graham Bell's "speaking telegraph" through the invention of the microphone "so the man sending the message didn't have to shout each sentence three or four times in order to be heard above the interference."
- Invented and continuously improved the phonograph.
- Invented the first movie camera which he called a "Kine-to-phonograph," and with the help of George Eastman of Rochester, New York, made motion picture history.
- Improved the first x-ray tube and made it more readily available to medical doctors everywhere.
- Discovered the right metal/chemical combination to make the storage of electricity in batteries efficient, effective, and durable.
- Designed a cement production system that enabled plants to make five times the amount of cement previously produced.
- Watched his whole fortune go up in flames when his largest factory and research lab burned to the ground.

Although his oldest son was devastated and felt responsible, Edison responded, "Oh shucks, it's all right. We've just got rid of a lot of old rubbish. I'm 67, but I'm not too old to make a fresh start. Where's your mother? Get her over here, and her friends too. They'll never see a fire like this again!"

- Although a pacifist, Edison helped defeat the German U-boats of World War I through a whole series of anti-submarine inventions including a device to enable quick maneuvers, antitorpedo nets, smoke cloud machines, and sonic detection devices.

- At age 84 he fell ill and, realizing he would not be able to continue his laboratory work, Thomas Alva Edison died on Sunday, October 18, 1931. At the time he was working to free the U.S. from foreign dependence on rubber through the development of a special strain of goldenrod which he had increased from 5% to 12% composition of rubber.

Just the thought of so many projects and the thousands of experiments they represent can be exhausting! No wonder Edison bristled at the notion of accomplishment through anything but hard work.

Jesus urged Christians to consider the high "cost" of discipleship. To follow Him means commitment of the most complete kind. He once told His followers, "Anyone who loves his father or mother more than Me is not worthy of Me; anyone who loves his son or daughter more than Me is not worthy of Me; and anyone who does not take up his cross and follow Me is not worthy of Me. Whoever finds his life will lose it, and whoever loses his life for My sake will find it" (Matthew 10:37–39).

In 2 Corinthians 11, Paul lists the many afflictions and difficulties he had to face because of his faith. His apostleship challenged, Paul was forced to lay out his credentials. In doing so he said, "Are they [the other apostles] servants of Christ? (I am out of my mind to talk like this.) I am more. I have worked much harder, been in prison more frequently" (2 Corinthians 11:23ff). Paul accomplished a great deal in his lifetime. It came through the inspiration of the Holy Spirit and hard work.

Paul would be the last to boast about his effort or imply that apart from the Lord he could have accomplished anything. But his humility and the doctrine of the Holy Spirit working through the Word of God does not negate the importance of Paul's effort. He was God's chosen instrument to bring the Gospel to bear in the lives of the Gentiles. In 1 Corinthians 9 he compares his work to a runner who must condition himself for victory. The race is too important to lose.

Christian leaders who think they can serve the Lord "while saving their lives" for their own purposes have missed the point of the Lord's calling. To serve Him is to offer up our lives as a living and holy sacrifice.[5] You can't serve the Lord and live "as you please" anymore than a man can successfully keep a foot in a boat and on the dock at the same time. A decision must be reached or a fall is almost certain.

A work ethic of greatest integrity is required. Those who are to accomplish much for the Lord must be willing to give much. For this reason the Bible says, "Not many of you should presume to be teachers, my brothers, because you know that we who teach will be judged more strictly" (James 3:1).

While all of this sounds unappealing, perhaps even repulsive, Christian leaders discover quickly that the Lord turns everything around. When you give, you receive. When you love, you are loved. When you sacrifice, you are blessed. It is the way God works. Although Christian leadership requires sacrifice of time, effort, hobbies, and sometimes even friendships or close relationship to extended family, the Lord returns a harvest one hundred times as bountiful. It may come in a deeper, more loving relationship with your spouse, ministry companions who become like family, greater efficiency of time, greater wisdom, insight, or even speaking ability.

The Lord has been known to also open the windows of blessing and shower greater resources, opportunities, and rewards upon His faithful, sacrificial servants. As Paul described, He loves a cheerful giver and is able to "increase your store of seed and will enlarge the harvest of your righteousness. You will be made rich in every way so that you can be generous on every occasion, and through us your generosity result in thanksgiving to God" (2 Corinthians 9:10–11).

The message of the obscure prophet Hanani is proven true over and over in the lives of Christian leaders. "The eyes of the LORD range throughout the earth to strengthen those whose hearts are fully committed to Him" (2 Chronicles 16:9).

Two years before his death, Thomas Edison was awarded the Congressional Medal of Honor at a special dinner held in his honor. More than 500 guests attended the occasion, including President and Mrs. Hoover. Overcome with emotion and fatigue, the aged Edison faltered and had to be attended to by the president's personal physician. After recovering sufficient strength following several days of recuperation at the Henry Ford residence, Edison announced, "I am tired of all the glory, I want to get back to work."[6] Christian leaders would do well to remember that line and recite it often.

More Scriptural Insight

John 9:4–5	What was the point of Jesus' comment?
2 Thessalonians 3:6–15	What is Paul upset about?
Proverbs 6:6–11	What is the lesson of the lowly ant?

A Leader's Prayer

Time is short, Lord, and if I am to accomplish things of eternal significance I will need Your help. Like Peter in the garden of Gethsemane, I desire to do good, but the spirit is willing and the flesh is weak. Instill in my heart a greater spirit of faithfulness. Help me look beyond the interruptions, demands, deadlines, and long hours to see the souls of those for whom You died. I don't always need to see the results of my efforts, but sometimes it is necessary for the sake of my encouragement. Lord, I am richly blessed, not only in spiritual things, but in earthly things as well. Yet, Lord, You know that sometimes I am inclined to complain or to compare myself to someone who seems to work less and enjoy more. Gracious Savior, I desire to lay up treasures in heaven, not on earth. When a spirit of jealously rolls over me, be quick to remind me that this world is fleeting and its treasure is of only limited value. I desire to value more highly those things of eternal significance. Thank You for the high privilege to work on Your behalf, through Your Son, my Savior. Amen.

Notes

1. Matthew Josephson, *Edison*, (New York: McGraw Hill Book Company, Harold Ober Associates, Inc., 1959), 494.

2. Ibid., 410.

3. Ibid., 431.

4. Ibid.

5. See Romans 12:1

6. Matthew Josephson, 506.

Chapter Fifteen

Chuck Colson
Living with Tension

One area in which Christian leaders typically excel is in presenting and defending their cause. That skill is sharpened and honed through countless encounters, passing conversations, and the exercise of leadership.

Every week pastors are asked to step before their congregations and deliver a logical, well-organized, and illustrated message. Teachers and professors learn to prepare objectives, then develop presentations to accomplish their stated outcome. Institutional spokesmen must carry the torch for their cause, articulating its case for support. The apostle Paul's last words to his young prodigy were a call to sharpen communication skills:

> In the presence of God and of Christ Jesus, who will judge the living and the dead, and in view of His appearing and His kingdom, I give you this charge: Preach the Word; be prepared in season and out of season; correct, rebuke and encourage—with great patience and careful instruction. (2 Timothy 4:1–2)

Christian leaders are permitted to have varying degrees of administrative skill, limited knowledge of accounting techniques, and may be totally lacking in musical ability; but if they are to be successful, they must be better-than-average communicators.

This great strength can be a valuable asset when contending for the faith. It can be an Achilles' heel if used to destroy those who disagree with an approach or direction that falls within the area of human judgment. Christian leaders who use their God-given skill of communication to unbraid and destroy those who oppose their leadership style will never be great in the kingdom of God. The temptation is great. Like Clint Eastwood's portrayal of the confident street cop facing down an inferior punk, our sinful nature whispers, "Go ahead, make my day." Before the critic has finished his first sentence, we have analyzed his argument, predicted his conclusion, and formed a three-part airtight rebuttal.

In my opinion, the character trait that most often separates the great leader from the above-average leader is the ability to avoid needless conflict. Please note carefully the word *needless*. There are occasions when the Gospel demands not only conflict, but our very lives in defense of the truth that leads to eternal life. Most conflict that stalls, impedes, and frustrates ministry, however, is not the Gospel-imperative kind. Critics of leadership style are not to be equated with opponents of the Gospel. The enemy is Satan and those who promote false teaching. Critics of our leadership styles may be sent as the prods and goads of God, intended to keep our efforts honest, humble, and balanced.

The fact that such tension is found within the church should not shake our faith or cause us to wonder about the presence of the Holy Spirit among us. Chuck Colson describes it as the difference between the church of faith and the church of fact. In his thought-provoking book *The Body, Being Light in Darkness* he writes,

> Messy, ambiguous, imperfect? Sure it is. There is no per-
> fect or model church. But we should not despair—for at
> least two reasons. First, tensions allow for a variety of
> expressions which, often confounding human wisdom,
> reach people who might not otherwise be reached. ... Sec-
> ond, this dynamic may well save us all from the one fate
> worse than chaos: triumphalism. That is the very real
> temptation to believe that we have all the truth, thus con-
> fusing ourselves with the kingdom of God.[1]

In his book, Chuck Colson is writing about the church in the broadest sense, namely the diversity that exists in the Christian church across the world. Using the analogy of Paul in his letter to Corinth, Colson points out that the church is a body made up of many members with different functions.[2] It should not escape our notice that sickness and death most often come from disease that cripples and destroys the body from within. Medical experts would encourage a healthier lifestyle, eating habits, and exercise to maintain the body's natural immunities. The body called the church might benefit from the advice.

If we are to withstand attacks from within the body, and live with the tension in a way that does not produce debilitating stress, we need to establish lifestyles, eating habits, and exercise that maintain our spiritual defenses.

Refusing to engage in foolish arguments is a lifestyle choice promoted by Solomon and observed in the life of his father, David. Do you recall the times that God seemingly placed the deranged King Saul within the grasp of David and his wandering band of outlaws? In the cave of Engedi, while searching to kill David, Saul rested within arm's length of David's hiding warriors. Others offered to kill the madman for

David, but he would not permit it.[3] In the wilderness of Ziph, David sneaked into the camp of Saul during the night and took the spear and water jug laying next to the sleeping king. Again, David spared the life of his sworn enemy. On both occasions David reminded Saul that the Lord would judge between them. He was content to let the Lord avenge his wrong.

David's son Solomon learned the lesson well. In the wisdom of his proverbs we are reminded that those who gain anything by force will eventually lose it.[4] We are also taught that little is accomplished through argumentation with fools. In fact, we receive only more heartache and criticism for our effort.[5] Instead, we are advised to walk in our integrity and keep our tongue from saying things we will later regret.[6] We would do well to think long and hard before engaging our critics in useless and potentially harmful arguments. As Solomon advises:

> When words are many, sin is not absent, but he who holds his tongue is wise. The tongue of the righteous is choice silver, but the heart of the wicked is of little value. The lips of the righteous nourish many, but fools die for lack of judgment. The blessing of the LORD brings wealth, and He adds no trouble to it. A fool finds pleasure in evil conduct, but a man of understanding delights in wisdom. What the wicked dreads will overtake him; what the righteous desire will be granted. When the storm has swept by, the wicked are gone, but the righteous stand firm forever. (Proverbs 10:19–25)

By feeding on the Word in this way, Christian leaders are able to withstand the temptation to "give as good as they get." It may seem like difficult counsel, easily said but rarely done. Some are destined to learn this lesson the hard way, like coronary patients who found exercise routines impossible before surgery, but relatively easy after a brush with their own mortality. A near-fatal brush with an ill-willed critic may be necessary to bring Solomon's wisdom into better focus. Take heart, most spiritual leaders confirm that this is one aspect of the faith that tends to get easier with practice. Colson handles it with a sense of humor.

> As it has been said, he writes, "The church is like Noah's ark: The stench would be unbearable if it weren't for the storm outside. This is the church we have. And as imperfect and even repugnant as we find it at times, we need to acknowledge that it is through this church of fact that the truth is proclaimed and portrayed ... admittedly, the pettiness and failures, the division and discord, can be disheartening at times. What a sorry mess we mortals often make of things in the name of the church! But our comfort comes from God's promise that He will build His church—sometimes in extraordinary ways."[7]

More Scriptural Insight

Romans 12:14–21	Why is this good advice?
Acts 15:36–41	Did Paul act wisely or sinfully here?
1 Corinthians 1:10–17	How does this controversy compare to the things the church argues about today?

A Leader's Prayer

Lord, today I must ask for Your patience. I'm the kind of leader that likes unanimity, not only in the Word of God, but in all things. Help me to recall that You made us all different. We don't always see things the same way, nor is it required by Your Word. Help me to be respectful of those who disagree and patient with those who attack and try to draw me into needless controversy. Give me the courage to stand firm on those issues that are decided by Your Word. Lift me up in Your mercy and enable me to lead in such a way that Your concern for the lost would always be paramount in the things I do, plan, and promote. Help me, as a leader, to be sensitive to others who also lead and need encouragement for their tasks. Give me the grace needed to suppress my desire to criticize their leadership so long as it is done to Your glory. Remind me that different styles reach different needs and You desire all to be saved and come to the knowledge of the truth. Help me today to be a better, more effective leader of Your people. All this I ask boldly in the name of Jesus, my Lord and my Savior. Amen.

Notes

1. Charles Colson, *The Body—Being Light in Darkness,* (Dallas, TX: Word Publishing, 1992), 72. Used by permission. All rights reserved.

2. See 1 Corinthians 12.

3. See 1 Samuel 24.

4. See Proverbs 1:18–19.

5. See Proverbs 9:7–8.

6. See Proverbs 10:9ff.

7. Charles Colson, 73.

CHAPTER SIXTEEN

CAROL HOWER

Encouragement

Love does make up for us having to be apart. You can hang this on your wall and be reminded of your little lonely red-head in Texas who misses you with all her heart.

Me

y dear wife, Carol, wrote those words almost 25 years ago when we were young sweethearts attending a Lutheran college in Austin, Texas. We had each returned to our respective homes for the summer; Carol to Corpus Christi, Texas, and me, to Huntington, Indiana. She wrote her note on the back of a small round picture of two pixies kissing under the words "Love makes our burdens seem lighter."

That treasure, along with countless others, now resides in a cardboard file box in the back of an upstairs storage closet. We have three boxes like it, one each for our boys, Joshua and Jacob, and one that Carol and I share. Our box is filled with memorabilia of our relationship and the experiences of our 20 years as wife and husband.

Carol is right. Love makes our burdens seem lighter. And love makes up for having to be apart ... also for sickness, uncertainty, parental angst, for lives lived far from home, long hours, demanding schedules, for sacrifices great and small. No wonder the Bible says, "These three remain: faith, hope and love. But the greatest of these is love" (1 Corinthians 13:13).

It takes encouragement to succeed as a Christian leader. Few ever succeed without it, and it's beyond me why any would want to. Over the years Carol has written many notes of encouragement, sometimes on the back of a birthday card, but just as often on a loose sheet of paper tenderly placed under my pillow. She comes by it naturally; her folks called weekly throughout our seminary training and continued right on through those critical years in our first congregation. Now Carol returns the favor, flying to Texas as often as possible and calling faithfully to check on the condition of her mother, diagnosed with terminal cancer.

Like all couples, we've shared many experiences in our 20 years together. The feeling of inadequacy was so great in those early days. Everything was so new! I was a new husband, new father, and a new pastor living in a new location, all within a relatively short period of time. I actually felt sorry for those folks I married, buried, and baptized, feeling they deserved someone with a little more experience ministering to them at such crucial moments in their life. But then Carol's father would remind me that our little Michigan congregation had prayed for us to come and they were thrilled to have us serve them, no matter how ineffective I felt. It takes encouragement to be a Christian leader.

The Lord is good. He has always surrounded us with friends of encouragement. I am of the firm conviction that although it takes only four years to get through the seminary, it takes another 10 for congregational members to finish the training. Seminary professors who advise students to avoid close friendships with members of their congregations are sadly mistaken. No one can do effective ministry in a vacuum. How could David have survived without the friendship of Jonathan, and later, his mighty men of valor? They were friends to the end, and by them David's hand was strengthened.

The encouragement of friends broadens and matures us as faithful leaders. I was not raised in a home that readily embraced or was quick to express personal sentiment. Thanks to friends more sensitive than me, we now rarely leave each other's homes without forming a prayer circle, hand in hand and shoulder to shoulder. Don Wharton, a Christian singer and songwriter living in Nashville, is one of those friends who knows the value of encouragement. He wrote a truly great song with "Encouragement" as the title and theme.

So now I'm caught in an artist's dilemma;
Torn between two raging needs.
One is the need to make a living
While the other is the need to make you see

That life is beautiful
And life is good,
But life will never, never be easy
Like we sometimes wish it could.

But I believe we all were meant to succeed.
I believe we were all born to win.
You might stand alone at the top of the vict'ry stand,
But you get there with the love and support of your
*   friends.*

It takes a pat on the back.
It takes a hand to hold.
It takes some words of hope
That touch your heart and soul.

(Chorus) It takes encouragement.
Encouragement.
That fragile bridge between your dreams and
*   accomplishment.*
Surround yourself in this human experiment
With those who proudly wear the badge of
*   encouragement.[2]*

"Life is beautiful and life is good, but life will never, never be easy, like we sometimes wish it could." I don't know what moved Don to write those words, but much of his music is inspired by his love for his precious wife, Leslie. Like Don and Leslie, we have come to understand that life is never, never going to be easy like we sometimes wish it could.

When we were young and starting out, we fell into the trap of thinking if only circumstances around us changed, then life would be less hectic and more fulfilling. My first assignment out of the seminary was to a small congregation, averaging 60 worshippers a weekend. My salary was $6,800 and a parsonage. Carol gave up her teaching position (which incidentally paid more than my first assignment) and off we went to our first call. Despite our misgivings, the people were good and we prospered in their midst. Over the years we began to realize our happiness and fulfillment had little to do with our circumstance and a lot to do with our faith and attitudes.

Ten years ago Carol wrote a note that reflected that change.

I love you when I'm happy.

I love you when I'm sad.
And, gee, I even love you,
When I'm feeling kinda mad.
I love you when you're near me.
Or, when you're far away ...
And, Gosh, I'm glad I've got you—
Cause I love you more each day!

She signed it,

"Love bears all things!" 1 Corinthians 13:7 RSV
You're right to say our life isn't boring!
Our life together as parents is a challenge, one that we
must work together.
Thanks for being a faithful father, who loves and cares
for his family.
From the mother of your boys!

Encouragement is one of the chief reasons for New Testament worship. The writer of Hebrews wrote, "Let us hold unswervingly to the hope we profess, for He who promised is faithful. And let us consider how we may spur one another on towards love and good deeds. Let us not give up meeting together, as some are in the habit of doing, but let us encourage one another—and all the more as you see the Day approaching" (Hebrews 10:23–25).

The Bible consistently talks about things getting more and more difficult before the end of the world. For this reason the apostle says we are going to need each other more than ever as time marches on. It should not surprise us to see that Jesus modeled this behavior as His own suffering and crucifixion approached. Before going down to Jerusalem, He met His Father on the hill of transfiguration to discuss His "exodus"[2] which would occur in Jerusalem. He drew strength for the coming days from fellowship with the great prophets Moses and Elijah, as well as the companionship of his close friends: Peter, James, and John. Later, in the Garden of Gethsemane, He would repeat the experience, again asking Peter, James, and John to stay awake with Him in His hour of need.[3]

The proverb is wise that says, "A friend loves at all times, and a brother is born for adversity." When days are darkest, the light of encouragement burns brightest and is most needed. It takes encouragement to be a Christian leader.

More Scriptural Insight

Acts 4:36–37, 11:22–26	What was so special about Barnabas?
Romans 16:1–16	Why was so much Scripture "wasted" recalling people?
2 Corinthians 8:1–6	How did the people of Macedonia express encouragement?

A Leader's Prayer

Thank You, O Lord, for the encouragers of this world. It seems for every person called upon to lead, there are dozens who lend support in ways unnoticed. Before You, O Lord, the gift of service is more highly regarded than those who exercise authority. Grant that we might aspire to the high office of servanthood and encouragement. We especially thank You for songwriters and musicians who practice long hours and work tirelessly for the sake of our encouragement. We also offer our prayer for the many spouses who have quietly and effectively supported Christian leaders as encouragers. Bless and prosper those who quietly go about the work of writing thank-yous, remembering birthdays, visiting the elderly and infirm, those who embrace the calling of encouragement. Help us to see the need for encouragement more each day. Help us to uplift and encourage fellow Christians in the midst of their battles and heartaches. Let our pulpits reflect Your love for those who suffer and need the peace that the world cannot give. Through us encourage others and bring many to faith in Jesus Christ, our Lord. Amen.

Notes

1. Don Wharton, *enCOURAGEment,* Cassette and CD, (Nashville: Matrix Recording, 1993). Used by permission.

2. Luke 9:31—Luke uses this Old Testament word in the Greek version of his gospel to describe the coming release from bondage that would occur in Jerusalem.

3. See Matthew 26:36–46.

CHAPTER SEVENTEEN

ROBERT E. LEE
Gracious

On the gymnasium wall of the Lutheran seminary in St. Louis, you will find the words "Modest in victory. Gracious in defeat." It is a good motto for a Christian sports team. I wonder how things might improve if every graduating pastor made that simple phrase the defining quality of his Christian leadership.

To be gracious is to be Christlike. "The law was given through Moses; grace and truth came through Jesus Christ" (John 1:17). Few American heroes ever demonstrated this quality more consistently than Robert E. Lee, the commander of the Confederate forces during the tumultuous Civil War. "Modest in victory, gracious in defeat" would be a fitting epitaph for General Lee.

It should not surprise us that men of grace and courage are admired by both friends and enemies alike. In a conversation between the generals after the war, Lee commented on the visage of Meade saying, "Meade, years are telling on you; your hair is getting quite gray."

"Ah, General Lee," was Meade's prompt reply, "it is not the

work of years; you are responsible for my gray hairs!"[1]

For the months and years after the surrender at Appomattox, Lee's residence was so besieged by visiting soldiers, grateful Southerners, and worthy opponents that the general had to be shielded from the constant press of admirers. Lee's namesake, in his excellent collection of remembrances, letters, and historic documents, commented on the gracious nature of his father. "My father was gentle, kind, and polite to all and never willingly, so far as I know, refused to see anyone."[2]

In leading the Southern resistance, Lee's motive was not the defense of slavery, but a strong belief in the moral right of a state to establish its own laws. So highly regarded was Lee, a colonel in the U.S. army, Lincoln asked him to assume the place of the aged Scott, and lead the Union army.[3] He declined, resigned his commission, and returned to his beloved Virginia, praying for a peaceful outcome of the growing tensions. Even in his resignation to General Scott, Lee was characteristically gracious, "I have experienced nothing but kindness from my superiors, and a most cordial friendship from my comrades. ... I shall carry to the grave the most grateful recollections of your kind consideration, and your name and fame shall always be dear to me. Save in defense of my native State, I never desire again to draw my sword."[4]

Although his family owned slaves, the war for General Lee was about states' rights. At the height of the fighting, the confederate commander, as executor of his father's will, took time to fulfill its request, granting freedom to all the slaves and servants of their house.[5] When his own son, General W. H. F. Lee (Fitzhugh) was wounded and then captured, so loyal were Lee's own servants that one risked his life to "escape from his liberators," stole and returned to Lee a favorite family horse which had been confiscated for Union service.[6]

Lee's gentle character was quite remarkable, especially in

consideration of the life and death decisions he made for thousands of men. His letters and dispatches give evidence of a deep Christian faith. As an invocation of God's mercy, Lee called for a day of fasting and prayer.

> Soldiers! We have sinned against Almighty God. We have forgotten His signal mercies, and have cultivated a revengeful, haughty, and boastful spirit. We have not remembered that the defenders of a just cause should be pure in His eyes; that "our times are in His hands," and we have relied too much on our own arms for the achievement of our independence. God is our only refuge and our strength. Let us humble ourselves before Him. Let us confess our many sins, and beseech Him to give us a higher courage, a purer patriotism, and more determined will; that He will convert the hearts of our enemies; that He will hasten the time when war, with its sorrows and sufferings, shall cease, and that He will give us a name and place among the nations of the earth. (August 13, 1863)[7]

Lee gave all credit to his soldiers and subordinate generals who carried out his plans. When the formidable Andrew "Stonewall" Jackson, returning unexpected from a scouting expedition, was wounded by his own pickets, General Lee wrote, "You are better off than I am, for while you have only lost your left, I have lost my right arm." When Jackson's wounds turned more serious and he succumbed, Lee poured out his heart to his wife in a letter saying, "I know not how to replace him. God's will be done! I trust He will raise up someone to take his place."[8]

In perhaps one of the fiercest cavalry battles of the war, General J. E. B. Stuart, head of all Confederate cavalry, led three brigades of horsemen against the strength of Grant's army as they approached Richmond. Stuart, "the eyes and ears of General Lee," fell mortally wounded and soon died.

One of Lee's captains recalled the general's deep silence upon hearing the tragic news. Lee quietly reflected, "He never brought me a piece of false information," then turned away with tears in his eyes.[9]

General Lee's continuous praise of his soldiers and of the Southern people's sacrificial spirit endeared him as a leader. They considered it an honor to touch him or even his famous confederate-gray horse, Traveller. The admiration was well earned. In the worse weather, Lee would not relent to sleep in abandoned homes or even barns, reserving such shelters for use by the sick and wounded. In a show of solidarity with his troops, the general slept only in tents. Even after the surrender, on his way home to his wife in Richmond, the general stopped to visit his eldest brother and despite their strongest urging, when bedtime came, he returned to join his small band of men in a tent pitched by the roadside.[10]

Although eschewing the glory, and praising everyone else for any success achieved through his skilled leadership, Robert E. Lee willingly bore criticism alone. When it became obvious that further fighting would be suicidal, he made the unpopular decision to surrender without a fatal last stand. "I know they will say hard things of us," he stated. "They will not understand how we were overwhelmed by numbers; but that is not the question ... the question is, 'Is it right to surrender this army?' If it is right, then I will take all the responsibility."[11]

He bargained successfully with Grant to supply his starving men with rations, gained their pardon, and even permission for them to return to their farms and homes with their horses. A magnanimous Grant also allowed the hero of the South to return quietly to his home in Richmond. His son recalls that until the time of his death, General Lee was in constant receipt of lucrative offers of houses, lands, money, and prominent positions in various business ventures and institutions. His standard reply remained, "I am deeply grateful; I cannot desert my native State in the hour of her adversity. I must abide her fortunes, and share her fate."[12] He lived only five years more, dying October 12, 1870. He was 63 years old. His final years were spent restoring war-stricken Washington College in Lexington, Virginia, which was later renamed Washington and Lee University in his honor.

Gracious leadership is contagious. Lee used his considerable influence to help the people of the South accept the consequences of their defeat, saving them from what could have been more severe treatment from Federal troops. Grant was so impressed by Lee's spirit that when an indictment of treason was leveled against the leaders of the Confederacy, he insisted that the terms of the surrender granted amnesty to these officers as well as the troops they commanded.

Jesus urged we maintain a gracious spirit towards those who trouble us:

> You have heard it was said, "Eye for eye, and tooth for tooth." But I tell you, Do not resist an evil person. If someone strikes you on the right cheek, turn to him the other also. And if someone wants to sue you and take your tunic, let him have your cloak as well. If someone forces you to go one mile, go with him two miles. Give to the one who asks you, and do not turn away from the one who wants to borrow from you." (Matthew 5:38–42)

The Savior's words are in a section of the Bible we call "The Sermon on the Mount." His words do more than describe a different ethic. They are a three-chapter description of what it means to live as a child of God with a heavenly perspective. When he finished his instruction, Matthew observed, "The crowds were amazed at His teaching" (7:28). Gracious behavior is not expected and seldom taught.

The attitudes of which Jesus speaks are impossible to maintain without a change of heart. Lee's faith in Christ and his attempt to emulate his Savior is repeatedly evidenced in his correspondence. Consider his Christmas Day letter to his wife in 1862:

> ... I will commence this holy day by writing to you. My heart is filled with gratitude to Almighty God for unspeakable mercies with which He has blessed us in this day, for those He has granted us from the beginning of life, and particularly for those He has vouchsafed us during this past year. What should have become of us without His crowning help and protection? Oh if our people would only recognize it and cease from vain selfish boasting and adulation, how strong would be my belief in final success and happiness in our country![13]

Christians who have trouble being gracious should take note. Typically, those who show greatest appreciation for the grace of God are most gracious unto others. By contrast, Christians inclined to be vengeful, difficult, or who practice cunning are a walking indictment of a weak and immature faith.

Upon concluding the seven petitions of the Lord's Prayer, Jesus immediately expounded on the one requiring a gracious heart. He states in the strongest words, "If you forgive when they sin against you, your heavenly Father will also forgive you. But if you do not forgive men their sins, your Father will not forgive your sins" (Matthew 6:14–15). When Peter asked how many times a Christian had to be gracious, Jesus told him a story about a great king who had forgiven his debtor an enormous sum. When that same debtor was unforgiving of an insignificant amount, the master "turned him over to the jailers to be tortured, until he should pay all he owed."[14] Jesus was not talking money. As Christians who have been forgiven innumerable sins, we are to reflect the love of Christ in our attitudes toward others. We will be gracious by nature ... the new nature that lives by faith in Jesus.

More Scriptural Insight

Genesis 50:15–21	Why did Joseph's brothers fear him?
Matthew 5:23–26	How important is peace between people?
Luke 23:34	What motivated Christ to be gracious?

A Leader's Prayer

Lord, sometimes it is hard to be gracious. Open my eyes to see the value of a life that refuses to be bitter, vengeful, always keeping a growing list of wrongs suffered. Enable me to better appreciate Your gracious attitude towards me so that I can in turn be more gracious and kind to others. Thank You for the kindness of those around me. Bless my friends and those that encourage others through their consistent cheerful demeanor. Enable me to draw strength from their example and to emulate their faith in action. When difficult situations develop, remind me of my opportunity to be gracious, not in a false or superficial way, but sincere and glad. Help Christians to be a leaven of kindness in our often callous world. Enable me to see past the immediate difficulty so that I might maintain a better perspective on what is important and what is relatively unimportant. Don't let Satan or others under his influence entrap me with little hurts and insults. Thank You for the great gift of salvation and access to Your throne of grace through Jesus Christ my Lord. Amen.

Notes

1. Robert E. Lee, Jr., *Recollections and Letters of General Robert E. Lee, by His Son, Captain Robert E. Lee*, (New York: Konecky & Konecky, 1992), 154.

2. Ibid., 158.

3. Robert Paul Jordan, *The Civil War,* (Washington, D. C.: Special Publications Division of The National Geographic Society, 1969), 48.

4. Robert E. Lee, Jr., 25.

5. Ibid., 89–90.

6. Ibid., 100.

7. Ibid., 105–106.

8. Ibid., 94.

9. Ibid., 125.

10. Ibid., 155.

11. Ibid., 151.

12. Ibid., 170.

13. Ibid., 88.

14. See Matthew 18:21–35.

CHAPTER EIGHTEEN

TOM PETERS

Risk

My boys are athletes and enjoy wearing shirts that express their absolute commitment to victory. My oldest has a shirt with the message "We were all born crying. Some of us outgrew it." On the front, just above the pocket, the words "Risk It" are printed. It is impossible to be a great leader without risk, and those who have a low tolerance for failure would be better off finding someone to follow.

Solomon understood the principle of risk. He wrote,

> Whoever watches the wind will not plant; whoever looks at the clouds will not reap. As you do not know the path of the wind, or how the body is formed in a mother's womb, so you cannot understand the work of God, the Maker of all things. Sow your seed in the morning, and at evening let not your hands be idle, for you do not know which will succeed, whether this or that, or whether both will do equally well. (Ecclesiastes 11:4–6)

We could put Solomon's words on a T-shirt with the motto "Risk It" above the pocket! Every Christian leader knows exactly what Solomon meant. Unrestrained effort (spelled P-A-S-S-I-O-N) is a key ingredient in the recipe of achievement. The French Foreign Legion's willingness to risk is legendary. They live and die by the motto: "No Regrets!" The expanded theme is equally forceful, "If I fall—push me. If I stumble—pick me up. If I retreat—shoot me."

Perhaps no one better exemplifies that attitude than the tenacious business analyst Tom Peters. His books *Thriving on Chaos, In Search of Excellence* and *A Passion for Excellence* have been bestsellers. Each urges absolute commitment to excellence as perceived by the customer, and offers a defense for those oft misunderstood innovators of new technology.

Tom also writes a monthly column that is carried in many of the business journals of America. His April 1991 article entitled "Get Lucky—40 ways to shake the status quo and bring a little innovation into life" certainly grabs your attention. If your organization is stuck in a rut, or slipped into reverse, Peters suggests you try one of these ideas:

1. At bats. More times at the plate, more hits.
2. Try it. Cut the baloney and get on with something.
3. Ready, Fire, Aim! (Rather than ready, aim, aim, aim, aim. ...)
4. Anything worth doing is worth doing poorly. Courtesy of Johnsonville Foods CEO Ralph Staver, who reminds us that the first phone and airplane were nothing to write home about—but you have to start somewhere.
5. Read odd stuff.
6. Visit odd places. Want to "see" some speed? Visit CNN.
7. Make odd friends.
8. Hire odd people. Boring folks, boring ideas.
9. Cultivate odd hobbies. Raise orchids. Race yaks.
14. Applaud passion. "Dispassionate innovator" is an oxymoron.

15. Pursue failure. Failure is success's only launching pad.
    (The bigger, the better!)
16. Root out, "Not Invented Here." Swipe from the best!
18. Listen to everyone. Ideas come from anywhere.
19. Don't listen to anyone! Trust your inner ear.
20. Get fired. (More than once is OK.) If you're not pushing
    hard enough to get sacked, you're not pushing hard.
31. Spend half your time with "outsiders." Distributors and
    vendors will give you more ideas in five minutes than
    another five-hour committee meeting.
32. Spend half of your "outsider time" with wacko outsiders!
38. Start a "Corporate Traitors Hall of Fame." "Renegades"
    are not good enough; you need people who despise what
    you stand for!
40. Vary your pattern. Eat a different breakfast cereal. Take a
    different route to work.[1]

I think you get the idea. The only thing that happens when
you maintain the status quo is the status quo. A new goal
demands a new strategy and new strategies always provide
risks at no extra charge. When it comes to effective leadership, people can be divided into two camps—those who
thought and never did, and those who did and never thought.
Leaders of every stripe must free themselves from the fears of
failure, rejection, and loss.

How many ministries have been stymied in their mission
because they feared loss of support from the old guard, or loss
of esteem from their more conventional peers? Jesus had little
time for such "leadership" in the kingdom of God. He said,
"No one can serve two masters. Either he will hate the one
and love the other, or he will be devoted to the one and
despise the other. You cannot serve both God and money"
(Matthew 6:24) ... or your critics ... or your reputation ... or

your staunchest supporters ... or district supervisors ... or your pastor. Anytime others counsel a viewpoint that leads away from God or opposes His will, our response is clear, "We must obey God rather than men! ... We are witnesses of these things, and so is the Holy Spirit, whom God has given to those who obey Him" (Acts 5:29, 32).

I like the counsel of the radio pastor who was answering a question about overcoming adversity in life. The listener had asked what steps the pastor would recommend to extract himself from the financial sinkhole he was experiencing. The pastor asked if he were tithing.

> "How can I tithe when I owe so much money?" was the understandable response.
>
> "And how can I help you, if the Lord Himself is frustrating you?" came the reply of the preacher.

The pastor based his counsel on the clear words of Jesus in the Sermon on the Mount. "But seek first His kingdom and His righteousness, and all these things will be given to you as well" (Matthew 6:33). There is a risk in taking God at His word. In the matter of tithing the prophet even describes it as a "risk" or a "test."

> "Test me in this," says the LORD Almighty, "and see if I will not throw open the floodgates of heaven and pour out so much blessing that you will not have room enough for it. I will prevent pests from devouring your crops, and the vines in your fields will not cast their fruit," says the LORD Almighty. Then all the nations will call you blessed, for yours will be a delightful land," says the LORD Almighty. (Malachi 3:10–12)

Too many people do what seems logical without ever asking if it is godly. To "risk" by following the counsel of God is really no risk at all, not only in the matter of tithing, but also in the settlement of disputes, the establishment of a sound marriage, the nurture of children, the running of a Christian ministry or any other matter upon which the Lord has provided direction in His Word. When we worry too much about the consequence of choosing the narrow road, we are really struggling against the greatest and first commandment, "You shall have no other gods before Me" (Exodus 20:3). Restated by Jesus to mean, "Love the Lord your God with all your heart and with all your soul and with all your mind" (Matthew 22:37).

The apostle, like every Christian leader, faced tremendous pressure to conform. His response to his critics at Galatia, reveals his firm conviction. "Am I now trying to win the approval of men, or of God?" Paul wrote, "Or am I trying to please men? If I were still trying to please men, I would not be a servant of Christ" (Galatians 1:10). It was a calculated risk by Paul, and a costly one too. The cost for Paul, and all the apostles except John, was martyrdom. It is sad to admit, their deaths often came at the instigation, and sometimes the very hands, of religious zealots convinced they were doing God a favor. Not every risk has a happy ending, but every risk taken for the cause of Christ and the mission of salvation has an eternal consequence.

The risk of Christian leadership parallels the risk required to achieve in industry. In *A Passion for Excellence,* the book he co-authored with Nancy Austin, Peters quotes a number successful businessmen who all agree: "A really new idea at first has only one believer ... fanaticism is crucial ... whenever anything is being accomplished, it is being done, I have learned, by a monomaniac with a mission."[2]

Risk is a part of any effort with the potential to make a lasting and important difference in life. Unfortunately, very few are willing to risk, even for things of eternal consequence. Playing it safe and staying "within the box" seems to be the preferred method of operation. James E. Byrnes, U. S. Supreme Court justice, once said, "Too many people are thinking of security instead of opportunity. They seem more afraid of life than death."[3]

When Paul was confronted by a choice of life or death, he opted for life with all its risks, reasoning; "This would mean fruitful labor for me ... and convinced of this, I know I will remain and I will continue with all of you for your progress and joy in faith. So that through my being with you again your joy in Christ Jesus will overflow on account of me" (Philippians 1:22, 25–26). Life with Christ is worth the risks.

More Scriptural Insight

Ecclesiastes 9:10–12	How would you summarize Solomon's advice?
Daniel 3:16–18	Are the faithful always spared when they risk? Explain.
John 11:7–16	What was the risk for returning to Judea? What was the outcome?

A Leader's Prayer

Lord, when You called me to be a leader of Your people, I was not fully aware of the consequences. Sometimes, in my weak moments, I am tempted to complain that the risk is not worth the effort, the pain, the rejection, and the loneliness of leadership. I take great comfort in the example and victory of Your Son, my Savior, Jesus. Help me to remember that a crown of life awaits those who are faithful until the end. In the interim, be quick to strengthen me for the task of leading. I don't ask that You make my way easy, but stand by my side to encourage and uphold me with Your powerful Spirit. I want to serve You and be faithful to Your calling. Help me to be more discerning of Your will so that I might know when to risk and when not to. Lord, as You know, there is always great pressure to conform. Jesus was asked not to heal on the Sabbath, to submit to godless authority, and to succumb to the devil's temptation in order to avoid the consequence of our salvation. Thank You for my salvation so dearly won, and enable me to gladly lead those for whom You sacrificed Your Son upon the cross. To You alone be all glory, honor, and praise. Amen.

Notes

1. Tom Peters, *St. Louis Business Journal,* April 8–14, 1991, 2C. © 1991 TPG Communications. All rights reserved. Reprinted with permission.

2. Tom Peters and Nancy Austin, *A Passion for Excellence—The Leadership Difference,* (New York: Random House, 1985), 135.

3. Howard E. Ferguson, *The Edge—the guide to fulfilling dreams, maximizing success and enjoying a lifetime of achievement,* (Cleveland: Getting The Edge Company, 1991), 5–14.

CHAPTER NINETEEN

MARTIN LUTHER
Tenacity

My wife, Carol, and I both enjoy the adventure known as "antiquing." We are not purists by any means. We have been known to arise early on a Saturday morning to enjoy breakfast out and several hours of "garage sale shopping." Often we return empty-handed or may have spent only $2.50 on sweatshirts Carol presents to young children of fellow staff members. The reward is in the "fun of the hunt" regardless of the outcome.

Since we live in Missouri, we also have opportunity to pass through small farming communities where hand-painted signs advertise "antiques" or "flea market" down this street or side road. When time allows, we often stop.

I have long searched for a simple picture of Abraham Lincoln like the one that hangs in the eighth grade room of our Christian school. While Carol is busy looking at plates and furniture, I am off in the recesses of the shops looking at old pictures and dusty books. Most of the autobiographies and leadership books in my library have been secured in this fashion.

This past summer we made the rounds through some country stores in a nearby small town. While Carol was looking through a box of Currier & Ives plates, I descended a set of rickety stairs into a small and dimly lit basement. There on the wall hung two classic items—not Mr. Lincoln, but an old picture of Martin Luther and a framed Navy recruitment poster from World War II. Carol's father is retired from the Navy and volunteers as a tour guide on the aircraft carrier *Lexington* in Corpus Christi. I knew the poster would be a great gift.

The picture of Luther was in excellent condition. Dated 1902, it was done in black and white. Storm clouds roll behind him as he looks resolutely and determined to the heavens. When we checked out, I asked the store owner how long Martin had been hanging on the basement wall? He glanced down at the picture and responded, "Is that who he is?" I wondered if he thought the picture had come with the frame! The 15 dollar price tag reflected his lack of appreciation for what is now one of our prized possessions.

The picture reflects the character I most respect about the great reformer. It shows the depth of his tenacity and the strength of his resolve.

The depth of Luther's integrity is perhaps best seen in the confrontation he had with representatives of Rome at the Diet of Worms. His elector, Frederick, reminded Emperor Charles of his coronation oath that no German would be tried outside of Germany, and that no citizen could be condemned without a public hearing. Worms was the place chosen for the trial of Luther. He was charged as a heretic who openly opposed the pope and his teachings. At the hearing, 25 of Luther's books were presented as evidence against him. Luther openly acknowledged the writings as his own. Portions were read aloud to show how they disagreed with the teachings of

Rome. Luther was asked if he would defend them, or publicly recant any of the positions he had taken.

The accused asked for time to weigh his answer. In the interest of fairness, Emperor Charles and John Eck, the pope's emissary, granted Luther 24 hours to render his decision. The next day, April 18, 1521, dawned warm and humid, but the large meeting room was packed to capacity. After dividing his writings into three categories, Luther defended the first two stacks as representing the historic faith of the church which none could deny.

Concerning the third group he said, "In these, I attacked certain persons whom I thought to be enemies of the Gospel. I admit that I may have used unkind language here and there. For this I apologize. But I can't take back what I have said in defending God's truth. If I did, then sin and evil would increase their power. Show me from the Bible where I have taught falsely. If you can, then I will be the first to burn my books. Your majesty, I put myself in your hands. Please do not let my enemies make you angry at me without a good reason."[1]

After a private consultation, it was determined that Luther had not really answered the question. He had not retracted anything but only asked his accusers to highlight areas of concern. Luther was told to end his debating of Scripture and give a simple answer—"Do you or do you not recant your books and the errors in them?"

There would be no further discussion, no further debate. Luther now spoke the words for which he is most remembered:

> Since your Majesty and your lordships want a simple, clear and true answer, I will give it, neither horned or toothed. Unless I am convinced by the teachings of Holy Scripture or by sound reasoning—for I do not believe either the pope or councils alone, since they have often made mistakes and have even said the exact opposite

about the same point—I am bound by the Scriptures I
have quoted and my conscience is held captive. I cannot
and will not recant anything, for to go against conscience
is neither safe nor right. God help me. Here I stand, I can
do not other! Amen.[2]

Tenacity is a necessary trait for Christian leadership. As
any leader can tell, there is constant and unending pressure to
compromise. Well-intentioned people and even Christian
friends often counsel compromise, believing the outcome justifies the action. Despite the high cost, and the threats of ruin,
Christian leaders must stand firm in their Christian resolve.

Jesus once told His disciples, "Do not be afraid of those
who can kill the body but cannot kill the soul. Rather, be
afraid of the One who can destroy both soul and body in hell.
Are not two sparrows sold for a penny? Yet not one of them
will fall to the ground apart from the will of your Father. And
even the very hairs of your head are all numbered. So don't be
afraid; you are worth more than many sparrows" (Matthew
10:28–31).

The Lord builds two arguments. First, we should realize
that compromise of God's Word makes no sense. If we believe
that God is the creator of heaven and earth, and that no one
succeeds or fails without His favor, why would anyone ever
knowingly oppose His will? The truly wise will always side
with the Lord for His protection and for the strong support
that He can provide. It is sheer foolishness to oppose the
greater to appease the lesser.

Secondly, Jesus reminds us that the Lord knows our plight.
The Lord, in fact, concerns Himself with much more trivial
matters—the care of sparrows and the counting of hair. If He
cares about such insignificant matters, it stands to reason He
will not leave or forsake us in issues of greater consequence!

Stand your ground. The Lord's wisdom turns the whole

world upside down. To decide a matter because it has the certain approval of those in control will eventually result in failure if it is not God's will. Conversely, to do what seems destined for certain failure, if it is clearly the will of the Lord, will succeed despite all that stands against it!

The Christian leader must stand in truth even if he stands alone. This position is guaranteed to produce times of loneliness and criticism. It is clearly not the approach most will choose. Yet, tenacious integrity is what sets godly leaders apart from well-intentioned, but lackluster populists who live lives of low achievement and few accomplishments.

The words of the prophet Hanani to the obscure Asa, king of Israel, should be seared on the heart of every Christian leader. "The eyes of the LORD range throughout the earth to strengthen those whose hearts are fully committed to Him. You have done a foolish thing, and from now on you will be at war" (2 Chronicles 16:9). Earlier in his reign, when outnumbered and without hope, Asa had turned to the Lord and stood in his integrity. The Lord granted him a great victory over superior forces. But at the time of the prophet's rebuke, Asa, now a wealthy and more secure king, had rejected the Lord and tried to buy national security from a foreign and ungodly power. It was his undoing.

The godly leader is a tenacious leader. He is willing to travel the less traveled roads, knowing that the Lord provides.

Luther, and the Christian world, would discover the wisdom of his stand at Worms. Later that same year, he would write his most well-known Christian hymn "A Mighty Fortress Is Our God." The third stanza reveals the source of Luther's tenacity.

Though devils all the world should fill, All eager to devour us
We tremble not, we fear no ill, They shall not overpow'r us.

This world's prince may still Scowl fierce as he will,
He can harm us none! He's judged; the deed is done;
One little word can fell him.

More Scriptural Insight

Psalm 37	Don't worry when men of this world seem to succeed in evil.
1 Samuel 15:17–35	Consider the outcome of King Saul's compromise.
1 Peter 4:12–19	Difficulty in the cause of Christ should not surprise us.

A Leader's Prayer

Lord, You know how lonely Christian leadership can be. When I stand with You, I sometimes see even my closest friends and other Christian leaders distance themselves, or urge my compromise. During such soul-searching times, be close, Lord. I don't want to walk a lonely path of my own making, but I am willing to walk with You. Help me to find peace in the clarity of Your Word, and then grant me the strength to follow its counsel. I thank You for those who have gone ahead, for their example. Help me take courage and to remember I am not alone. Like You reminded Elijah, I'm sure there are others who have "not bent the knee to Baal." Keep me from self-pity and help me find happiness in service to You. There is much to do and great satisfaction in doing it for You. Keep me always close to Your heart. In the name of the Lord and giver of life, Jesus Christ. Amen.

Notes

1. Frederick Nohl, *Martin Luther, Hero of Faith,* (St. Louis: Concordia Publishing House, 1963), 65.

2. Ibid, 66.

CHAPTER TWENTY

RUTH BELL GRAHAM
Unconditional Love

Have you noticed there are special moments in life which people enjoy but rarely do? Things like

Making homemade soup.

Taking walks in the rain.

Saying bedside prayers with teenagers.

Taking as many pictures of the second child as they did their first.

Hugging their spouse.

Eatting a meal by candlelight.

Dropping by the house of a friend just to say hi.

Using the camcorder.

Sending postcards.

Leaving love notes under pillows.

Stopping for ice cream.

Bringing flowers home for no reason.

Pulling taffy or making popcorn balls.

Singing songs with friends at the piano.

All of these "little things" are the stuff of which love is

made. Christian leaders sometimes run the danger of being too busy about "important" things to make the time for such trivial pursuits. How many families must crash and burn before we realize the simple truth of the Bible: "Love never fails. But where there are prophecies, they will cease; where there are tongues, they will be stilled; where there is knowledge, it will pass away. ... These three remain: faith, hope and love. But the greatest of these is love" (1 Corinthians 13:8, 13).

Christian leaders are not immune from heartache of the worst kind. Many of the great ones felt it: Abraham, Isaac, Jacob, Eli, Samuel, David, and his wise son Solomon. They all felt the heartache of a wayward child. Those closest to us are best positioned to inflict the wound. Often it is not an intentional blow, but accidentally caused by a child's pursuit of goals and dreams at variance with the Gospel. Christian leaders have often "suffered much" and "paid the price" for the very things their loved ones may momentarily or even permanently reject. The pain is not unlike the rejection the Lord must have experienced when Adam and Eve pursued the enticement of forbidden fruit. It always hurts to see those you love pursue their destruction.

How is a Christian leader to handle such prodigals? Some well-intentioned friends will surely help recall the passage,

> If anyone sets his heart on being an overseer (pronounced: "Christian leader"), he desires a noble task. Now the ["Christian leader"] must be above reproach, the husband of but one wife, temperate, self-controlled, respectable, hospitable, able to teach, not given to drunkenness, not violent but gentle, not quarrelsome, not a lover of money. He must manage his own family well and see that his children obey him with proper respect. (If anyone does not know how to manage his own family, how can he take care of God's church?). 1 Timothy 3:1–5

Does Paul mean that if our families fall, we are disqualified for service? This cannot be the correct interpretation, less the Lord Himself be deemed guilty for the failure of the first family. The Lord is holding us accountable for our behavior. Faithful leadership must be demonstrated first in our home before we exercise spiritual authority over others. How can we lead others spiritually if we are not demonstrating "temperate, self-controlled, respectable, and hospitable" behavior in our home? We demonstrate faithful leadership when our families evidence Christ in their lives. We have special opportunities to demonstrate faithful leadership when our families succumb to an assault of Satan and wander from the fold.

Evangelist Billy Graham and his wife, Ruth, know from experience the challenge of this special kind of adversity. Two of their five children were "spiritual wanderers" who strayed for a time from the fold of faith. In her book *Prodigals and Those Who Love Them,* Ruth provides counsel for those experiencing the anguish of a child gone astray.

Survival and successful intervention mean knowing the difference between "our part" and "God's part."

> "We mothers" she writes, "must take care of the possible, and trust God for the impossible. We are to love, affirm, encourage, teach, listen and care for the physical needs of the family. We cannot convict of sin, create hunger and thirst after God, or convert. These are miracles, and miracles are not in our department!"[1]

She capably expresses the difference in a poem she wrote called "For All Who Knew the Shelter of the Fold." Notice the past tense in the title. Ruth is contemplating the plight of those outside the shelter.

For All Who Knew the Shelter of the Fold

*For all
who knew the shelter of the Fold,
its warmth and safety
and the Shepherd's care,
choosing instead to fare
out into the cold,
the night;
revolted
by guardianship,
by Light;
lured
by the unknown
eager to be out
and on their own;
freed
to water where they may,
feed
where they can,
live as they will:
till
they are cured,
let them be cold,
ill;
let them know terror;
feed them thistle,
and thorn;
who chose
the company of wolves,
let them taste
the companionship wolves give
to helpless strays;
but, oh! let them live—*

wiser, though torn!
And wherever,
however, far away
they roam,
follow
and
watch
and
keep
Your stupid, wayward, stubborn
sheep
and someday
bring them Home![2]

Unconditional love is a special quality of exceptional Christian leaders. You can be Christian without it. You can be a leader without it. But to be a truly great and Christlike leader you must have the mind of Christ. He did not wait for us to make the first move. What does the Bible say? "At just the right time, when we were still powerless, Christ died for the ungodly. Very rarely will anyone die for a righteous man, though for a good man someone might possibly dare to die. But God demonstrates his own love for us in this: While we were still sinners, Christ died for us" (Romans 5:6–8).

We should not give up hope. Moses tried his best to free the children of Israel while still a member of Pharaoh's court. When he discovered that his own people had no special love or respect for him, he fled from the entire mess into the Sinai desert. He was to discover the truth of Psalm 139,

> Where can I flee from Your Spirit? Where can I flee from Your presence? If I go up to the heavens, You are there; if I make my bed in the depths, You are there. If I rise on the wings of the dawn, if I settle on the far side of the sea,

even there Your hand will guide me, Your right hand will hold me fast. (Psalm 139:7–10)

While demonstrating unconditional love for the wayward, we can rest assured God has not discontinued His involvement. Prodigals can never flee beyond His reach. Although it would be wrong to call pursuit of aberration all part of God's wonderful plan, He can and often does use the experiences of aberration for the benefit of His wayward children. In commenting on Moses' flight from Egypt, Ruth Graham noticed how God used His experience for good.

Moses' Wanderings Weren't All for Naught

*Moses' wanderings weren't
all for naught;
Wandering, he learned the
wilderness firsthand;
And later through this
Devastation brought
His brethren from bondage to
the Promised Land.*[3]

Everyone needs the unconditional love of the Lord who can turn a wrong decision into a blessing. It should be easier for us than experience proves. When the Ephesians demonstrated a self-righteous attitude, Paul reminded them of God's grace in their life.

> As for you, you were dead in your transgressions and sins, in which you used to live when you followed the ways of this world and of the ruler of the kingdom of the air, the spirit who is now at work in those who are disobedient. All of us also lived among them at one time, gratifying the cravings of our sinful nature and following its desires and thoughts. Like the rest, we were by nature

objects of wrath. But because of His great love for us, God, who is rich in mercy, made us alive with Christ even when we were dead in transgressions—it is by grace you have been saved. (Ephesians 2:1–5)

More Scriptural Insight

Luke 15:11–32 What evidence is there of unconditional love?
Matthew 5:43–48 What point is Jesus making?
Matthew 18:21–35 What does it mean to "forgive from the heart"?

A Leader's Prayer

Lord, the frustrations of love can sometimes get to a Christian. People take advantage of our love, and that can hurt. We are not omniscient, nor do we readily know how our love should best be expressed. We wonder, "Should we comfort, or confront?" Help us to leave more to Your care and to allow time for You to help. Keep our focus more on our own behavior, rather than the behavior of others. Enable us to express heartfelt, sincere love in the most difficult situation or relationship. Keep us from insincerity, smiling politely because it is our duty or expected of our position. Teach us to love like You love, unconditionally and willingly. Let people see in the exercise of our leadership an acceptance of their value as Your child. Enable us to be of assistance to those whose needs are within our ability to help. In all situations keep our thoughts on You so that we might reflect Your love. In Jesus' name. Amen.

Notes

1. Ruth Bell Graham, *Prodigals and Those Who Love Them,* (Colorado Springs: Focus on the Family Publishing, 1991), 81. Used by permission.

2. Ibid., 15.

3. Ibid., 37.

CHAPTER TWENTY-ONE

CHARLES SWINDOLL
A Sense of Humor

The famous preacher Henry Ward Beecher once said, "A person without a sense of humor is like a wagon without springs—jolted by every pebble in the road." The Bible understands the value of joy in the life of God's people. Consider the following insights:

"The joy of the Lord is your strength." (Nehemiah 8:10)

"You have made known to me the path of life; You will fill me with joy in Your presence, with eternal pleasures at Your right hand." (Psalm 16:11)

"All the days of the oppressed are wretched, but the cheerful heart has a continual feast." (Proverbs 15:15)

"A cheerful heart is good medicine, but a crushed spirit dries up the bones." (Proverbs 17:22)

"I will turn their mourning into gladness; I will give them comfort and joy instead of sorrow." (Jeremiah 31:13)

"When they saw the star, they were overjoyed." (Matthew 2:10)

"My soul glorifies the Lord and my spirit rejoices in God my Savior." (Luke 1:46–47)

The chief casualty of the fall was eternal death and everlasting separation between the Lord and the people of His creation. One of the symptoms of that condition is the loss of joy in life.

To Eve the Lord said, "I will greatly increase your pains in childbearing" (Genesis 3:16). Every time a birth occurs, our wives and daughters are reminded of sin's consequence. To Adam the Lord said, "By the sweat of your brow you will eat your food until you return to the ground, since from it you were taken; for dust you are and to dust you will return" (Genesis 3:19). Not a pretty picture! But wait, look again. Sin brought pain, sweat, and death, but God's response always brings recovery, restoration, and joy!

Joy is a tangible blessing. If it isn't breaking out somewhere in your life, you probably don't have it! In the life of Chuck and Cynthia Swindoll joy is a Harley-Davidson motorcycle. "I know, I know ..." comments Chuck, "it doesn't fit our image. Who really cares? We stopped worrying about our image years ago. ... We are having more fun than anybody can imagine (except fellow Harley riders). One of the best things about the whole deal is that those guys and gals down at the bike shop don't have a clue who we are. We have finally found a place in our area where we can be out in public and remain absolutely anonymous. If anybody down there happens to ask our names, we'll just tell 'em we're Jim and Shirley Dobson. Those Harley hogs don't know them either."[1]

It is a grave mistake (as in dying before your time), to believe that the power of the Gospel has no positive effect until our death. (Swindoll believes too many die at 30 but the corpse isn't buried until 60 or 70.) According to the Bible the power of the Gospel takes effect when the Holy Spirit enters our life and transforms our world. John did not say, "I write these things to you who believe in the name of the Son of God so that you may *one day in the future* have eternal life." No, he wrote, "... so that you *may know* (as in today!) that you have eternal life." You have it now, and if we have it now our lives ought to reflect the joy. As the Christmas hymn says,

No more let sin and sorrow grow,
Nor thorns infest the ground!
He comes to make His blessings flow,
Far as the curse is found!
Far as the curse is found!
Far as, far as, the curse is found!

If death no longer has any power over us, why do so many live as though Jesus was beaten and the tomb still holds His dry bones? That's an excellent question. One for which the best-selling author has an answer.

> When I was a teenager, the most popular business advertisements in magazines read: "Send me a man who reads." As much as I value reading and applaud the resourcefulness of those who pore over the pages of good books, I think today's slogan should be: "Send me one whose attitude is positive, whose heart is full of cheer, whose face shouts, yes!"

> Some critics would be quick to point out that our times do not lend themselves to such an easygoing philosophy. They would ask, "Under these circumstances how could I be anything but grim?" To which I reply, "What are you doing *under* the circumstances?" Correct me if I'm wrong, but isn't the Christian life to be lived *above* the circumstances?[2]

If Christians are to live lives that reflect the Gospel freedom we have in Christ, then the lives of Christian leaders should especially reflect the "peace that the world cannot give[3] ... the peace of God, which transcends all understanding" (Philippians 4:7).

We have long known that psychosomatic illnesses are real. A person who constantly worries, frets, and stews over problems can make himself sick. Studies are also beginning to confirm the truth Solomon shared 1,000 years before the birth of Christ. "A cheerful look brings joy to the heart, and good news gives health to the bones" (Proverbs 15:30) and, "A man's spirit sustains him in sickness, but a crushed spirit who can bear?" (Proverbs 18:14).

Like all insurance carriers these days, those responsible for the benefits of our clergy roster have been stressing proactive health care and "wellness" since the mid-1980s. In their May 1984 publication, the Christian professionals of our denomination were alerted to the well-documented story of Norman Cousins, for 35 years the editor of Saturday Review magazine. In his best-selling book *Anatomy of an Illness as Perceived by the Patient,* Cousins describes his remarkable recovery from a paralyzing illness. After being told his chances of recovery were one in 500, he asked and received permission to treat his own illness. Cousins moved from his hospital bed to a nearby hotel where he began a treatment that consisted of massive doses of vitamin C, and an analysis of stress as a health issue. He took the time to resolve long-standing disputes in primary relationships and prescribed a "laugh time" for two hours every day. He spent time watching funny movies and discovered "the more I laughed the better I felt." His symptoms disappeared and he returned to work. Did it last? He continued his research on the benefits of laughter and stress reduction, wrote his book 10 years later, and began lecturing in medical schools across the country.

But is such a joyful spirit fitting for a Christian leader? Swindoll has considered this question and has a definitive answer.

> My vocation is among the most serious of all professions. As a minister of the gospel and as senior pastor of a church, the concerns I deal with are eternal in dimension. A week doesn't pass without my hearing of or dealing with life in the raw. Marriages are breaking, homes are splitting, people are hurting, jobs are dissolving, addictions of every description are rampant. Needs are enormous, endless, and heartrending.
>
> The most natural thing for me to do would be to allow all of that to rob me of my joy and change me from a person who has always found humor in life—as well as laughed loudly often—into a stoic, frowning clergyman. No thanks.
>
> Matter of fact, that was my number-one fear many years ago. Thinking that I must look somber and be ultraserious twenty-four hours a day resulted in my resisting a call into ministry for several years. Most of the men of the cloth I had seen looked like they held down a night job at the local mortuary. I distinctly remember wrestling with the Lord over all this before He pinned me to the mat and whispered a promise in my ear that forced me to surrender: "You can faithfully serve Me, but you can still be yourself. Being My servant doesn't require you stop laughing." That did it. That one statement won me over. I finally decided I could be one of God's spokesmen and still enjoy life."[4]

No competent Christian leader would argue that life is "a bowl of cherries" or the great problems of life should be ignored, shrugged off, or treated lightly. Remember, "There is a time for everything, and a season for every activity under heaven. ... a time to weep and a time to laugh, a time to mourn and a time to dance" (Ecclesiastes 3:1, 4). Solomon, who encouraged the establishment of a joyful spirit, also spoke of discretion in its use. "Like one who takes away a garment on a cold day, or like vinegar poured on soda, is one who sings songs to a heavy heart" (Proverbs 25:20). The apostle Paul likewise urged us to be discerning in our behavior. "Rejoice with those who rejoice; mourn with those who mourn. Live in harmony with one another" (Romans 12:15–16).

Swindoll urges Christians to maintain a gospel perspective especially in the tough times. We are always a people of victory. For Christians the best is always yet to come. "Weeping may remain for a night, but rejoicing comes in the morning" (Psalm 30:5). How fitting, Swindoll reflects, that we should live in a country that declared its independence with an acknowledgment of this divine intention! The immortal words of Thomas Jefferson still intrigue me, he writes:

> We hold these Truths to be self-evident; that all Men are created equal, that they are endowed by their Creator with certain unalienable Rights; that among these are Life, Liberty, and the Pursuit of Happiness.

"For many, however," Swindoll concludes, "happiness is a forgotten pursuit. A dream that has died."[5] It needn't be a lost pursuit. How strong is the gospel truth in your heart? How firmly do you cling to the promises of God to never leave you nor forsake you?[6] Swindoll reminds us that the Lord never wavers and His promises can be trusted. His quotation of Ella Wheeler Wilcox's powerful poem is a fitting call to action based on those promises.

The Winds of Fate

One ship drives East and another drives West
With the selfsame winds that blow.
'Tis the set of the sails
And not the gales
Which tell us the way to go.

Like the winds of the sea are the ways of fate,
As we voyage along through life:
'Tis the set of a soul
That decides the goal,
And not the calm or the strife.[1]

More Scriptural Insight

Kings 18:22–29   How would you describe the mood of Elijah?

John 2:1–11   Why water into wine and not a resurrection or healing?

John 16:17–22   What is the point of comparison between birth and joy?

A Leader's Prayer

Lord, Your ways are inscrutable and wise. Help me to see the humor in life and to maintain childlike faith. Keep me from all temptation to overestimate my own importance or to act in a self-righteous manner. Enable me to accept my own foibles and laugh at my mistakes. Never let the devil lead me to despair over my sins and failures. Keep me fully focused on the victory of the opened tomb and the defeat of Satan. When he attempts to depress me with accusations and mocking, remind me to laugh at his efforts and recall his defeat. O Lord, keep me from having fun at other people's expense and enable me to see their hurtful remarks as harmless and empty words. Never let bitterness occupy even a corner of my heart, and let the full glory of salvation drive all darkness from my life. Let Your peace fill my heart and restore unto me and all Christian leaders the joy of our salvation, in Jesus Christ. Amen.

Notes

1. Charles Swindoll, *Maybe It's Time to Laugh Again*, (Dallas, TX: Word Publishing, 1991), 191.

2. Ibid., 20.

3. See John 14:27.

4. Charles Swindoll, 13

5. Ibid., 49

6. See Hebrews 13:5

16. Charles Swindoll, 45; quoted from Ella Wheeler Wilcox, "The Wind of Fate," in *The Best Loved Poems of the American People*, compiled by Hazel Felleman, (Garden City, NY: Garden City Books, 1936), 364.

CHAPTER TWENTY-TWO

HARRIET TUBMAN
Looking Out for Others

S ometimes the best stories come from the most unexpected sources at the most unpredictable times. Recently the
Lutheran pastors of Missouri were gathered for an annual
conference to discuss changes in our official reconciliation
process. In other words, denominational officials were about
to walk us through new grievance procedures for settling
relational problems between pastors and their congregations
and between pastors and other pastors.

These conferences are never much fun and the subject
matter of this one had a cringe factor of nine on a scale of one
to 10. A high-ranking official of synod was making the
keynote presentation, and since he is a personal friend and a
member of our congregation, I had little choice but to attend,
sit close to the front, and show my support. ... Okay, so I did-
n't sit close to the front, but I promised Carol I would listen
and appear interested.

He began by setting aside his presentation to "tell a little
story" he had heard recently from a colleague who was a staff

member of our Commission on Theology and Church Relations. Things did not look promising. We were about to hear a story, told by a serious-minded denominational official, which he had heard from an even more serious-minded theological expert. I was beginning to sweat.

The story began:

I'm disgusted with my brother;
I am positively sore,
I have never been so angry
With a human being before.
He's everything detestable
That's spelled with A through Z,
He deserves to be the target
Of a ten-pound bumble bee.

I was grabbing my yellow pad and writing furiously at this point.

I'd like to wave a magic wand (he continued)
And make him disappear,
Or watch a wild rhinoceros
Attack him from the rear.
Perhaps I'll cook a pot of soup
And dump my brother in;
He forgot today's my birthday!
Oh, how could he ... he's my twin.

The history of strained relations can be traced through time to the first family. The two young men at odds with each other were brothers. (This comes as no surprise to us parents.) The older brother despised his younger brother because he seemed to be treated with greater favor. It wasn't favoritism by parents creating the jealousy however; the Lord Himself seemed to bless the life of the younger brother more than the life of the older. The Lord (as James would later write) is not partial. He simply will not foster a wrong spirit by encouraging a bad attitude. Instead, the Lord told Cain to get his act together, and do the right thing. Then the Lord promised he'd experience the same blessing his brother Abel enjoyed.

We all know the choice Cain made. Rather than do the right thing, he decided to eliminate the competition and took the life of his brother, *even after his personal conversation with the Lord.* Christians are not immune from the temptation to oppress, hate, and even eliminate those who are different.

I grew up in the 1950s, attended high school during the 1960s and saw firsthand the battle for social equality by blacks in America. Many, both black and white, paid the highest price for joining in the fray. It should not surprise us that many of the leaders who boldly stepped to the front during those critical days came from the Christian church. The courage needed to take the beatings, endure the abuse, and overcome the reign of terror was extraordinary, requiring divine grace and favor.

As in nearly all great campaigns, there were heroes that inspired and encouraged us by their previous example. The life of a former slave named Harriet Tubman was often recalled as a model of leadership in difficult times. Even as a student I loved history and to this day have a strong recollection of a television program hosted by Walter Cronkite in the 1960s called "You Are There." Through the magic of television Walter would transport us back in time and we could listen as he interviewed great people of history. I still remember his interview with Tubman, a well-known conductor on the Underground Railroad. The "Railroad," as it was called, was nothing more than a well-organized chain of concerned people who provided shelter and food to runaway slaves heading North to freedom. Harriet organized the safest trips of her day. Although she lived at a different time and was of a different culture and race, I have always admired her courage and determination to help others at the risk of her own life. She was a leader in every sense of the word.

After her own daring escape from a Maryland plantation in 1849, Tubman made it her mission in life to rescue others from the same fate. In her book on the role of women in the Civil War, Ina Chang honors Harriet's contribution to the cause of freedom. "She made nineteen trips," Chang wrote, "mostly to Maryland and Delaware, to lead runaways northward. The slaves in the area called her 'Moses,' after Moses of the Bible, who led his people out of slavery and to the Promised Land."[1]

In total it is believed Harriet led no fewer than 300 slaves to freedom, supported along the way by abolitionists and Northern sympathizers. She demonstrated unusual courage, continuing her forays despite an offer of $40,000 by slaveholders for her capture. When the Civil War erupted, Harriet again stepped forward and was formally attached to the Union Army in South Carolina, serving as a cook, nurse, and scout for raiding parties. She was able to infiltrate the enemy's cities and towns and through consultation with sympathetic black slaves was able to map exact army placements, river mines, and rebel plans.[2] She recalls the rescue of one black woman who boarded the Union gunboat, "with a steaming pot of rice on her head, a pig slung across her back, and three or four children clinging to her dress. Another brought along a black pig she called Jeff Davis, named for the confederate president."[3]

She lived to a ripe old age of 92 and was honored by the city of Auburn, New York, which erected a monument to her courageous leadership during the life and death struggle against slavery. Although she received no formal education and was never able to read or write, Harriet became a true national treasure and often spoke words of encouragement and conviction for the cause of the downtrodden. "At a women's rights meeting in Rochester, New York, in the 1880s, she told her audience, 'Yes ladies, I was a conductor on the Underground Railroad for eight years, and I can say what most conductors can't say—I never ran my train off the track, and I never lost a passenger!' "[4]

Harriet was never greatly rewarded for her selfless life of heroism. After the war she worked tirelessly in a home which the city of Auburn established for the care of impoverished Negroes. As long as she was able, she worked as a cook and continued to speak from place to place, providing for her needs and the needs of others. Two books were written about her life by admirers with all proceeds to help support her cause and to provide for her care in old age. Harriet never sought recognition nor objected to her difficult life. She was proud to have lived for the purpose of helping others.

Helping others is an important part of the overall role of a leader. To exercise leadership there must be others in need of direction, inspiration, and guidance. Leadership by definition can never be exercised in a vacuum. In my younger days (before my blood thinned), when asked where I would like to serve as a pastor, I used to respond, "The boundary waters between Canada and the United States, but the wolves, the moose and the northern pike don't need saving." Leadership of any kind assumes provision for the needs of people. Christian leadership assumes leaders will serve people by making provision for their greatest need, the establishment and nurture of an active and viable Christian faith.

Jesus is the head of the church because He provided for its

greatest need. Leadership is not always exercised by extroverts who stand on high platforms rallying people with stirring words of rhetoric. Jesus exercised His leadership through servanthood. Isaiah uses very vivid language to describe the means by which Jesus achieved the honor of Lord and head of the body of Christ.

> He was despised and rejected by men, a man of sorrows, and familiar with suffering. Like one from whom men hide their faces he was despised, and we esteemed him not. Surely he took up our infirmities and carried our sorrows, yet we considered him stricken by God, smitten by him, and afflicted. But he was pierced for our transgressions, he was crushed for our iniquities; the punishment that brought us peace was upon him, and by his wounds we are healed. We all, like sheep, have gone astray, each of us has turned to his own way; and the LORD has laid on him the iniquity of us all. He was oppressed and afflicted, yet he did not open his mouth; he was led like a lamb to the slaughter, and as a sheep before her shearers is silent, so he did not open his mouth. (Isaiah 53:3–7)

Jesus was not motivated by the prospects of personal acclamation. He didn't offer His service because one day His followers would wear tiny crosses on gold chains around their necks, hang His portrait above the piano in the formal living room, and gather weekly in large buildings to recall His exploits. He stepped out for only one reason. Without His help everyone was destined for certain and eternal death.

Christian men are called to exercise that same attitude of leadership in their homes. In his counsel to husbands, Paul urges men to love their wives, "As Christ loved the church and gave Himself up for her to make her holy, cleansing her by the washing with water through the word, and to present her to Himself as a radiant church, without stain or wrinkle or any other blemish, but holy and blameless. ..." (Ephesians 5:25).

This kind of leadership to cure a "singular" problem is so unusual Paul calls it, "a profound mystery" (Ephesians 5:25). Likewise, leadership by a husband in a Christian home is not to be exercised for the purpose of dominance, self-promotion, or personal recognition. If it is Christlike leadership, it will be offered in humble service for the benefit of his wife and children, like Christ offered Himself as a servant and sacrifice for the church.

If such a spirit is expected of those who exercise leadership in the primary relationship of the home, how much more should it be a model of Christian leadership for those who would lead the church for which Christ died?

More Scriptural Insight

Proverbs 24:10–12	What warning is made to those who fail to get involved?
Matthew 11:16–19	What does the last line of verse 19 mean in this context?
James 2:1–10	What does the Lord have to say about favoritism?

A Leader's Prayer

Lord, I come to You for help and guidance in the exercise of leadership. Like You did for Abraham, Moses, Joshua, Samuel, David, and others, You have done for me. You, for reasons known only to Yourself, have reached down and claimed me as Your child, and raised me up as a leader of Your people. I know that this was not done for my sake alone, but for the sake of others in the Kingdom whom You love and desire to serve. Give me a servant's spirit and a discerning heart to lead in accord with Your desires. I recall others that You also called to leadership, men such as Samson and Saul, also the many wicked kings of Judah and Israel, and Judas, one of the Twelve. These forgot their calling and became self-centered and useless in the Kingdom. Keep me from the sin of arrogance and selfishness. Let my life be wholly offered in service to You and the people of Your choosing. Forgive my mistakes, renew and establish my leadership to the glory of Your name and promotion of the gospel of salvation through Jesus, my Lord, who is the head of the body, His church. Amen.

Notes

1. Ina Chang, *A Separate Battle—Women and the Civil War,* (New York: Scholastic Inc., 1991), 12.

2. Earl Conrad, *Encyclopedia Americana,* "Harriet Tubman," (New York: Americana Corporation, vol. 27), 203.

3. Ina Chang, *A Separate Battle,* 55–56.

4. Ibid., 13.

CHAPTER TWENTY-THREE

JAMES DOBSON
Love Must Be Tough

Perhaps no other layman of our generation has had a more important and positive impact on the American Christian church and our society than Dr. James Dobson of Focus on the Family Ministries. Even his opponents would have to admit that his books, tapes, videos, and radio program have been molders and shapers of public opinion.

How could a layman gain the ear of so many in such a short period of time? Bible-believing Christians might quote David's reflection on that subject, "In Your hands are strength and power to exalt and give strength to all" (1 Chronicles 29:12). Nonbelievers might attribute his prominence to his first book, *Dare to Discipline.* The book and its practical advice struck a chord with parents who were choking on permissive models of child rearing. He has written almost a dozen best-sellers since *D.T.D* and has guided millions to common sense, biblical solutions for relational problems of every sort.

163

"Why," you might ask, with so much counsel on such a wide range of topics, "Why have you chosen to focus on Dobson's counsel about the exercise of tough love?" Obviously, I believe the single greatest need in the church today is for courageous leadership. The pulpits are filled with passive leaders who have committed themselves and their ministry to abide "faithful" to the inerrant Word, but that was only half of the Lord's counsel to Joshua.[1] For many, the hardest part of courageous leadership is the exercise of tough love. Whether a relational strain exists between husband and wife, parent and child, pastor and parishioner, or between people on a Christian staff, the exercise of tough love is necessary for the restoration and ultimate health and happiness of the relationship. Dobson's book on the subject, *Love Must Be Tough—New Hope for Families in Crisis,* is the best I have found in providing practical suggestions for the inspired counsel of Paul, "Speaking the truth in love, we will in all things grow up into Him who is the Head, that is, Christ" (Ephesians 4:15). Love without truth is not true love, and truth without love is of absolutely no effect.

What is tough love and why is it so hard to administer? Tough love is taking a stand for what is true and right and requiring our relationships be established on that basis. Relationships that ignore the truth, suppress the truth, or distort the truth can never be healthy. It doesn't matter if the relationship is personal or professional, it must be based on personal integrity and mutual respect. By contrast, too many relationships are abusive or built on appeasement for the sake of peace, a compromise that will in the end only make matters worse. As Dobson points out in an opening chapter,

> Attempts by one side to "buy off" an aggressor or offender appear to represent peace proposals, but they merely precipitate further insult and conflict. World War II might

have been prevented and fifty million lives saved if British Prime Minister Neville Chamberlain and other national leaders had understood the folly of appeasement in 1936–39. Every time they offered Adolf Hitler another Czechoslovakia to tranquilize his lust for domination, they only fed his disdain for them and their armies. Hitler's interpretation of their yearning for "peace in our time" as evidence of weakness and fear enticed him to ever greater audacity. Finally, it became necessary to fight what Winston Churchill called the most preventable war in modern times. That is where appeasement leads, whether in affairs of state or affairs of the heart."[2]

The truth of Dobson's observation is valid from both the perspective of the staff member and the perspective of a staff leader. The staff member who allows a director to run over him with no regard for integrity and honesty will receive more of the same until the condition completely deteriorates and self-destructs. Likewise, the administrative leader who hesitates to hold staff members accountable and is unwilling to discipline, correct, and even dismiss people that lack integrity and commitment will only increase the aberrant behavior by acceptance of the unacceptable. Far too many ministries are frustrated by the gridlock that comes from failure to hold one another accountable to Christian standards and Christian behavior.

What happens when accountability becomes a part of the formula? There are two possibilities and both of them lead to restored unity. First, the one who is acting contrary to the spirit and counsel of God, when confronted, may recognize it, admit their error, and return to committed unity under Christ.

But what happens when there is no admission of error and the staff member challenges the accusation? That too is good, clarifying the issue under question. (Light has a way of seeping through the cracks, and folks are quickly drawn to it.) If the presumption has no factual basis, the matter can be quickly clarified and the relationship quietly restored. If the presumed wrong is proved but denied or defended, accountability will eventually bring an end to the behavior, or an end to the one who refuses correction. In either case unity is restored, although regrettably at the expense of those who deny their error and refuse correction. The result of disunity in a Christian relationship is too high to just look the other way. It is also contrary to Christ's will for the church. Jesus prayed, "May they be brought to complete unity to let the world know that You sent Me and loved them even as You have loved Me" (John 17:23).

True to the scriptural admonition to "speak the truth in love," Dr. Dobson cautions that tough love *is still love:*

> You must be careful not to behave in unloving ways. Remember that with God's help, you are attempting to build new bridges to this disrespectful, trapped partner. Don't burn them before they reach the other shore. Don't call him names, except to label his harmful behavior for what it is. Don't try to hurt him with gossip or even embarrassing truth ... and don't forget that your purpose is to be tough, yes, but loving as well.[3]

When Christians are united virtually anything is possible. The creator imbued us with the potential to achieve the extraordinary when united with other people. Seeing this potential put to sinful use in the building of the tower of Babel, the Lord reflected, "If as one people speaking the same language they have begun to do this, then nothing they plan to do will be impossible for them" (Genesis 11:6). He tells the church to use the power of unity for good. "Live a life worthy of the calling you have received. Be completely humble and gentle; be patient, bearing with one another in love. Make every effort to keep the unity of the Spirit through the bond of peace" (Ephesians 4:1–3). Unity that grows from authentic Christian living is the only kind of unity that lasts.

If you were to talk to Jim Dobson, you would soon realize that his dedication to relationships based on truth and integrity has not been lately learned. It is a commitment which precedes his own experience by generations. He repeatedly credits the godly example of his parents, his extended family, and grandparents as his wellspring of attitudes and values. "Throughout my childhood," he once wrote, "I had watched him (his father) at home where it was impossible for him to hide his true character. Never once did I see him compromise with evil or abandon the faith by which he lived. His character had been like a beacon to me, illuminating my way."[4]

He learned the life-changing power of tough love by personal experience. It also came at the hand of his father.

> I will long remember and be indebted to his words of tough love back in 1969. I was running at an incredible speed, working myself to death, just like every other man I knew. Although my activities were bringing me professional advancement and the trappings of financial success, my dad was not impressed. He had watched my hectic lifestyle and felt obligated to express his concern. He did so in a letter which included the following paragraph:
>
> *I have observed that the greatest delusion is to suppose that our children will be devout Christians simply because their parents have been or that any of them will enter into the Christian faith in any other way than through their parents' deep travail of prayer and faith. But this prayer demands time, time that cannot be given if it is all signed and conscripted and laid on the altar of career ambition. Failure for you at this point would make mere success in your occupation a very pale and washed-out affair indeed.*[5]

If tough love is essential to strong relationships and the Christian mission, why is it so rare? Perhaps we fear rejection or the loss of a friend. Solomon reminds us that our enemies, not our friends, ignore self-destructive behavior. "Better is open rebuke than hidden love. Wounds from a friend can be trusted, but an enemy multiplies kisses" (Proverbs 27:5–6). Christian leaders that find it impossible to establish and maintain accountability in the exercise of leadership will not lead for long.

More Scriptural Insight

1 Samuel 15:12–23	What is more important to the Lord than worship?
1 Corinthians 5	Who is to hold whom accountable?
Galatians 2:11–16	Why did Paul correct the behavior of Peter?

A Leader's Prayer

Gracious Lord, loving Savior, You never ask us to do something that You were not willing to do on our behalf. We have seen in the gospels how it was necessary for You to correct Your disciples when they argued who was greatest. When Peter was disrespectful and in error, You rightfully called him to account. Help us to lead in a spirit of gentleness but firmly also. Remind us of our duty to the kingdom of heaven so that none would be lost through timidity or the ineffectiveness of ministry clouded by dissension and disunity. Send Your Holy Spirit in special measure upon all who lead that they might exercise wisdom and faithfully use the Scripture to "teach, rebuke, correct, and train others in righteousness." In matters of adiaphora, enable all who lead to pursue unity with integrity and to be authentic Christians. When compassion is called for, enable us to administer it with sincere concern. When hard decisions are required, give us the courage to act decisively for the greater good of the Kingdom. Help us to do all we can to maintain the unity of the Spirit in the bond of peace through Christ Jesus. Amen.

Notes

1. The Lord counseled Joshua to be faithful and strong and courageous as a leader of God's people. See Joshua 1 for the details of the exchange between the Lord and Joshua.

2. James Dobson, *Love Must Be Tough—New Hope for Families in Crisis*, (Dallas: Word Book Publishers, 1983), 24. Used by permission. All rights reserved.

3. Ibid., 65.

4. Gloria Gaither, *What My Parents Did Right*, including, "A Lifetime of Friendship" by James Dobson, (Nashville: Star Song Publishing Group, 1991), 69.

5. Ibid., 71–72.

CHAPTER TWENTY-FOUR

ABRAHAM LINCOLN
Objectivity

When a country is rebellious, it has many rulers,
but a man of understanding and knowledge
maintains order. (Proverbs 28:2)

Leadership is more art than science, more heart than mind. Gifted leaders have an innate ability to manage conflicting sentiments, sympathize with divergent views but not be overly influenced by them. Out of turmoil they bring clarity. Like a beacon piercing thick fog, they provide direction. Unconvinced by the influence of friends, or the intimidation of enemies, they maintain their objectivity. It is a sign of good leadership that everyone is equally frustrated and pleased with their course.

Abraham Lincoln exhibited extraordinary leadership in an era of unparalleled need. The emotions and opinions of his day were extreme and by the end of his tenure they had forever etched their lines in his furrowed visage. In the midst of unrelenting pressure he could not be pressured, and in the face of extreme opinion he kept his balance. Lincoln had a knack for diffusing crises through self-effacement and affirmation of good. He was, as Solomon described, "a man of understanding and knowledge" able to bring order out of chaos and establish leadership in time of rebellion.

He was a man to be trusted. When he spoke, it was not to impress and soothe his critics. Time and time again he remained true to himself and the principles upon which he had campaigned and been elected. His speech at Gettysburg was made from the heart, spoken without regard for expectation. Only two minutes long, it was over before the photographer could adjust his cumbersome equipment and take his picture. The next day many reporters treated his efforts with disdain.

> The Chicago Times said, "The cheek of every American must tingle with shame as he reads the silly, flat, and dishwatery utterances of the man who has to be pointed out to intelligent foreigners as the President of the United States!"
>
> In Harrisburg (Pennsylvania), the Patriot Union refused to print the speech saying, "We will skip over the silly remarks of the President."
>
> Others showed uncharacteristic insight. "The dedicatory remarks of President Lincoln will live among the annals of man," wrote the Chicago Tribune.[1]

Written in cursive on unlined paper, the 269 words of his original speech took only one sheet. (Later signed copies were more neatly composed over several pages.) Commemorative events such as the dedication of the Gettysburg battlefield were typically day-long affairs and speeches were rarely short. Edward Everett preceded Lincoln. His credentials were formidable as former secretary of state, congressman, senator, governor of Massachusetts, president of Harvard, and professional orator. Although Everett was considered the greater speaker and invited to make the keynote address, his two-hour speech has been long since forgotten. Lincoln's remarks, by contrast, are memorized and recited by children to recall the great and terrible sacrifice of those days.

How ironic that in his remarks Lincoln wrote, "The world will little note, nor long remember what we say here ..." And how prophetic his closing line, "We here highly resolve that these dead shall not have died in vain; that this nation, under God, shall have a new birth of freedom; and that government of the people, by the people, for the people, shall not perish from the earth." Lincoln's oratory judgment proved exactly right, causing even Edward Everett to write, "I should be glad if I could flatter myself that I came as near to the central idea of the occasion, in two hours, as you did in two minutes."[2]

Lincoln's good judgment far exceeded matters of public address. With Lee's surrender only a month away, the Thirteenth Amendment abolishing slavery passed, and his reelection a resounding success, Lincoln was in a position to assert his authority and humble the Confederacy, a popular notion held by many whose families had been touched by personal loss. Instead, Lincoln remained objective and plotted a more difficult course of restoration and reunification.

When political sense called for rewarding the victors and punishing the defeated, Lincoln called for neither. The wisdom of his second inaugural address is legendary, "With malice toward none; with charity for all; with firmness in the right as God gives us to see the right, let us strive on to finish the work we are in; to bind up the nation's wounds; to care for him who shall have borne the battle, and for his widow, and his orphan, to do all which may achieve and cherish a just and lasting peace among ourselves, and with all nations."[3]

In the exercise of leadership, Lincoln charted a steady and consistent course down a path deemed best for all, friend and foe alike. Although he is often called "The Great Emancipator," Lincoln made no secret of the fact that slavery was secondary to his main goal of maintaining the Union. Let there be no doubt, Lincoln opposed slavery and often said, "He who would be no slave, must consent to have no slave. Those who deny freedom to others, deserve it not for themselves; and, under a just God, cannot long retain it."[4] But, as his famous "House Divided" speech revealed, Lincoln's primary motive for resolving the slavery issue was unity. "This government cannot endure permanently half slave and half free." He said, "I do not expect the Union to be dissolved—I do not expect the house to fall—but I do expect it will cease to be divided. It will become all one thing, or all the other."[5] In a letter to Horace Greeley of the New York Tribune, Lincoln reiterated his position, "My paramount objective in this struggle is to save the Union, and is not either to save or to destroy slavery. If I could save the Union without freeing any slave, I would do it; and if I could save it by freeing all the slaves, I would do it; and if I could save it by freeing some and leaving others alone, I would also do that."[6]

It was his honest integrity that commended Lincoln to his nation. Frederick Douglass, the most influential black leader of his day, differed with Lincoln on many points but admired the president for the clarity of his positions and the respectful way he treated those who opposed him. "In all my interviews with Mr. Lincoln," Douglass said later, "I was impressed with his entire freedom from popular prejudice against the colored race. He was the first great man that I talked with in the United States freely, who in no single instance reminded me of the difference between himself and myself, of the difference of color, and I thought that all the more remarkable because he came from a state where there were black laws."[7]

Lincoln maintained his commitment to do what seemed right, even if sometimes his decisions seemed contradictory. Northern generals were often frustrated by his tendency to be lenient with deserters. "The generals always wanted an execution carried out before it could be brought before the president," a friend observed. "He was as tenderhearted as a girl."[8] Of course, Lincoln saw it differently. Certainly large numbers of court-martialed soldiers were executed for cowardice in the face of the enemy, but when the president could think of a good reason to pardon, he didn't hesitate. "If almighty God gives a man a cowardly pair of legs, how can he help their running away with him. ... It rests me, after a hard day's work that I can find some excuse for saving some poor fellow's life."[9] He was even known to grant pardon to enemy soldiers when the appeal came from home. When two women from Tennessee requested the release of their husbands from a Union prison, Lincoln granted their request but admonished the advocates, "You say your husband is a religious man: tell him when you meet him, that I say I am not much of a judge of religion, but that, in my opinion, the religion that sets men to rebel and fight against their government, because as they think, that government does not sufficiently help some men to eat their bread on the sweat of other men's faces, is not the sort of religion upon which people can get to heaven."[10]

The apostle Paul knew what it was like to feel tugged and pressured to take a popular position rather than the heat that comes from standing for truth. In his letter to the church of Galatia, he strongly challenged those succumbing to the pressure of legalists. In reference to the integrity of his own witness Paul asked, "Am I now trying to win the approval of men, or of God? Or am I trying to please men? If I were still trying to please men, I would not be a servant of Christ" (Galatians 1:10).

Leadership requires discernment and a commitment to integrity. Without it confusion reigns as special interests compete for attention and support. Capable leaders consider all sides of the issue and affirm that which is right even if it's the least popular of all the choices. Jesus had choices to make. During His trial before Pontius Pilate, the governor urged Jesus to contribute to His own defense. When the Lord remained silent, Pilate was amazed. "Do you refuse to speak to me? ... Don't you realize I have power either to free you or to crucify you?" (John 19:10). John even tells us that from then on Pilate tried to set Jesus free but to no avail. Why didn't Jesus cooperate with His would-be benefactor? We needn't speculate about the answer. John records Jesus' own thoughts on the subject the day of His triumphal entry into Jerusalem. While everyone else rejoiced, Jesus said, "Now My heart is troubled, and what shall I say? 'Father, save Me from this hour'? No, it was for this very reason I came to this hour. Father, glorify Your name" (John 12:27–28).

When the time came for Jesus to choose between expediency and the will of His Father, He never wavered. "My Father," He prayed, "if it is not possible for this cup to be taken away unless I drink it, may Your will be done" (Matthew 26:42). The consequence of His decision was well known before He made it. He would die so that we might live. As He once told His disciples, "Greater love has no one than this, that he lay down his life for his friends" (John 15:13).

Great leaders will continue to make their decisions on the basis of what is right not what is expedient, most popular, or safest. Many a besieged leader has taken comfort in Lincoln's well-known statement, "If I tried to read, much less answer, all the criticisms made of me, and all the attacks leveled against me, this office would have to be closed for all other business. I do the best I know how, the very best I can. And I mean to keep on doing this, down to the very end. If the end brings me out all wrong, ten angels swearing I had been right would make no difference. If the end brings me out all right, then what is said against me now will not amount to anything."[11]

Leaders of integrity understand and appreciate the difficulty of maintaining objectivity in a very subjective world.

More Scriptural Insight

1 Samuel 13:1–14	What should Saul have done differently?
2 Chronicles 10:1–17	What was the mistake of Rehoboam?
Acts 5:17–32	On what basis did the apostles decide their course of action?

A Leader's Prayer

Lord, I am not necessarily brave or courageous. The choice between expediency and right is more difficult than it appears. I sometimes wonder what good can come from conflict when compromise looks so enticing. I am often surrounded by friends and enemies with strong bias and personal opinion. Strengthen me to know Your will and stiffen my resolve to abide faithful. Thank You, Lord, for the example of those who have gone before. Give me the ability to set aside personal consideration in favor of the pursuit of righteousness. Raise up others to support, encourage, and help in the difficult task of leading in the midst of controversy. Forgive past mistakes and enable me to learn the great value of doing that which is right, godly, and best for all. This I pray in Jesus' name. Amen.

Notes

1. Frank Latham, *Abraham Lincoln—Immortals of History,* (New York: Franklin Watts Inc., 1968), 135.

2. Ibid., 135.

3. Keith Jennison, *The Essential Lincoln,* (New York: Franklin Watts Inc., 1971), 218.

4. Russell Freedman, *Lincoln a Photobiography,* (New York: Scholastic Inc., 1987), 135.

5. Keith Jennison, 41.

6. Ibid., 194.

7. Russell Freedman, 104.

8. Ibid., 105.

9. Ibid., 105.

10. Keith Jennison, 215.

11. Paul Lee Tan, *Signs of the Times,* (Chicago: R. R. Donnelley and Sons, Inc., 1990), 294.

CHAPTER TWENTY-FIVE

WALTHER P. KALLESTAD
Influence

influence (in'floo uns), n.,v., —**enced,** —**encing.** —n. 1. power of persons or things to act on others. 2. power to produce an effect without using coercion: *A person may have influence by his ability, personality, position, or wealth.* 3. person or thing that has such power, —v. have power over; change the nature or behavior of: *The moon influences the tides.*

Leadership is influence. Those words greet Walt Kallestad each day he enters his office and sees them inscribed under a picture which hangs there. In his latest book Walt acknowledges that effective leadership is often exercised by unlikely people in unlikely places. Our parents, wives, children, and friends all exercise the most powerful kind of leadership as they influence us through supportive relationships.

Walt has been the senior pastor of Community Church of Joy for the past 15 years. During that time, the church has grown from 200 to 7,000 members and is perhaps the largest

Lutheran church in North America. Walt's leadership ability
has become well-known as the Lord continues to enlarge his
sphere of influence beyond his own church body to include
Christians of every denomination.

We can assume Walt has his critics. The voices are loud and
the efforts never-ending that attempt to thwart leadership's
positive influence. It is not surprising so few leaders emerge to
succeed in their chosen field. Someone summarized it well in
the Ten Commandments for Leadership:

1. People are illogical, unreasonable, and self-centered.
   Love them anyway.
2. If you do good, people will accuse you of selfish, ulteri-
   or motives. Do good anyway.
3. If you are successful, you win false friends and true
   enemies. Succeed anyway.
4. The good you do today will be forgotten tomorrow. Do
   good anyway.
5. Honesty and frankness make you vulnerable. Be honest
   and frank anyway.
6. The biggest people with the biggest ideas can be shot
   down by the smallest people with the smallest ideas.
   Think big anyway.
7. People favor underdogs but follow only top dogs. Fight
   for a few underdogs anyway.
8. What you spend years building may be destroyed
   overnight. Build anyway.
9. People really need help but may attack you if you do
   help them. Help them anyway.
10. Give the world the best you have and you'll get kicked in
    the teeth. Give the world the best you have anyway.

(Author Unknown)

Walt knows about overcoming adversity, and he has experienced the miraculous power of God in the most personal

way. In 1975, Walt was attending the Institute on Church Growth at Garden Grove Community Church in California. During a Friday morning session of the conference, the speaker was interrupted by a man who announced an emergency phone message awaited Walt Kallestad. His young son Patrick had fallen into the swimming pool at the home of friends and was discovered unconscious and not breathing. As he rushed to the parking lot, Dr. Robert Schuller, the conference host, caught up to ask about the nature of the emergency. Dr. Schuller prayed quickly that a miracle would save Patrick's life. As Walt rushed to the hospital, Dr. Schuller returned to the conference and called the whole assembly to prayer on behalf of the Kallestad's young son.

At the hospital Walt and his wife, Mary, embraced with tears as they awaited the outcome of Patrick's emergency treatment. Their prayers and Mary's explanation were interrupted by the good news that Patrick had fully recovered. Patrick's lungs had miraculously cleared, and there was no indication of brain damage. After a night in the hospital the Kallestads took Patrick directly to the closing service of the conference, and at the altar they rededicated their family to the service of Christ and His church. Walt points to this incident as the day he decided to seek ordination and make ministry a lifelong career.

> "The skeptics," Walt recalled, "those who want things to be scientifically provable—challenged my decision by asking, 'But what if Patrick had died or had suffered severe brain damage?' My response was that the 'what ifs' in life are impossible to deal with. I believed with all my heart, then as now, that God would have worked in a dynamic and profound way in my life regardless of the outcome. God's power, love, joy, peace and encouragement are not circumstantial; rather, they are 'certain and substantial.' "

"I have learned," Walt continues, " 'Why' is the wrong question. 'God, why did this have to happen?' That's impossible to answer. It's the 'What' question that's more helpful and purposeful. 'God, what can I do now that this event has happened in my life?' And also, 'Loving Lord, what do you want to do in and through me.' "

"The deepest desire since that time has been to spend the rest of my life caring for people and enthusiastically telling the world how wonderful and great God is. I have asked God to take of my time, talents, and finances to help people discover God's love for them. People everywhere need to know what God's promise means: 'No eye has seen, no ear has heard, no mind has conceived what God has prepared for those who love him.'" (1 Corinthians 2:9)[1]

The conviction that Walt and Mary have for their gospel ministry is infectious and rare. The Greeks have a word for it. They call it *enthousiasmos*, which literally means, "possessed by God." Typically, as people grow older, enthusiasm slips away. Like the time-worn German proverb says, "He who has burned his mouth blows on his soup." During our youth, opportunities look enormous while the obstacles and dangers go unnoticed. But once we've "been burned," we become more and more cautious until caution replaces enthusiasm altogether. Like helium slowly escapes from a child's balloon, our enthusiasm leaks away. Only the fortunate maintain their youthful enthusiasm into midlife and beyond. Those who remain "possessed by God" have a decided advantage.

The prophet wrote:

Do you not know? Have you not heard? The LORD is the everlasting God, the Creator of the ends of the earth. He will not grow tired or weary, and His understanding no one can fathom. He gives strength to the weary and increases the power of the weak. Even youths grow tired and weary, and young men stumble and fall; but those who hope in the LORD will renew their strength. They will

soar on wings like eagles; they will run and not grow
weary, they will walk and not be faint. (Isaiah 40:28–31)

Enthusiasm is the key to influence, an important leadership quality. Without it leaders could not ignite the fire of
desire in the heart of another. Without enthusiasm there
would be no risk takers. For Kallestad, "Risk is not careless
action. Risk is faith in action." In his book *The Everyday
Anytime Guide to Christian Leadership,* Walt builds on Robert
Schuller's well-known phrase, "It takes guts to leave the
ruts."

"Effective leaders," Walt believes, "are people of great
faith. The essence of faith is risk. A leader constantly risks
going where the possibility of failure is greater than the
potential for success. The movie *Columbus 1492* contained a
great line for leaders. Columbus had a nautical map for the
journey; however, he and his crew sailed beyond the map.
They sent a message back to headquarters with the report,
'We have sailed beyond the map; please send further instructions.'" Walt concludes, "Leaders are always going off the
map."[2]

Jesus, as the head of the whole Christian church on earth,
established a model of leadership by example. He led through
humility and achieved victory through sacrifice. The church
does His bidding not out of fear, for our certain salvation was
assured on the cross. Christians risk everything, even their
lives, because He first loved us and gave His life on our
behalf. Christians live to be Christlike as an expression of love
for all that He has done. The influence of His leadership lives
on.

In the upper room Jesus girded His waist with a towel,
washed the dirty feet of His disciples, and then reminded
them, "You call Me 'Teacher' and 'Lord,' and rightly so, for

that is what I am. Now that I, your Lord and Teacher, have washed your feet, you also should wash one another's feet. I have set you an example that you should do as I have done for you. I tell you the truth, no servant is greater than his master, nor is a messenger greater than the one who sent him. Now that you know these things, you will be blessed if you do them" (John 13:13–17).

Our forgiveness was accomplished on the cross. Our guarantee of heaven was assured by the empty tomb. Our leadership training was completed by example. "As I have loved you, so you must love one another. By this all men will know that you are My disciples, if you love one another" (John 13:34–35).

More Scriptural Insight

2 Kings 5:1–14   How many examples of influence can you identify?
Ephesians 6:1–9   What should motivate all Christian influence?
1 Peter 3:1–6   How are wives able to influence obstinate husbands?

A Leader's Prayer

Lord, I have only one life and it is fleeting like the morning dew, like a shadow it will pass quickly. Enable my example to be a godly influence upon young and old alike. Help me realize how people observe not only what I say, but how I act. Make me a cause of joy and encouragement among fellow Christians disheartened by the narrow and difficult path they walk. Let my witness also be a light to those who remain in the shadow of death. Extend the sphere of my influence only to the degree that I bring honor to Your name. Let my leadership gifts be sharpened and useful in my own home. Enable me, by Your grace, to be a Christian influence to my spouse and children, to my grandchildren, and to all their friends.

Grant that there would be no difference between my public witness and the reality of my life. Let all that I do be sincere and honest without any motive except to draw others to You, the author and perfecter of faith. Grant it, Lord, for Jesus' sake. Amen.

Notes

1. Walther Kallestad, *Turning Financial Obstacles into Opportunities,* (Burnsville, MN: Prince of Peace Publishing, Inc.), 1987, 21.

2. Walther Kallestad, *The Everyday Anytime Guide to Christian Leadership,* (Minneapolis: Augsburg Fortress), 1994, 55.

CHAPTER TWENTY-SIX

CARL FERDINAND WILHELM WALTHER
Discernment

The miracles of Scripture were awe-inspiring events. Just imagine walking on dry ground between two towering walls of water, or seeing fire from heaven consume Elijah's altar on Mount Carmel. Nebuchadnezzar was astonished by the survival of Shadrach, Meshach, and Abednego. God's miracles have a way of making ordinary people feel extraordinarily small. After Jesus calmed a devastating storm, Mark tells us, "[The disciples] were terrified and asked each other, 'Who is this? Even the wind and the waves obey him?' " (Mark 4:41). First they were terrified by the storm; moments later they were terrified by *the One greater than the storm!* The boat must have felt pretty small. Sinful men were suddenly confined to close quarters with a sinless and all-powerful Savior—that would be terrifying.

No less awesome is the way Jesus was able to correctly assess situation after situation, always saying and doing just the right thing. His powers of discernment were incredible.

When the woman caught in adultery was thrown at His feet, Jesus knew just what to do. He began writing on the ground with His finger and invited the one with no sin to cast the first stone. Did He write the secret sins of those ready to cast the stones? That would be terrifying.

When He met the woman by the well, she was shocked that He, a Jewish teacher, would talk to her, a Samaritan woman. He was kind to her, even though He revealed complete knowledge of her sinful life. To what end? She became an effective missionary to her entire village. Who would have guessed it? Most righteous men would have kept their distance!

Jesus knew exactly when to be compassionate and when to be tough. He is the Living Word, "... sharper than any double-edged sword, capable of dividing soul and spirit, joints and marrow; correctly judging the thought and the attitudes of the heart."[1] When the self-righteous young man approached Jesus confident of his own goodness, Jesus knew exactly what to say. "If you want to be perfect," Jesus told him, "go, sell your possessions and give to the poor, and you will have your treasure in heaven. Then come, follow Me" (Matthew 19:21). Matthew tells us the young man went away sad because he had great wealth. How did Jesus know? How did He *always know* when to be tough, and when to be compassionate?

Every godly leader will tell you how they pray for discernment. When Solomon was offered the opportunity to "name it and claim it," he asked for a discerning heart. It pleased God that he resisted the obvious temptations: wealth, long life, and power over his enemies. Wisdom, the Lord acknowledged, was the key to every other blessing.

Obtaining a position of leadership is infinitely easier than exercising it wisely. Most godly leaders would gladly be compassionate or even tough, if only they knew which to choose. To be wise requires more than knowledge. Wisdom is much more complex. The true mark of wisdom is discernment, knowing when and how to apply knowledge to improve a given situation.

C. F. W. Walther is a great model of discernment. Largely unknown outside Lutheran Christian circles, C. F. W. is considered the father of confessional Lutheranism in America. It was Walther who restored confidence among the immigrants of 1839, when the immorality of their spiritual leader, Martin Stephan, was exposed. Through the exercise of godly wisdom, he was able to restore trust among the laity and bolster the shattered confidence of their pastors. He built bridges of mutual respect to other confessional German Lutherans already in America. A man of many talents, he solidified that unity through the publication of two journals, *Der Lutheraner,* for the education and edification of the whole church; and 10 years later, *Lehre Und Wehre,* a scholarly journal established for the publication of professional essays by the clergy. As if that weren't enough, Walther helped organize a new Lutheran synod, served as its first president, and established, taught, and guided the work of the new synod's seminary.

Dr. Walther wrote many doctrinal treatises, but is probably best known for the classic work "Law and Gospel," a compilation of his seminary lectures on the proper exercise of the pastoral office. The lectures were largely about discernment. Walther told his students, "Now, a teacher and preacher must be trained in these two things and possess the skill and experience in them; viz., he must both rebuke and crush the obstinate, and again, he must be able to comfort those whom he has rebuked and crushed, lest they despair utterly and be swallowed up by the Law."[2]

Walther was able to do what he taught. When an influential segment of immigrants questioned the authenticity of the pastors and their congregations, Walther agreed to debate their spokesman, an attorney by the name of Marbach. On the basis of God's Word, the historic confessions of the church, the writings of respected pastors and those of Ambrose and Augustine, Walther established his case. In recounting the incident the historian has written, "The evidence was so clear and convincing that, after the conclusion of the first disputation, Marbach declared himself in agreement with the five paragraphs which had been debated, and testified to this by subscribing the record of the proceedings which was kept."[3] But Walther's goal was not only to win the debate, he desired to restore the unity. The following day attorney Marbach made the statement, "(1) I acknowledge that the Christian church is present here; (2) I have been extricated from my fundamental error; (3) the true Lord's Supper is present here; (4) there only remains for me the question whether I can take part in it."[4] Dr. Walther immediately instructed his previous opponent on the grace and mercy of God and by his kindness won and restored the heart of his adversary.

Walther was often at the center of controversy. His namesake and son, Pastor Ferdinand Walther, struggled for success and acceptance in his early ministry, often letting the discouragement overcome him. While he sympathized with his son, Walther would not allow him to continue in his melancholy without challenge. After quoting comforting Scriptures and assuring him of his love and prayers, Ferdinand Sr. wrote, "Here, too, we have enough trouble, as you can imagine. Because I must always wield the pen, I am especially vulnerable when a storm arises. However, I will not allow the devil to triumph over me. I know that the devil raves and rages against us just because we are in his way. Even if he would find a Judas among Christ's disciples, that will not help him but will only harm him and help us. Even if the world and false church should laugh at us, 'he who laughs last laughs best.' "[5] This counsel against discouragement was a constant theme in his correspondence to spiritual leaders. In another letter he wrote, "Do not be downhearted because of your controversies! If you could establish your doctine without such controversies, then it would surely not be the pure Word of God. ... Be on guard against the spirit of grief, for that is not the Holy One, no matter how holy and pious he pretends to be; but the Holy Spirit is a spirit of joy."[6]

While on a visit to Europe in 1860 to regain his health, Walther contemplated the value of unity with diversity. The church, he reminded his peers, has been called to unity, not legalistic uniformity. "We are," he wrote, "in spite of all the jealous concern for our unity in doctrine and faith, free, nevertheless from every inquisitorial spirit, which can so easily convert the fraternal bond into oppressive shackles. ... We subscribe wholeheartedly to the well-known maxim *in necessarilis unitas, in dubiis lertas, in omnibus caritas* (in essentials unity, in doubtful things liberty, in all things charity). ... Our union," he said, "stipulates agreement in ceremonies only insofar as this unity is required for the confessional rites of our church. Unity in practice is of great value to us, to be sure, but only insofar as the unhindered edification of the church depends upon a common foundation and faithfulness to the Confessions requires it."

Walther refused to exercise leadership through mandate, a temptation which entraps so many religious leaders. He believed in the power of the Word and remained poised between law and gospel, confrontation and compassion, unity and liberty, expressed always in love. Leadership of his kind requires knowledge of the Word, which leads to confidence, which enables discernment, which is the spirit of Christ.

More Scriptural Insight

1 Kings 3:16–28	What characteristics did Solomon expect to discern?
Proverbs 3:13–26	What are the benefits of godly wisdom and discretion?
James 1:19–27	How will you know a wise person when you see one?

A Leader's Prayer

Gracious Lord, almighty God, receive my prayer and bless me according to Your mercy. Lord, I have often prayed for courage, good health, and the energy necessary to carry out my Christian duties. I realize, Lord, that these are not enough. Equip me with Your discerning spirit. Help me to use my knowledge, strength, and authority in ways that would honor You and further the cause of the Gospel. Surround me with the counsel of godly people to help me in my task. Give me humility and a desire only to do Your will in each and every issue I must decide. Keep me from succumbing to the temptation of mandating change without concern for those who may not understand or have a position different from my own. Keep my mind open to consider all possibilities except any which would compromise the Christian faith or bring shame to the Gospel. Above all, let Christ's love be seen in all I do and say. Bless the efforts of all who would answer the call to Christian leadership. Bless especially those who lead Your little ones closer to a knowledge and love for You, Father, Son, and Holy Spirit. Amen.

Notes

1. Hebrews 4:12, literal translation.

2. C. F. W. Walther, *Law and Gospel*, Reproduced from the German edition of 1897 by W. H. T. Dau, (St. Louis: Concordia Publishing House, 1946), 99.

3. Carl S. Meyer, *Moving Frontiers*, (St. Louis: Concordia Publishing House, 1964), 141.

4. Ibid., 141.

5. Carl S. Meyer, *Walther Speaks to the Church—Selected Letters,* (St. Louis: Concordia Publishing House, 1973), 89.

7. Ibid., 38.

CHAPTER TWENTY-SEVEN

THOMAS JEFFERSON
Communication

Effective communication is a challenge to the success of any would-be leader. Consider the movie mogul Sam Goldwyn, who came to America from Poland. No one would dispute his success, but Goldwyn's knack for abusing the English language has nearly eclipsed his professional reputation. His fractured phrases have become known as Goldwynisms:

- A verbal contract isn't worth the paper it's written on.
- Include me out.
- I may not always be right, but I'm never wrong.
- It's more than magnificent—it's mediocre.
- I read part of it all the way through.
- If I could drop dead right now, I'd be the happiest man alive.
- Anyone who goes to a psychiatrist ought to have his head examined.
- For your information, I'd like to ask a question.
- Going to call him William? What kind of name is that? Every Tom, Dick and Harry is called William!

- Yes, my wife's hands are very beautiful. I'm going to have a bust made out of them.[1]

Not every leader is a great communicator nor is every orator a great leader, but for leadership to succeed, communication must occur. The life of Thomas Jefferson demonstrates the point.

Thomas Jefferson was many things: a fine architect, a true friend, a devoted husband, dedicated father, an excellent horseman, a skilled negotiator, an accomplished musician, an advocate for universal education, a champion for emancipation, well read, and multilingual. But if it were not for his exceptional ability to communicate the great truths of our founding fathers, we might not even know his name. Jefferson was not even listed among the 56 delegates to attend the First Continental Congress of September 5, 1774. Neither would he have attended their second meeting in May of 1775, had it not been for an upheaval in Virginia that kept their chosen delegate homebound.

It was an era of extraordinary talent and huge egos. John Adams' fiery rhetoric was without equal. Fellow Virginians, Patrick Henry and Colonel George Washington, were highly regarded militarists, while the reputations of Benjamin Franklin, John Hancock, and Benjamin Harrison had established them as intellectual giants. "Jefferson discovered that each delegate considered himself a 'great man, an orator, a critic, a statesman' and was intensely jealous of his imaginary reputation. Amid the animosities that were taking root, Jefferson displayed a great political gift—an ability to win and hold the friendship of remarkably opposite men, without compromising his own principles."[2]

But Jefferson possessed a talent greater than his ability as a reconciler, his gift to record profound thoughts in simple but majestic prose brought him quickly to the fore. After British attacks in the North made war inevitable, Jefferson was assigned to a committee of five to draft a declaration of independence.

The members selected were: Jefferson, Adams, Franklin, Roger Sherman, and R. R. Livingston. Franklin was ill and neither Sherman nor Livingston were known for their literary talent, leaving the task of drafting the document to Adams or Jefferson. Jefferson deferred to the senior Adams who refused the honor for three reasons which he later recalled. "Reason first—you are a Virginian, and a Virginian ought to appear at the head of this business. Reason second—I am obnoxious, suspected and unpopular. You are very much otherwise. Reason third—you can write ten times better than I can."[3]

A wise man once said, "When something can be read without effort, great effort has gone into its writing." No finer compliment could be paid to Jefferson and the document which would become known as The Declaration of Independence. Although the document in whole went through considerable editing at the hands of the delegates, the opening arguments were so well established that little editing occurred until the actual listing of grievances against King George III of England.

Jefferson's intent was to place before mankind a statement on the purpose and limits of government made on the basis of such overwhelming common sense that all would be compelled to agree. Thus, basing his arguments upon what he believed were divine intentions, he wrote;

> When in the course of human events it becomes necessary for one people to dissolve the political bands which have connected them with another, and to assume among the powers of the earth the separate and equal station to which the laws of nature and of nature's god entitle them, a decent respect to the opinions of mankind requires that

they should declare the causes which impel them to the separation.

We hold these truths to be self-evident, that all men are created equal; that they are endowed by their Creator with certain unalienable rights; that among these are life, liberty, and pursuit of happiness; that to secure these rights, governments are instituted among men, deriving their just powers from the consent of the governed; that whenever any form of government becomes destructive of these ends, it is the right of the people to alter or abolish it, and to institute new government, laying its foundation on such principles, and organizing its powers in such form as to them shall seem most likely to effect their safety and their happiness ....

Jefferson's words crystallized the passion which had been raging in the hearts of the colonists. Despite the fact that July 2 was the date when the fiercely debated vote for independence was passed, July 4 is forever considered the birthday of American Independence. It was not until the fourth that Jefferson's declaration was formally ratified by official vote. The importance and power of communication are demonstrated by the tradition of celebrating the later date.

Communication is no less important in Christian ministry. It was for the Gospel that people labored, sacrificed, and even died. The church was not established by Christ to obtain riches, achieve high honor, or conquer nations. It was for the sake of the message that the apostles were martyred. When commanded to stop speaking about Christ, their response was immediate. "Judge for yourselves whether it is right in God's sight to obey you rather than God. For we cannot help speaking about what we have seen and heard" (Acts 4:19–20).

If the Gospel is so important as to die for, it only makes sense that we should communicate it in the most effective manner. To be sure, those who proclaim the Gospel can expect divine assistance. Paul, a master of the written word, relied heavily on the Lord. "When I came to you, brothers, I did not come with eloquence or superior wisdom as I proclaimed to you the testimony about God. For I resolved to know nothing while I was with you except Jesus Christ and Him crucified. I came to you in weakness and fear, and with much trembling. My message and my preaching were not with wise and persuasive words, but with a demonstration of the Spirit's power, so that your faith might not rest on men's wisdom, but on God's power" (1 Corinthians 2:1–5). It is certainly more important to be faithful though perhaps awkward than to be articulate and wrong. But Paul never argued that less than his best was acceptable when representing Christ and the Gospel.

When it comes to communicating the spoken word, God's measure is truth, but the measure of the audience is presentation. The effective communicator must care about both. We have all heard people rave about well-delivered messages even though they contained obvious, even heretical errors. Conversely, many a fine message falls on "deaf ears" because the speaker fails to present it in an interesting and confident manner.

In the movie *Planes, Trains, and Automobiles,* Steve Martin has had his fill of John Candy's endless and meaningless gibberish. At his breaking point, Martin unleashes a five-minute speech about the pain he has endured during the time the two have been forced to coexist.

> Didn't you notice on the plane, when you started talking, eventually I started reading the vomit bag? Didn't that give you some sort of clue, like, "Hey, maybe this guy is not enjoying it?" Everything is not an anecdote. You have to discriminate. You choose things that are funny or mildly amusing, or interesting. You're a miracle! Your stories have none of that! They are not even amusing, *accidentally!* ...

> I could tolerate any insurance seminar. For days I could sit there and listen to them go on and on with a big smile on my face. And when they'd say, "How can you stand it?" I'd say, "Cause I've been with Dale Griffith. I can take anything!" ... And by the way, when you are telling these little stories. Here's a good idea: *have a point*! It makes it so much more interesting for the listener!

The Gospel of Christ deserves better. As Solomon reflected in his conclusion to Ecclesiastes. "Not only was the Teacher wise, but also he imparted knowledge to the people. He pondered and searched out and set in order many proverbs. The Teacher searched to find just the right words, and what he wrote was upright and true. The words of the wise are like goads, their collected sayings like firmly embedded nails—given by one Shepherd" (Ecclesiastes 12:9–11).

The words of the wise are like goads, they motivate and encourage others to action. They are like well-driven nails, able to unite people in such a way that goals are achieved and division is not easily accomplished.

Speeches and well-written documents have been known to change the course of history. After the Declaration of Independence was ratified, George Washington had it read aloud to his troops in New York. Civilians there, when they heard it, pulled down the leaden statue of George III and melted it into bullets.[4] Inspired by the words of Thomas Jefferson, the American forces overcame enormous odds and obtained the victory. In the Gospel of Jesus Christ there is an even greater outcome at stake. Paul wrote, "I am not ashamed of the gospel, because it is the power of God for the salvation of everyone who believes: first for the Jew, then for the Gentile. For in the gospel a righteousness from God is revealed, a righteousness that is by faith from first to last, just as it is written: 'The righteous will live by faith" (Romans 1:16).

No wonder so many Christian pastors begin their messages with the quotation, "May the words of my mouth and the meditation of my heart be pleasing in Your sight, O LORD, my Rock and my Redeemer" (Psalm 19:14).

More Scriptural Insight

Exodus 4:10–16   What was Moses' problem and God's solution?

Mark 13:9–13   What help is promised when required by adversity?

2 Peter 3:14–18   How did Peter assess the writings of Paul?

A Leader's Prayer

Gracious Lord, I find it all too easy to relate to the communication inadequacies of Moses! The important task of effective communication far exceeds my abilities, even my God-given abilities. Lord, help me to understand that You often intend to accomplish great things through meager talents. I desire to be useful in Your kingdom, Lord, not for the sake of my own reputation, but for the sake of the lost and for the benefit of the Kingdom. Allow the splendor of the Gospel to be seen in contrast to the earthen vessel which contains it. I realize the importance of the Gospel and count greatly on Your promise to empower my words through the Holy Spirit. As You enabled Moses, David, Elijah, Paul, and Peter so empower my witness for the salvation of the lost and the strengthening of the saved. Give greater clarity to my understanding so that each word might be always true and plain spoken. As Thomas Jefferson inspired others to independence, use my words of encouragement to inspire others to receive the freedom obtained through Christ upon the cross. In His name I pray. Amen.

Notes

1. Richard Lederer, *Anguished English—An Anthology of Accidental Assaults upon Our Language,* (New York: Dell Publishing, 1987), 129–31.

2. Thomas Fleming, *The Man from Monticello—An Intimate Life of Thomas Jefferson,* (New York: William Morrow and Company, 1969), 246.

3. Ibid., 251.

4. Ibid., 263.

CHAPTER TWENTY-EIGHT

STEPHEN R. COVEY
Personal Integrity

I once heard a motivational speaker explain how "attitude affects altitude." He contended that people are restricted in their ability to excel more by internal limits than by external obstacles. It's like the pastor who found his Arizona congregation difficult to motivate. He complained that Arizona winters were so nice, heaven didn't interest them, and the summers were so hot, hell held no fear!

According to Steve Covey, author of *The Seven Habits of Highly Effective People,* it is possible to change personal limitations, but it must be done "inside-out."

> Inside-out is a process—a continuing process of renewal based on the natural laws that govern human growth and progress. It's an upward spiral of growth that leads to progressively higher forms of responsible independence and effective interdependence.

> I have had the opportunity to work with many people—wonderful people, talented people, people who deeply want to achieve happiness and success, people who are searching, people who are hurting. I've worked

with business executives, college students, church and civic groups, families and marriage partners. And in all of my experience, I have never seen lasting solutions to problems, lasting happiness and success, that came from outside in."[1]

Covey believes there are no shortcuts. Lasting change, which results in true greatness, is a matter of personal character established on integrity. Anyone can achieve a singular victory and grab momentary glory, but those who would be regarded as truly great must be great "inside out." Covey puts so clearly into words what years of frustration and futility have taught many a leader. We have all attended many conferences and workshops on the "how-tos" of better leadership and organizational techniques. While there is benefit in learning the "how," it is not nearly as valuable as learning the "why."

Win Arn, the well-known analyst of ministry trends in America, recently predicted the failure of what he calls "Willow Creek clones." He correctly pointed out that while many pastors were busy imitating the activities of the successful Barrington, Illinois, congregation, they were actually missing the point. It is not "what" Willow Creek does that leads to their success, *it is why they do what they do* that leads to their ultimate success. By the time many have learned the techniques that bring growth, Willow Creek has changed and is no longer doing the things these imitators spent so much time learning! They grow because their motive and their mission is not a superficial one. They grow because they never stop asking the deeper questions: "How can we reach unchurched people? How do unchurched people think? What do unchurched people think of the church? What are the hurts and pains of the unchurched people? How can the Christian community help unchurched people overcome their problems and draw them to Christ?"

If Covey is right about the impossibility of lasting solutions based on external, quick-fix solutions, it follows that everyone who has enjoyed lasting success, happiness, and the respect of their peers has accomplished it based on what Covey calls "personal or character ethic." He makes his point with a striking analogy.

> To focus on techniques is like cramming your way through school. You sometimes get by, perhaps even get good grades, but if you don't pay the price day in and day out, you never achieve true mastery of the subjects you study, or develop an educated mind.

> Did you ever consider how ridiculous it would be to try to cram on a farm—forget to plant in the spring, play all summer and then cram in the fall to bring in the harvest? The farm is a natural system. The price must be paid and the process must be followed. You always reap what you sow; there is no shortcut.[2]

There are no shortcuts. If successful leaders had a quarter for every time they have been asked "the secret of their success," most could retire to the country club of their choice. Those who ask are implying that there is some simple idea, some simple formula, that if applied in any situation will result in great achievement. Recent trends in continuing education are partly to blame for the rise of the "quick-fix" mentality. Many successful leaders are likewise guilty of "boiling down" *the secrets of their success* to 12, 10, even six "keys" which can be heard at their workshop, purchased on audiocassette recordings encased in a handsome plastic binder, or watched on their just-released video. Not everyone is buying it.

Covey points out, "As I travel around the country and work with organizations, I find that long-term thinking executives are simply turned off by psych up psychology and "motivational" speakers who have nothing more to share than entertaining stories mingled with platitudes. They want substance; they want process. They want more than aspirin and Band-Aids. They want to solve the chronic underlying problems and focus on the principles that bring long-term results."[3]

What are the Seven Habits ® Covey has observed in highly effective people?

1. Be Proactive.®
2. Begin with the End in Mind.®
3. Put First Things First.®
4. Think Win Win.®
5. Seek First to Understand, Then Be Understood.®
6. Synergize.®
7. Sharpen the Saw.®

Knowing the Seven Habits® is the easy part, putting them into practice is what separates leaders from wannabes. As Albert Gray writes in his essay *The Common Denominator of Success,* "Successful people have the habit of doing the things failures don't like to do. They don't like doing them either, necessarily, but the disliking is subordinated to the strength of their purpose."[4]

Inside-out leadership is biblical leadership with a new name. Jesus warned His followers to be careful of false teachers who outwardly appeared harmless, but inwardly were ravenous wolves. "Watch out for false prophets. They come to you in sheep's clothing, but inwardly they are ferocious wolves. By their fruit you will recognize them. Do people pick grapes from thornbushes, or figs from thistles? Likewise every good tree bears good fruit, but a bad tree bears bad fruit. A good tree cannot bear bad fruit, and a bad tree cannot bear good fruit. Every tree that does not bear good fruit is cut down and thrown into the fire. Thus, by their fruit you will recognize them" (Matthew 8:15–20).

The Lord cares a great deal about personal integrity. The end does not justify the means, as is shown in the life of Saul. Saul's continual compromise led to God's eventual rejection and the selection of David as the future king of Israel. In perhaps the best known of his failures, Saul was understandably slow to admit his compromise. It was not his first, but it would be his last moral failure as king of Israel.

Instructed by the prophet Samuel, Saul was to utterly destroy the Amalekites for their rejection of God and their cowardly attack against the stragglers during Israel's wilderness wandering.[5] Instead of following the counsel of the Lord, Saul spared the best of the spoil and Agag, king of the Amalekites. When confronted, Saul tried in vain to excuse his behavior by saying, "The soldiers took sheep and cattle from the plunder, the best of what was devoted to God, in order to sacrifice them to the LORD your God at Gilgal" (1 Samuel 15:21). Samuel didn't debate the truth of Saul's questionable explanation. His rebuke reveals just how highly the Lord regards personal integrity:

> Samuel replied: "Does the LORD delight in burnt offerings and sacrifices as much as in obeying the voice of the LORD? To obey is better than sacrifice, and to heed is better than the fat of rams. For rebellion is like the sin of divination, and arrogance like the evil of idolatry. Because you have rejected the word of the LORD, he has rejected you as king."

> Then Saul said to Samuel, "I have sinned. I violated the LORD's command and your instructions. I was afraid of the people and so I gave in to them. Now I beg you, forgive my sin and come back with me, so that I may worship the LORD."

> But Samuel said to him, "I will not go back with you.
> You have rejected the word of the LORD, and the LORD has
> rejected you as king over Israel!" (1 Samuel 15:22–26)

Saul's confession came too late to be believed. One of the saddest verses of Scripture says, "Samuel mourned for him. And the LORD was grieved that He had made Saul king over Israel" (1 Samuel 15:35). It hurt Samuel to be so harsh but the Lord had seen enough. There was something wrong with Saul that went deeper than his outward action; something was wrong at the core.

Personal integrity is not as common among leaders as we would wish. The Christian integrity of which Jesus spoke, and for which Saul was rejected, requires a rescue described by Paul in Romans. "When I want to do good, evil is right there with me. For in my inner being I delight in God's law; but I see another law at work in the members of my body, waging war against the law of my mind and making me a prisoner of the law of sin at work within my members. What a wretched man I am! Who will rescue me from this body of death? Thanks be to God—through Jesus Christ our Lord!" (Romans 7:21–25). Good habits are built slowly over time. We will never be completely free from our "old self" but Jesus is there to restore, renew, and enable.

Covey's conclusion is apropos and agrees with Paul's. "It's obviously not a quick fix," he writes. "But I assure you, you will feel benefits and see immediate payoffs that will be encouraging. In the words of Thomas Paine, 'That which we obtain too easily, we esteem too lightly. It is dearness only which gives everything its value. Heaven knows how to put a proper price on its goods.'"[6] Paul called it fighting "the good fight of faith" which, in the end, results in the "crown of righteousness which the Lord, the righteous Judge, will award to me on that day—and not only to me, but also to all who have longed for His appearing" (2 Timothy 4:7–8).

More Scriptural Insight

Psalm 37:12–20	How are the righteous distinguished from the wicked?
Matthew 19:16–26	What was lacking in the life of this good man?
1 Corinthians 9:24–27	Why does Paul continue to exercise self-control?

A Leader's Prayer

Lord, there is so much to learn and I wonder if I will ever master my profession. It even seems the more I learn, the more confused I become. Not everyone follows the same road to success. There are many ways to lead, teach, encourage, and motivate. The choices can be confusing. But Your call to obedience and integrity is clear and equally applies to all. I know that "obedience is better than sacrifice." A pure heart is of greater importance than honor, and righteousness more highly prized than praise. Lord, grant me a clean heart and renew a right spirit within me. Restore unto me the joy of Your salvation and grant me Your Holy Spirit. It is an age-old prayer, and still a necessary one. Uphold me in my integrity and arouse my conscience to always know and do Your will. Whether I succeed or fail, let my life be a living witness to You. This I pray through Jesus Christ, my Lord. Amen.

Notes

1. Stephen Covey, *The Seven Habits of Highly Effective People—Powerful Lessons in Personal Change,* (New York: Simon & Schuster, 1989), 43. Excerpts used with permission of Covey Leadership Center, Inc., 3507 N. University Ave., P.O. Box 19008, Provo, Utah 84604-4479. Phone: (800) 331-7716.

2. Ibid., 22.

3. Ibid., 42.

4. Stephen Covey, *Personal Leadership Application Workbook,* (Provo, UT: Covey Leadership Center, 1991), 2.

5. See Deuteronomy 25:17–19 and Exodus 17:8–16.

6. Stephen Covey, *The Seven Habits of Highly Effective People*, 62.

CHAPTER TWENTY-NINE

ULYSSES SIMPSON GRANT
Knowing Your Strengths

I n a hierarchical system every person tends to rise to his level of incompetence ... or so the Peter Principle says. The theory is based on the notion that those who succeed at their jobs will always be noticed and offered greater responsibility until they reach the limits of their abilities. The conclusions of such a theory are equally interesting. 1) In time, every post tends to be occupied by an employee who is incompetent to carry out its duties. 2) Work is accomplished by those employees who have not yet reached their level of incompetence.

Although uncertain, the Peter Principle was surely postulated by an oppressed underachiever, chaffing at the leadership of perceived incompetence. If there are only two types of employees: 1) Those who understand what they do not manage, and 2) Those that manage what they do not understand, the author of the Peter Principle must have considered himself one of the former managed by the latter!

While the theory validates every employee's frustration with management, if it were true no organization could achieve its purpose or even endure for long. Although amusing, it is a flawed theory. It assumes abilities are static and without the potential for growth. To accept it you must also believe people will always be promoted who demonstrate great ability. Experience has shown neither premise to be true.

The apostle Paul Principle establishes a completely different theory of management. In the kingdom of the Lord, strength is weakness, and weakness is perceived as strength!

> To keep me from becoming conceited because of these surpassingly great revelations, there was given me a thorn in my flesh, a messenger of Satan, to torment me. Three times I pleaded with the Lord to take it away from me. But He said to me, "My grace is sufficient for you, for My power is made perfect in weakness." Therefore I will boast all the more gladly about my weaknesses, so that Christ's power may rest on me. That is why, for Christ's sake, I delight in weaknesses, in insults, in hardships, in persecutions, in difficulties. For when I am weak, then I am strong. (2 Corinthians 12:7–10)

A quick review of great biblical leaders will show that Paul's experience was the norm rather than the exception. God is in the habit of choosing incompetents and down-and-outers for significant roles in His army.

Abraham sometimes lied about his wife to protect his own hide.

Jacob lied to his father and deceived his brother to gain an inheritance.

Judah, who slept with prostitutes, once accused his daughter-in-law of harlotry.

God chose an Egyptian prisoner to save the world from a coming famine.

Moses offered five excuses before accepting God's call to leadership.

Gideon was the least son, of the least clan, of the least tribe in Israel.

Saul was painfully shy when chosen to be king.

David was at first overlooked when Samuel asked to see all the sons of Jesse.

If it seems weakness and insignificance are preferred attributes of the Lord, you are not far from right. Paul not only observed this principle at work, he also explained it. "God chose the foolish things of the world to shame the wise; God chose the weak things of the world to shame the strong. He chose the lowly things of this world and the despised things— and the things that are not—to nullify the things that are, so that no one may boast before him" (1 Corinthians 1:27–29).

Ulysses S. Grant, according to the apostle Paul Principle, was a sure candidate for greatness. When Lincoln's call to defend the Union came, Grant was a broken man, living in Galena, Illinois, working to support his family in the leather shop of his father. "He struck neighbors as a sad man—taciturn, shabby, and stooped."[1]

Some people, it seems, are made for a certain task in history. Unnoticed before and unsuccessful after, they distinguish themselves as the right person for a specific time when no one else would do. General Ulysses S. Grant was such a man.

James Russell Lowell called him, "One of those still plain men that do the world's rough work."[2] "Lyss," as his dad called him, was raised the oldest son of a leather tanner. His early years were undistinguished. He was not an especially good student but he was admired for his dogged determination, self-reliance, and an uncanny ability to maintain control over the most difficult of horses. "An Ohio farm boy, he graduated from West Point 21st in his class of 39, a quiet and unassuming fellow. 'Nobody would have picked him out as one who was destined to occupy a conspicuous place in history,' recalled a classmate."[3]

The same determination that broke horses, broke enemy lines and brought the young officer success on the battlefield, including several citations for bravery during the Mexican campaign. Later, that same unswerving spirit would make him the most highly regarded general in the Northern army. More than one biographer has explained Grant's success by quoting his explanation for the victory at Vicksburg. "One of my great superstitions, had always been when I started to go anywhere, or to do anything, not to turn back, or stop until the thing intended was accomplished." When his men were flooded out of their position by a sudden rise in the Mississippi River, he reasoned, "There was nothing left to be done but to go forward to a decisive victory."[4] That is precisely what he did. Lincoln appreciated his determined spirit more than most. When newspapers criticized Grant for the large number of casualties at Shiloh,[5] Lincoln's rebuttal was simple and direct, "I can't spare this man—he fights!"[6]

Unfortunately, our perception of Grant is clouded by the smoke and haze of his eight years as the 18th president of the United States. Although not personally accused, his cabinet was smeared by one scandal after another. There was also the matter of his drinking. Whether his "battle with the bottle" was ever won is disputed, he had developed an unwelcome reputation in Galena, that dogged him throughout the war and into the White House. Like Lincoln before him, the newspapers took special delight in attacking the presidential office with outrageous accusations and extreme caricatures. Lacking the clarity of war, the political arena proved more troublesome for President Grant than did Robert E. Lee or the entire Confederate army. Out of his element, Grant was easy prey for unscrupulous men who, for personal gain, took advantage of his simple trust in the chain of command.

Time has afforded a better perspective. U. S. Grant was not

a successful farmer,[7] businessman, or even a great president; he was a courageous soldier, a gifted leader of men, and a highly respected general. Most believe if it were not for the less-than-courageous leadership of Grant's predecessors, the war might have ended much sooner. Lincoln said of him, "Grant is the first general I have had. You know how it has been with all the rest. They wanted me to be the general. I am glad to find a man who can go ahead without me."[8]

The apostle Paul Principle is also seen in Grant's greatest moment, the surrender at Appomattox. Ever since his decisive victory at Fort Donelson early in the war, General U. S. Grant had been known as General "Unconditional Surrender" Grant—the terms he required when Confederates sought a truce. Appomattox would be uncharacteristically different.

Lee's men were outnumbered, starving, and decimated after the long siege of Petersburg, which had been his final defense of the Confederate capital, Richmond. When the city fell, Lee retreated, hoping to regroup and continue the fight. Grant moved quickly to keep Lee from strengthening his resistance. Realizing the hopelessness of his situation and to spare the South any more pain, Lee accepted Grant's call for surrender. It was Palm Sunday, April 9, 1865. Grant's military haste brought him to this historic moment without benefit of his entourage. Dressed in his field uniform with muddy trousers tucked into his muddy boots, he wrote the terms of surrender himself and presented them to the impeccably dressed southern general. Lee was surprised one last time. Instead of the reprisals he anticipated, Grant asked only that the Confederate army stack its weapons and go home. When Lee asked if the men could take their horses with them, Grant agreed for the sake of their farms. Lee, in turn, offered immediate release of all remaining Union prisoners since food even for his own men was scarce. Grant was again generous, sending 25,000 rations to Lee's army. But the troops didn't wait for the order to be filled, following the lead of their general, they entered the Confederate camps and emptied their haversacks of beef, bacon, and biscuits.

Three days later, Lee's army of 28,231 men stacked their rifles in Appomattox square and returned to their homes. As they entered the square, the spirit of mutual respect was now demonstrated by the rank and file. "From early morning until late afternoon, the saluting soldiers of the South marched past the saluting Union soldiers, stacked their rifles and tattered Confederate flags and started home."[9]

The apostle Paul Principle requires mercy and grace, recipient becomes dispenser. Explaining this aspect of the principle, Paul wrote, "Christ Jesus came into the world to save sinners—of whom I am the worst. But for that very reason I was shown mercy so that in me, the worst of sinners, Christ Jesus might display His unlimited patience as an example for those who would believe in Him and receive eternal life" (1 Timothy 1:15–16).

The humble origins and failure in Grant's early life may explain his gracious and wise treatment of his enemy in defeat. Those who rise from humble origins and past failure have the advantage when it comes to managing success. They are the first to realize that except for the Lord's favor, circumstance, and the right opportunities, there is often little difference between success and failure. Few would doubt that Lee was the better general, but due to military might, repeating rifles, industrial strength, and the sheer numbers of new recruits, the North was at last victorious. Grant had suffered his share of defeats, and like Paul, had experienced patience and mercy when so many called for his removal. At Appomattox, the former failure extended a hand of mercy to the recently fallen.

More Scriptural Insight

1 Chronicles 17:16–27   To what did David attribute his greatness?

Psalm 127   According to Solomon what is the essential element of success?

Galatians 6:6–10   Summarize Paul's concluding comments to the Galatians.

A Leader's Prayer

Heavenly Father, grant me a more determined spirit, fully committed to a life of useful service. I realize, Lord, that I am not gifted in every area. Make me more willing to admit my shortcomings, first to myself, and then to others. Open my eyes to see that we are made for dependence as well as independence. Give me a gracious and willing spirit to receive help and advice from others. Also enable me to recall my failures without embarrassment so that I might be more gracious to others who struggle and fail. Like the apostle Paul, help me to see the value of admitting my weakness so that my life will be available for a display of Your power. In success, let it be the name of Christ that is honored. Make me more sensitive to those around me who may be encountering personal setbacks and frustrations similar to those General Grant experienced while in Galena. Comfort all Christians with constant knowledge that our ultimate worth was determined upon the cross. In You we have received our value. We do not despair too greatly over our failures, or rejoice too greatly over any success we may experience. All glory, honor, and praise belong to You and You alone for You found me, saved me, and gifted me to lead Your people. To You, O Lord, I offer my praise. Amen.

Notes

1. Robert Paul Jordan, *The Civil War*, (Washington, D. C.: National Geographic Society, 1969), 36.

2. Ibid., 210.

3. Ibid., 63.

4. David Donald, *Ulysses Simpson Grant,* The Encyclopedia Americana, (New York: Americana Corporation, 1963), vol. 13, 136.

5. Shiloh was the bloodiest battle to be fought on American soil up to that time. Grant was surprised by the Confederates but quickly regrouped and mounted a counteroffensive which routed the enemy, killing their commanding general. News of the casualties shocked both North and South alike; 10,700 Confederates and over 13,000 Union troops died in just two days of fighting.

6. Frank B. Latham, *Immortals of History: Abraham Lincoln,* (New York: Franklin Watts, Inc., 1968), 107.

7. His father-in-law gave Grant 80 acres of land outside of St. Louis which he unsuccessfully attempted to farm before the war. He called the place "Hard Scrabble" and after four years abandoned the idea. After an equally unsuccessful effort at real estate, Grant moved his family to Galena, Illinois, where he returned to work in his father's leather shop.

8. Russell Freedman, *Lincoln, A Photobiography,* (New York: Scholastic Incorporated, 1987), 107.

9. William Zinsser, *Mercy at Appomattox,* The Reader's Digest, (Pleasantville, NY: Reader's Digest Inc., vol. 145, no. 872, December 1994), 93–96.

CHAPTER THIRTY

CAPTAINS MERIWETHER LEWIS
AND WILLIAM CLARK
A Spirit of Adventure

The easy roads are crowded,
and the level roads are jammed;
The pleasant little rivers
with the drifting folks are crammed.
But off yonder where it's rocky,
where you get a better view;
You'll find the ranks are thinning,
and the travelers are few.

Where the going's smooth and pleasant
you will always find a throng.
For so many—it's a pity—
seem to like to drift along.
But the steps that call for courage,
and the task that's hard to do
In the end results in glory
for the never wavering few. (Unknown)

t's a pithy little poem and has much to say about leadership. Those who live to the glory of the Lord will wince over the last two lines, but they will experience the same lonely quest. All great endeavors, Christian or otherwise, require an explorer's heart for adventure and tolerance for adversity.

Jesus said, "Anyone who does not take up his cross and follow Me is not worthy of Me. Whoever finds his life will lose it, and whoever loses his life for My sake will find it" (Matthew 10:38–39). To most reasonable people, terms such as "cross bearing" and "loss of life" have an element of risk associated with them. Peter confirmed the obvious when he wrote, "Dear friends, do not be surprised at the painful trial you are suffering, as though something strange were happening to you. But rejoice that you participate in the sufferings of Christ, so that you may be overjoyed when His glory is revealed. If you are insulted because of the name of Christ, you are blessed, for the Spirit of glory and of God rests on you. If you suffer, it should not be as a murderer or thief or any other kind of criminal, or even as a meddler. However, if you suffer as a Christian, do not be ashamed, but praise God that you bear that name" (1 Peter 4:12–15).

Jesus spoke of "walking the narrow path" and said few find it. Robert Frost called it walking the "road less traveled." To those familiar with the Lord's analogy, Frost's words have special meaning.

Two roads diverged in a yellow wood,
And sorry I could not travel both
And be one traveler, long I stood
And looked down one as far as I could
To where it bent in the undergrowth;

Then took the other, as just as fair,
And having perhaps the better claim,
Because it was grassy and wanted wear;
Though as for that passing there
Had worn them really about the same,

And both that morning equally lay
In leaves no step had trodden black.
Oh, I kept the first for another day!
Yet knowing how ways leads to way,
I doubted if I should ever come back.

I shall be telling this with a sigh
Somewhere ages and ages hence:
Two roads diverged in a wood, and I—
I took the one less traveled by,
And that has made all the difference.[1]

Walking the road less traveled requires a spirit of adventure and involves risks and effort most are unwilling to accept. Captains Meriwether Lewis and William Clark accepted the risks and undertook the adventure.

I have the good fortune of living very close to the confluence of the Missouri and Mississippi rivers. It is truly a beautiful part of God's creation and an important historic site. Whenever I cross one our city's great bridges, I think of the incredible journey made by these two explorers. Rivermen accompanied them as far as North Dakota but fewer than 30 crossed Montana and the mountains to reach the Pacific Ocean. What they accomplished was thought impossible. By today's measure, their journey crossed 10 states, and passed through Indian territories occupied by many different and unpredictable tribes. Most were hospitable, even helpful, others were antagonistic, suspicious, or opportunists who considered the expedition a potential source of great gain. The explorers dealt with each tribe in a friendly but firm manner, always with a show of strength to avoid being considered easy prey.

If the trip up the river was hazardous,[2] the trip over the

Rockies was life threatening. Their horses often fell, "packs and all" rolling end-over-end down the steep terrain. Away from the plains and their bounty, food got scarce. They survived by trading trinkets and knives to the Indians for powdered fish, corn meal and dogs—not hot dogs, but the four-legged variety. Although Clark ate the latter by necessity only, Lewis wrote in his journal, "For my own part, I have become so perfectly reconciled to the dog that I think it an agreeable food and would prefer it vastly to lean venison or elk."[3]

All this, and an overland return, they accomplished in just over two years from May 13, 1804, through September 24, 1806. In his introduction to Lewis and Clark's published journals,[4] John Bakeless remarks, "The success of the Lewis and Clark Expedition was due to the remarkable qualities of leadership possessed by these two officers. They traversed North America from St. Louis to the Pacific Coast and returned, taking a woman and a newborn baby with them.[5] ... All this they accomplished with only one Indian fight and with the loss of only one man—from disease. ... It may be well to point out that Lewis and Clark led, without friction of any kind, a group of three races: their own white men; the Negro slave, York; and the Indian girl, Sacagawea, not to mention her half-breed baby."[6]

Their journey, recorded in meticulous detail and the voluminous maps produced by Clark, was invaluable to men such as President Thomas Jefferson, whose world view included great knowledge of Europe and the eastern seaboard but little reliable information about the rest of the North American continent. Although other, more traversable routes were later discovered through the Rocky Mountains, Lewis and Clark's expedition helped the fledgling American government comprehend the value of this country when negotiating treaties and land acquisition from the English, French, and Spanish empires.

The expedition also served notice to the many Indian tribes

Lewis and Clark encountered. Not only were they told of the coming westward expansion, some Indians, including a prominent chief, made the journey east, including a visit to Washington, D. C. You can imagine the stories they told when they returned to their native tribes three years later.

The sheer danger of the excursion from the elements, raging rivers, Indians, bears, mountain lions, lack of food, and their uncharted mountain crossing could be equated to the technical challenge of modern man's journey into space. With primitive gear and methods they survived the odds. (Before their last thermometer broke they recorded temperatures of 70 degrees below freezing!) We can only imagine their satisfaction upon completion of the hazardous journey.

The explorers had hoped to find return passage on any one of the many ships known to visit the Pacific Coast. "Although the *Lydia*, a ship out of Boston, was in the area during November of 1805 and aware of the possible presence of the overland expedition, the two never met. "The captain did not find them, though a few signal guns would certainly have attracted the explorers' attention. *Lydia* stood off and on the Pacific Coast till August 1806, by which time Lewis and Clark were nearly home. Soon after they left Oregon, one copy of their message[7] fell into the hands of the brig's captain, who carried it to Canton (China) where an American copied it and sent a copy to Boston. The *Lydia* herself reached Boston in 1807, nearly a year after Lewis and Clark had returned."[8]

A sense of adventure is required by all who would offer their life as a "living sacrifice" to the Lord. As James puts it, "Now listen, you who say, 'Today or tomorrow we will go to this or that city, and spend a year there, carry on business and make money.' Why, you do not even know what will happen tomorrow. What is your life? You are a mist that appears for a little while and then vanishes. Instead, you ought to say, 'If it is the Lord's will, we will live and also do this or that' " (James 4:13–15). Biblical leaders have demonstrated a willingness to step out, unaware of the future but willing to follow the Lord's leading.

Abraham was successful and 75 years old when God invited him to follow.

Moses was content as a shepherd before he encountered the burning bush.

Gideon was in hiding when the recruiting angel called him into military service.

The young shepherd David would become a hero, an outlaw, and finally a king.

Nehemiah gave up a king's palace to rebuild Jerusalem.

Peter, James, and John were mending nets, enjoying a secure and predictable life.

When they accepted the mantle of leadership, they had no idea how their lives would change. So it is with everyone who follows Christ's leading. The writer of Hebrews wrote, "And what more shall I say? I do not have time to tell about Gideon, Barak, Samson, Jephthah, David, Samuel and the prophets, who through faith conquered kingdoms, administered justice, and gained what was promised; who shut the mouths of lions, quenched the fury of the flames, and escaped the edge of the sword; whose weakness was turned to strength; and who became powerful in battle, and routed foreign armies. ... The world was not worthy of them" (Hebrews 11:32–38).

Life in service to the Lord is unpredictable at best but never, never, no never without adventure.

More Scriptural Insight

Ruth 1:6–18	What might have motivated Ruth's courage?
Luke 9:57–62	What is the purpose of Jesus' dialog?
Hebrews 11:13–16	What distinguished the heroes of faith?

A Leader's Prayer

Lord, I have often sung, "Where You lead, I will follow." It is easier to sing than do. Like Peter, my spirit is willing but my flesh is weak. I desire to suffer all ... except maybe the loss of friends, the scorn of enemies, and the loneliness that comes from following an unpopular course. I willingly offer all I have ... except maybe a tenth of my income, my weekends, and control of my schedule. Why is it, Lord, that while I am in worship, the sacrifice and commitment seem so right and my heart is so willing, but often, before I finish the day, the demands of life and my own skepticism steal my spiritual resolve? I know the heart of the father who once responded so honestly, "Lord, I do believe; help my unbelief!" Help my unbelief, Lord. Resolve my fears and give me greater courage to accept the adventure, putting one foot in front of the other until life's walk is done. Thank You for the privilege of leadership and the opportunity to live my life in gratitude for all that You have done for me. In the name of Jesus, my Lord and Savior. Amen.

Notes

1. Robert Frost, *You Come Too,* (New York: Henry Holt and Company, 1992), 84.

2. In one day on June 14, 1805, Lewis escaped a grizzly bear attack by wading into the river and drawing his sword, then stumbled upon a cougar guarding her lair, and was charged by three bull buffaloes!

3. John Bakeless, "The Journals of Lewis and Clark," (New York: Mentor Books, 1964), 288.

4. Both Lewis and Clark were required to keep detailed journals as a condition of the government-financed expedition.

5. The woman was an Indian squaw acknowledged as a skilled interpreter who, unknown to either explorer, was pregnant before the journey began. She delivered her child without any help, and causing no delay in the expedition! Amazed, Lewis wrote, "In about an hour the woman arrived with her newborn babe and passed us on her way to the camp, apparently as well as she ever was."

6. John Bakeless, Introductory remarks, xi.

7. Before departing on their homeward journey, Lewis and Clark posted a letter of their excursion in the cabin they had constructed near the mouth of the Columbia. It included the names of those on the expedition and the date of their arrival and departure. Other copies were left with friendly Indian tribes who were asked to place them in the hands of white traders who may visit the coast by ship.

8. John Bakeless, footnote, 296.

CHAPTER THIRTY-ONE

THEODORE ROOSEVELT

Try

It was an incredible undertaking, requiring 14 years of Herculean effort and nearly a million dollars. But what seemed ridiculous in concept is now a highly regarded national shrine. Now, on the 6,200 foot wilderness peak called Mount Rushmore, there appear the images of George Washington, Abraham Lincoln, Thomas Jefferson, and Theodore Roosevelt. These were not the originally intended visages. Doane Robinson, a South Dakota historian, submitted a proposal to increase tourism and attract money to the state's economy. He suggested the carving of three great western legends: Kit Carson, Jim Bridger, and John Colter on the austere peak. The chosen sculptor, John Gutzon Borglum, opposed such blatant commercialism and argued that such an undertaking ought to honor men of colossal reputation and national significance.

The scope of the project from start to finish is beyond simple description. My son once carved a duck from a bar of soap for a school project. I'm not sure if a duck was our original design or just our final option, but I do remember the frustration and hours that went into that effort. What I can't imagine is the vision and skill that went into the Mount Rushmore effort. Working from a scale model, Borglum blasted away tons of surface rock before finding stone suitable for sculpting. Washington's chin, for example, began 30 feet back from the original surface, and Teddy Roosevelt's forehead required the removal of 120 feet of surface rock! We could step back a pace or two and examine our Dial-duck, but Borglum was strapped to a rope dangling over 20-foot-long noses, 18-foot-wide mouths, and eyes 11 feet across!

The sculptor was 60 years old when the project began, and after his death on March 6, 1941, it was left for his son to finish. When Doane Robinson first proposed the concept in 1923, he could not have anticipated the extraordinary outcome. Mount Rushmore has become world renown and stirs the pride of every true American.[1]

How does one qualify for such immortal recognition? It is doubtful that Washington, Jefferson, Lincoln, nor Roosevelt ever felt worthy of such a monument. They nonetheless paid a great price for their inclusion. Theodore Roosevelt spoke for them all when he said, "No man is worth his salt who is not ready at all times to risk his body, to risk his well-being, to risk his life, in a great cause."[2]

Roosevelt certainly qualifies as a "larger than life" individual. His accomplishments are extraordinary. He achieved greatness in so many different spheres it is hard to believe he was only one man of less than average life span.[3] Besides being the 26th president of the United States, Theodore

- Mastered taxidermy at the age of 13.
- Graduated with honors from Harvard.
- Established a cattle ranch in the Bad Lands of North

Dakota.

- Survived the sudden death of his wife and mother on the same day.[4]
- Published dozens of magazine articles on a wide variety of topics.
- Wrote the definitive work on the naval war of 1812.
- Wrote a number of best-selling historic books on the Wild West.
- Served as the United States Civil Service Commissioner, introducing the concept of qualified testing for government employment.
- Served as head of the Police Commission for New York City.
- Was appointed assistant secretary of the Navy.
- Was made a lieutenant colonel in the 1st U. S. Volunteer Cavalry, later promoted.
- Became a war hero who led the assault against the fort of San Juan in Cuba during the Spanish American War.
- Served as governor of New York.
- Was elected vice president, became president after McKinley's assassination.
- Was reelected president by the largest margin of victory ever achieved.
- Negotiated and undertook the building of the Panama Canal.
- Was awarded the Nobel Peace Prize for mediation in the Russo-Japanese War.
- Founded the Boone and Crocket Club for the promotion of adventure and the preservation of wildlife.
- Established countless conservation efforts for future generations, including the establishment of a federal parks program.

- Completed several exhaustive safaris to Africa and Brazil to secure specimens for American museums.
- Helped train soldiers for World War I, which claimed the life of his youngest son, Quentin.

Roosevelt achieved all this despite childhood asthma so severe no one expected him to survive. Unable to attend regular school, he was forced to cope in an age before inhalants and modern medications. Perhaps his early struggle was responsible for a work ethic not easily dissuaded. I have long admired his own explanation,

> It is not the critic that counts, not the one who points out how the strong man stumbles or how the doer of deeds might have done better. The credit belongs to the man who is actually in the arena; whose face is marred by dust and sweat and blood; who strives valiantly; who errs and comes short again and again; who knows the great enthusiasms, the great devotions, and spends himself in a worthy cause; who at best knows in the end the triumph of high achievement; and who at the worst, if he fails, at least fails while daring greatly, that his place shall never be with those cold timid souls who know neither victory nor defeat. ...
>
> Far better it is to dare mighty things, to win glorious triumphs, even though checkered by failure, than to take rank with those poor spirits who neither enjoy much nor suffer much because they live in the gray twilight that knows neither victory nor defeat.[5]

Roosevelt endured his share of defeats and had more than his share of critics. It wasn't defeat that concerned him as much as apathy. He described himself as an average man who worked harder at it than the average man. It never got too complicated for President Roosevelt. Once, when asked how an ordinary man could be so popular with the people, he simply replied, "I get things done. Americans like that."[6]

He kept it simple when it came to values also. His most popular book of all was one published after his death entitled *Letters to His Children.* This aspect of his life caused one biographer to write, "No more virtuous or clean-living man ever existed; the temptations which wreck the lives of so many human beings simply did not exist for him. Though somewhat indifferent to formal theology, he was an earnest practicing Christian, deeply concerned for his own moral and spiritual decency and that of his children."[7]

A wise father once told his son that it was a grave mistake to withhold his effort because there was someone who could do the thing better, bigger, or faster. "Do what you can," was his counsel. It is still good advice. The Lord compares us only against the talent, skill, and resources of our blessing. He doesn't ask us to do better, bigger, or faster things. He only asks us to be faithful. The apostle described God's standard when he wrote, "Men ought to regard us as servants of Christ and as those entrusted with the secret things of God. Now it is required that those who have been given a trust must prove faithful" (1 Corinthians 4:1–2).

Faithfulness is its own standard. What is faithful for one may be too little or too much for another. Although tempted by our human nature, we are not to compare the Lord's expectation of us to others. Neither should we complain because His expectation of Christian leaders seems so great. The Lord makes no apologies for high expectations. He once told a story to illustrate this point,

> Suppose one of you had a servant plowing or looking after the sheep. Would he say to the servant when he comes in from the field, "Come along now and sit down to eat"? Would he not rather say, "Prepare my supper, get yourself ready and wait on me while I eat and drink; after that you may eat and drink"? Would he thank the servant

because he did what he was told to do? So you also, when you have done everything you were told to do, should say, "We are unworthy servants; we have only done our duty." (Luke 17:7–10)

While the Lord has high expectation, He also possesses great compassion and understanding. A verse in Psalm 103 has always held special comfort because it provides a significant glimpse into the heart of God. The psalmist wrote, "As a father has compassion on his children, so the LORD has compassion on those who fear Him; for He knows how we are formed, He remembers that we are dust" (Psalm 103:13–14). It is the same kind of reality that caused the Lord to put the rainbow in the sky and promise not to flood the earth again on account of man. After all, He acknowledged, "every inclination of his heart is evil from childhood" (Genesis 8:21).

It should not surprise us that those closest to Jesus failed Him at His hour of greatest need. Knowing human nature and the power of temptation, Jesus showed the same divine understanding toward His dearest friend, Peter.

"Simon, Simon, Satan has asked to sift you as wheat. But I have prayed for you, Simon, that your faith may not fail. And when you have turned back, strengthen your brothers." But he replied, "Lord, I am ready to go with you to prison and to death." Jesus answered, "I tell you, Peter, before the rooster crows today, you will deny three times that you know Me." (Luke 22:31–34)

He "knows our frame," understands when we fail, but expects us to learn from the experience and use it to "strengthen your brothers."

We are all tempted to complain, even the best of us. Missionary Henry C. Morrison, who returned from Africa on the same boat as Roosevelt's African expedition, had been on the African mission fields for 40 years. When the ship entered

New York harbor, Roosevelt was received with great fanfare including a boat armada. For a moment Morrison thought he, not Roosevelt, deserved the reception, but then a small voice came to him whispering, "Henry—You're not home yet."

More Scriptural Insight

Job 19:13–27   Despite enormous setbacks, what was the attitude of Job?
Ecclesiastes 9:10–12   Describe the advice of Solomon.
Philippians 4:10–13   What gave Paul the courage to try?

A Leader's Prayer

Lord, I am not necessarily good at many things, but this I know, "Most of what I try will fail, and what succeeds, others will criticize." I am only human and such an outcome sometimes makes it hard to give Your work an honest effort. Overcome my resistance and help me to see it is not so much the outcome but the effort that pleases You. Lord, I appreciate Your understanding of human failing. We are a people of two natures, flesh and spirit. I confess I often feed the flesh and starve my spirit. Give me food that nourishes my faith and causes me to attempt greater things, relying on Your aid to accomplish all that You desire to accomplish through me. Remind me that I am not alone. "Greater is He who is in me than he who is in the world." Lord, I believe, help Thou my unbelief! All this I pray through the precious blood-bought merit of Jesus Christ, my Lord. Amen.

Notes

1. Charles Panati, *Extraordinary Origins of Everyday Things*, (New York: Perennial Library, Harper and Row, 1987), 282–84.

2. Peggy Anderson, *Great Quotes from Great Leaders*, (Lombard, IL: Celebrating Excellence Publishing Co., 1990), 9.

3. Theodore Roosevelt, born in New York City in 1858, died January 6, 1919, at the early age of

60 years.

4. The tragedy occurred on February 14, 1884, when his wife died in childbirth. His mother died of typhoid fever 12 hours later. His father also died at a young age while Teddy was enrolled at Harvard.

5. The quote is from a personal file on famous quotes gathered over the years. Although it is one of Roosevelt's more famous statements and appears in many books, I am unable to determine the occasion when it was first used.

6. Clara Ingram Judson, *Theodore Roosevelt,* (Chicago: Follett Publishing Company, 1953), 194.

7. Edward Wagenknecht, *Theodore Roosevelt,* The Encyclopedia Americana, (New York: Americana Corporation, 1964), vol. 23, 684–86.

CHAPTER THIRTY-TWO

Audie Murphy
Perspective

If you can keep your head when all about you
  Are losing theirs and blaming it on you,
If you can trust yourself when all men doubt you,
  But make allowance for their doubting too;
If you can wait and not be tired by waiting,
  Or being lied about, don't deal in lies,
Or being hated, don't give way to hating,
  And yet don't look too good, nor talk too wise:

If you can dream—and not make dreams your master;
  If you can think—and not make thoughts your aim;
If you can meet with Triumph and Disaster
  And treat those two impostors just the same;
If you can bear to hear the truth you've spoken
  Twisted by knaves to make a trap for fools,
Or watch the things you gave your life to, broken,
  And stoop and build 'em up with worn-out tools:

If you can make one heap of all your winnings
  And risk it on one turn of pitch-and-toss,
And lose, and start again at your beginnings
  And never breathe a word about your loss;
If you can force your heart and nerve and sinew

235

To serve your turn long after they are gone,
And so hold on when there is nothing in you
Except the Will which says to them: "Hold on!"

If you can talk with crowds and keep your virtue,
Or walk with kings—nor lose the common touch,
If neither foes nor loving friends can hurt you,
If all men count with you, but none too much;
If you can fill the unforgiving minute
With sixty seconds' worth of distance run,
Yours is the Earth and everything that's in it,
And—which is more—you'll be a Man, my son![1]

Rudyard Kipling's famous poem is a fitting tribute to Audie Murphy and such who display great leadership in times of severe testing. Murphy, the most decorated American soldier of World War II, survived the worst battles of the entire war from North Africa, to Sicily, to the landing at Anzio, the invasion of Normandy, Alsace, the Siegfried Line, and finally Germany itself. In one seven-week period Murphy's division suffered over forty-five hundred casualties. Several times his company was all but destroyed.

Murphy's platoon developed a reputation for no-holds-barred combat. Known as the "grave yard regiment," they spent the entire war on the front line, leading patrols and reconnoitering the enemy positions under cover of darkness. Everyone in his original unit, including Murphy, was either killed or severely wounded. Some were wounded repeatedly. An orphan from Texas, Murphy declined furlough stateside until the campaign was finished. His closest friends and literally hundreds of replacements died by his side during his two and a half year tour-of-duty. Despite hospitalization for malaria, concussions from artillery, repeated shrapnel wounds, and a crippling bullet wound, Murphy survived. He was officially credited with having killed, captured, or wounded 240 enemy soldiers, several times single-handedly holding off entire units while his men recovered their wounded or retreated from a trap of enemy crossfire. For his bravery and leadership Murphy, a buck private, rose to the rank of first lieutenant and was awarded 21 medals of honor, including the highest military decoration, the Congressional Medal of Honor.

But perhaps more amazing than his physical survival was Murphy's ability to withstand the horrors of war on such a personal level day in and day out. Hand-to-hand combat, mine fields, machine gun fire, mortar attacks, and the constant hammering of artillery can destroy a person in more than one way. Front-line battle fatigue took its toll, and a good number of men suffered complete emotional breakdowns. Without warning or preference, it would strike seasoned veteran and new recruit alike. Nothing is more devastating than the violent death of those you love, but each time Murphy was able to regain his perspective and reaffirm the mission.

At the conclusion of his autobiography *To Hell and Back*, Murphy reveals the depth of his despair, and his attempt to gain a new perspective at the end of hostilities.

> When I was a child, I was told that men were branded by war. Has the brand been put on me? Have the years of blood and ruin stripped me of all decency? Of all belief?

> Not of all belief. I believe in the force of a hand grenade, the power of artillery, the accuracy of a Garand. I believe in hitting before you are hit, and that dead men do not look noble.

But I also believe in men like Brandon, and Novak, and Swope, and Kerrigan; and all the men who stood up against the enemy, taking their beatings without whimper and their triumphs without boasting. The men who went and would go again to hell and back to preserve what our country thinks right and decent.

My country. America! That is it. We have been so intent on death that we have forgotten life. And now suddenly life faces us. I swear to myself that I will measure up to it. I may be branded by war, but I will not be defeated by it.

Gradually it becomes clear. I will go back. I will find the kind of girl of whom I once dreamed. I will learn to look at life through uncynical eyes, to have faith, to know love. I will learn to work in peace as in war. And finally—finally, like countless others, I will learn to live again.[2]

Maintaining a balanced perspective whether in war or in the day-to-day exercise of Christian leadership is no easy task. The enemy is especially good at infiltrating our lines. In order to fend off the intended hurts and subtle attacks of those he uses, we are tempted to withdraw from the very people we lead. Near the war's end, Murphy's sensitivities were all but lost. "I am concerned with the individual only as a fighting unit," he wrote. "If his feet freeze, I will turn him over to the medics. If his nerves crack, I will send him to the rear. If he is hit, I will see that his wound is treated. Otherwise, I look upon him as a unit whom I must get to the front and in battle position on schedule."[3]

Effective leaders must maintain a high degree of objectivity to accomplish the overall mission, not allowing the roller coaster of human emotions to overly influence their decisions. This is probably the weakest link in the armor of most Christian leaders. Concern for others is what has drawn us to positions of leadership in the Lord's army. And because the mission is accomplished by people and on behalf of people, sensitivity is a helpful quality. The key to a healthy balance is found in the model of Jesus.

From the cross He could look upon His own executioners and pray, "Father, forgive them, for they do not know what they are doing" (Luke 23:34). Even when His closest friends deserted Him, Jesus was able to see past their action to the reason for their action. "The spirit is willing, but the body is weak" (Matthew 26:41).

Jesus' perspective enabled Him to complete the mission, despite the nonsupport of those for whom He labored. He was able to rise above the attacks of His enemies and the confusion of His friends to follow the will of His Father. The dimensions of Christ's leadership are beyond mortal man. One of the most haunting of the messianic prophecies is from Isaiah, "I have trodden the winepress alone; from the nations no one was with Me" (Isaiah 63:3). All alone, He was left to personal prayer and visitation with His heavenly Father. At the moment of His greatest need, even His Father left Him.[4]

Christlike leadership still requires intense prayer and time with the Lord through the use of His means of grace, His Word and Sacraments. Few (if any) can go it completely alone. Wise Christian leaders will enlist the aid of other mature Christians to support, encourage, and enable them.

Kipling's poem effectively describes the great challenge of leadership. Only with the help of the Lord and the support of Christian friends can you "keep your head when all about you are losing theirs and blaming it on you!"

More Scriptural Insight

Numbers 12	What led to the rebellion and how did Moses handle it?
Matthew 11:2–14	How would you describe John's ministry?
Ephesians 6:10–20	Describe the main points of Paul's counsel.

A Leader's Prayer

Gracious Father, I am not up to the standards of Your Son, my Savior, Jesus. How He withstood the attacks of His enemies and the immaturity of His friends is beyond me. In fact, I identify more with the immature disciples than with the constant and mature leadership of Your Son. Yet, You have placed me in leadership. You have asked me to maintain Your perspective for the work that is before us. Help me to both understand and accomplish all that You wish to be accomplished. Keep me from cynicism and indifference. Help me maintain my sensitivities while rising above the insults and attacks of Satan. Surround me with mature and faithful fellow Christians for I need their support and encouragement. Also enable me to be supportive of others whom You have called out from among Your people. Let me be the first to honor and encourage their efforts to offer their lives in willing service to You and those for whom Christ died. In all things let Your name be honored and Your praise be sung, through Christ Jesus, my Lord. Amen.

Notes

1. Rudyard Kipling, *Rudyard Kipling's Verse—The Definitive Edition,* (Garden City, NY: Doubleday, Doran and Company, Inc., 1945), 578.

2. Audie Murphy, *To Hell and Back,* (New York: Grosset and Dunlap Publishers, 1949), 273–74. Used by permission.

3. Ibid., 253.

4. See Matthew 27:46.

CHAPTER THIRTY-THREE

WALTER A. MAIER
Change

Someone once said, "Leaders are people who help others make the transition from the past to the future." It only sounds easy. It takes a special kind of person to "think outside of the box." Leadership within the body of Christ may be the hardest of all.

Christian organizations tend not to be known for their innovative spirit as much as their ability to uphold time-tested standards. Christians wrongly equate the mission to the unchangeable nature of Christ, who is "the same yesterday, today, and 'yes' forever."[1] He is the same, but that sameness doesn't mean predictability! Even the historic Athanasian Creed describes a dynamic Trinity, "The Father incomprehensible, the Son incomprehensible, and the Holy Spirit incomprehensible."

The apostle Paul preached a "changeless Christ to a changing world" by adapting his *modus operandi* to the culture and attitudes of his target audience. He wrote,

> Though I am free and belong to no man, I make myself a
> slave to everyone, to win as many as possible. To the Jews
> I became like a Jew, to win the Jews. To those under the
> law I became like one under the law (though I myself am
> not under the law), so as to win those under the law. To
> those not having the law I became like one not having the
> law (though I am not free from God's law but am under
> Christ's law), so as to win those not having the law. To the
> weak I became weak, to win the weak. I have become all
> things to all men so that by all possible means I might
> save some. I do all this for the sake of the gospel, that I
> may share in its blessings. (1 Corinthians 9:19–23)

Why is change so hard? The well-known futurist Joel Barker believes that people are resistant because when change occurs (or as he puts it, "when the paradigm shifts"), everyone goes back to zero. What he means, of course, is that change "levels the playing field" between the rookie and the veteran. In fact, those heavily invested in the former way of thinking and doing are actually at a disadvantage.

The organist/choir director who acknowledges the validity of contemporary Christian music is immediately no better (maybe even worse off) than a young graduate. Suddenly decades of leading mass choirs, brass quartets, handbells, and expertise on the pipe organ become insignificant. New instruments and changing musical styles necessitate new ways of doing things. Electronic drum pads, keyboards, and computer-programmable synthesizers require rethinking, retraining, and diminish the importance of former skills—skills that were acquired only through years of hard work.

It is understandable (and very typical) for established directors to simply oppose the change on the basis of lofty and important-sounding rhetoric. Lack of expertise is disguised as concern for heritage, or the innovations are discredited as "inferior." Suddenly preserving one's heritage becomes the mission, and music, once intended to serve the Gospel, becomes an end in itself. Instead of "being all things to all people," the inflexible church asks people outside its traditions to "adapt, adopt, or look elsewhere."

Music isn't the only tradition challenged by change. Television has made education a more visual process, requiring teachers to incorporate more visuals: overheads, object lessons, videos, dramas, and printed outlines to help students learn. Despite these obvious changes, most Christian ministries have done little to vary their traditional method of teaching. Why? The more invested we are in the old ways of doing things, the more resistant we are to change. That is why seminary professors and pastors are such static creatures. They have paid huge "dues" to achieve their positions and aren't willing to quickly endorse those things that would render their investment insignificant. The same could be said for farmers, lawyers, engineers, secretaries—virtually any profession that must do business with an ever-changing clientele.

Paradigm pioneers are people willing to adapt to change, finding new and effective ways to achieve success in a fast changing world. They are especially rare in any society established upon tradition and the communication of old values. Almost always innovation and change are advocated by those on the institutional fringe. The closer one gets to the center of a social order, the more protective they become of the present system—but not Walter A. Maier.

Maier emerged as a paradigm pioneer from the most unlikely of settings. As an Old Testament professor of a confessional seminary, no one expected him to be innovative or act as a catalyst for change, but that is exactly what happened. Although heavily invested in the present, Maier was driven by possibilities for the future.

His education was classic and intense. Maier attained his Ph.D. in the field of Semitic Languages from no less a school than Harvard. His examination required proficiency in Sumerian, Babylonian, Hittite, Assyrian, Hebrew, and the Arabic language, also complete knowledge of Semitic literature, history, geography, and archaeology, not to mention expected competency in Greek, Latin, French, and German—a grand total of 10 languages. He not only achieved these incredible expectations, he graduated with honors in what was probably the most rigorous doctoral study in the most demanding institution of his day. Since its founding in 1636, many students had attempted the Ph.D. in this area, but by 1929 only 19 had ever succeeded![2] Even more amazing, Maier completed these studies while teaching full time at the prestigious Concordia Seminary of St. Louis. At the age of 29, Maier was the youngest professor in the history of the institution. No one was more "heavily invested" in the system than Dr. Walter A. Maier.

Impressive as his academic achievement was, it was not the thing which would distinguish Dr. Maier from other Christian leaders of his time. Before accepting the professorship, Maier had already demonstrated considerable leadership skills by reestablishing the financial viability of his denomination's youth association, enlarging its mission and focus. In just two years as its executive director, Maier doubled the league's membership and the number of congregational affiliates.[3] His newsletters were successful in mobilizing young and old alike. Under his direction, the league raised more than $200,000 (1920 dollars!) to rescue a floundering tuberculosis hospital in Wheat Ridge, Colorado. They also conducted an unprecedented and hugely successful European relief effort after World War I. This early success in motivating others provided a hint of his truly God-given strength.

Maier's special gift was an ability to communicate the Gospel in the most powerful and effective way. Jesus had people like Walter Maier in mind when He told His followers, "Anyone who has faith in Me will do what I have been doing. He will do even greater things than these, because I am going to the Father" (John 14:12). W.A.M., as Maier was called for his rapid fire, high energy teaching style, took the revolutionary invention of Guglielmo Marconi and put radio waves to work for Christ. By 1950 his was one of the most recognized voices in America. His weekly sermons were translated into 35 languages, aired from 55 different countries, and heard in 120 nations. It began with a simple low-power transmission from an attic on the seminary campus and steadily grew to an international network of 1,236 stations with a listening audience estimated at 20 million people worldwide.

As his well-known son and author, Paul Maier, described, "His voice often reached considerable intensity early in the sermon, violating the usual rule that radio speakers should use the volume level of a living-room conversation. The average rate of his fairly rapid delivery was 130–170 words per minute, and at times he introduced variety by raising pitch and volume as a thought cycle progressed, hitting the climax with emphasis, than tapering off for the denouement."[4] Some called it "prophetic boldness," but whatever the description, it remains a rare moment in the history of radio, and worldwide proclamation of the Gospel, by a here-to-fore unknown scholar.

His ability to personalize the often impersonal mode of radio was without equal. The Saturday Evening Post said, "The microphone becomes his audience, and to it he delivers his discourse, pointing his finger at it in stern warning, raising clenched fists toward it as he calls for penitence and spiritual rebirth, shaking his head at it intensely, as though it were the most miserable of sinners."[5]

Such a powerful force for change and progression from within such a staid institution also won the attention of critics. Life was too short and the cost too high for Maier to succumb to the pressure for conformity. As his son recalls, "If Maierian theology was 'traditional Lutheranism expressed in an untraditional manner,' it was only natural that he, as one of his church's leading progressives, should come under attack by the ultra-orthodox. Synod's ultra-orthodox were a dwindling splinter group, but a very vocal one. While they approved the Lutheran Hour speaker's battle with Modernism, they also censured him for addressing non-Lutheran groups and praying with them! Interpreting this as religious unionism, their heresy-hunting organ, The Confessional Lutheran, did Walter Maier the honor of attacking him. Naturally he made no reply, for he would not do battle with brethren of constricted mind."[6]

Abraham Lincoln once said, "Good things come to those who wait, but only the things left by those who hustle." Maier demonstrated a drive unequaled by his peers and misunderstood by his critics. He believed in his mission with consuming passion. His convictions were obvious; discerned in the certainty of his writing, the strength of his voice, and the integrity of his life. "Had a professional consultant been brought in, his criticism would likely have been: too much sermon by a person who uses his voice too forcefully, stressing too much the same message of salvation in Christ. Even the name 'Lutheran Hour' is wrong: too particularist, narrow, denominational. How can you expect a Methodist, or Catholic, or Quaker to listen to it?"[7]

Ecclesiastes 9:10 could serve as a fitting epitaph for Dr. Maier. "Whatever your hand finds to do, do it with all your might, for in the grave, where you are going, there is neither working nor planning nor knowledge nor wisdom." Tragically, at the early age of 56, the Lord called Dr. Walter Maier to his eternal and well-deserved rest. Expressions of sympathy from around the world inundated Dr. Maier's family and his radio headquarters. No greater comfort was received than that which Dr. Maier provided from beyond the grave. A prolific writer, he had already completed the devotionals for the 1950 and 1951 booklet *Day by Day*. As his family shared his devotional for the first Sunday after his death, they found the peace that only the Lord can provide. His meditation was based on the passage, "Our present sufferings are not worth comparing with the glory that will be revealed in us" (Romans 8:18). "What God ordains is always good," he wrote. "When we believe the Gospel of Christ's atoning death for our life; when we begin to realize that one moment in heaven is worth more than centuries on earth, we will understand that God let our Christ-dedicated dear ones meet death so that they could the longer enjoy the hallowed bliss and beauty with their Redeemer."[8]

Godly and blessed leader that he was, the ministry of Walter A. Maier continued with great vigor after his death. One of his own Old Testament students, an extremely bright and gifted speaker, eventually picked up the cloak of his fallen professor. Since 1955, until his retirement 35 years later, Dr. Oswald Hoffman continued the mission of proclaiming a "changeless Christ to a changing world." As demonstrated in the life of Dr. Maier, the marriage of progressive leadership to God's timeless truth is a powerful union rarely seen but so desperately needed in the church of our Lord.

More Scriptural Insight

Judges 4:4–15 What made Deborah a leader worthy of mention?
Luke 7:1–10 Describe the leadership traits of the Centurion?

Acts 17:15–33   How did Paul adapt his approach to the people of Athens?

A Leader's Prayer

Gracious Lord, most holy God, change is difficult. The uncertainty of change makes it difficult for leaders to step out with confidence, and difficult for others to trust them in uncharted waters. Help us to be open to new opportunities for the Gospel. Protect us from misplaced fears and keep our hearts focused on the true and only mission. Help us to know how best to honor past traditions and our godly heritage without being held captive by it. Encourage us to recall the great faith and sacrifice of previous generations so that we might be inspired to even greater acts of Christian service. Help us to think of ways to use the new technologies of science and industry for the cause of the Gospel. All creation is established to bring praise, honor, and glory to Your name. Bless courageous ministries with adequate support and, when a Christian leader falls, raise up another who will testify to Your grace with power and conviction, in Jesus' name. Amen.

Notes

1. See Hebrews 13:8.

2. Paul Maier, *A Man Spoke, A World Listened,* (New York: McGraw-Hill Book Company, 1963), 86–91.

3. Ibid., 56.

4. Ibid., 208.

5. Ibid., 207, from The Saturday Evening Post, June 19, 1948, 88.

6. Ibid., 259.

7. Ibid., 193.

8. Ibid., 372.

CHAPTER THIRTY-FOUR

COMPETITIVE SPIRIT
Michael Jeffrey Jordan

harles Schwab, the well-known industrialist, had a steel mill manager whose men were not producing their quota of work. Despite plant improvements and good wages, their production was the worst of those plants owned by Schwab.

"How is it," Schwab asked the manager, "that a man of your experience cannot bring this mill to full production?"

"I don't know," replied the frustrated manager. "I have coaxed the men and offered work incentives, but to no avail. I tried pushing and threatening them with penalties, but it made no difference. Mr. Schwab, I simply don't know what to do to get them to produce."

It was near the end of the day, and Mr. Schwab and the plant manager were completing a tour of the facilities. "Give me a piece of chalk," Schwab said. Then, turning to the nearest foreman he asked, "How many heats did your shift make today?" "Six," he answered. Without another word Schwab chalked a big figure "6" on the floor and walked away.

When the next shift came in, they saw the "6" and asked what it meant. The day foreman said, "The big boss was here today and asked how many heats we had made on our shift. When I told him, he wrote it down on the floor and walked away." The next morning Schwab walked through the plant again. The night shift had rubbed out the "6" and had replaced it with a "7." The day shift saw it too. They went to work to prove they were just as good as the night shift. When they quit that evening, an impressive "10" had been proudly scrawled on the floor. It wasn't long before the mill that had been trailing all others in production was producing more steel than any other company plant.

The way to get things done, Schwab firmly believed, was to stimulate competition. Not competition for pure financial gain, but in such a way as to create a desire to excel.

No one epitomizes the competitive spirit more than Michael Jeffrey Jordan. Describing his play, one commentator has written, "Michael Jordan floats above the rest of the NBA like a cloud, sometimes hurling down thunder and lightning, sometimes only a gentle rain of jump shots, the effects of which become cumulus. He is always overhead, hovering, so that what you see is what you are about to get. Players who have guarded him speak earnestly of trying to recognize these cloud formations and seeking shelter before they end up petrified in a state of permanent recoil on the walls of half the 12-year-old boys in America."[1]

Those closest to the game are in the best position to judge the competition. They regard Michael as simply the best. Consider these comments from the 1993 NBA championship issue of Sports Illustrated.

- "Is Michael Jeffrey Jordan simply the best basketball player in the history of the planet? No matter what you think of Jordan as a person, as a role model, as a shoe salesman, or even as a high-stakes gambler, you know the answer to that question: yes. A resounding yes."

- "Three-peat? Without Jordan the Bulls don't even peat."
- "Perhaps the most amazing thing about Jordan is the huge gap in sheer ability between him and his contemporaries."
- "There is no foil for Jordan, not even the shining Sun (a.k.a. Barkley)—for all of Barkley's belligerent brilliance, he was still out-scored by Jordan by an average of 14 points per game in the Finals."
- "The guy wins scoring titles, and he's one of the best defensive players of all time. That says it all."
- "As far as I'm concerned, Michael is Nureyev against a bunch of Hulk Hogans." (Bob Cousy, Boston Celtics)
- "Oscar (Robertson) was great defensively, when he wanted to be, but Michael is the Tasmanian devil."
- "Can't nobody have done better." (Dominique Wilkins, Atlanta Hawks)
- "The Bulls have not lost three games in a row since the beginning of the 1990–91 season, a statistic that is directly attributed to Jordan's competitiveness and drive."
- "The main thing to remember about Michael is that God only made the one."[2]

Everyone's entitled to an opinion. What gives these opinions such weight are the records that back them up.

1. 1984–85 Rookie of the year
2. 1987–88 Defensive Player of the year
3. 1991 MVP of the NBA finals
4. 1992 MVP of the NBA finals
5. 1993 MVP of the NBA finals
6. 1990–91 Overall Most Valuable Player of the NBA

7. 1991–92 Overall Most Valuable Player of the NBA
8. NBA best career scoring average, 32.6 pts./506 games
9. Led the league in scoring for seven consecutive seasons, 1986–93
10. Led his team to three consecutive NBA championships, 1991–93
11. Led the league in steals during the 1989–90 season
12. Named to the all-defensive NBA team for six consecutive years 1987–93

A competitive spirit is not a new concept—even for a Christian leader. Paul often used the metaphor of competition to describe the Christian way of life. He wrote to the church at Corinth, "Do you not know that in a race all the runners run, but only one gets the prize? Run in such a way as to get the prize. Everyone who competes in the games goes into strict training. They do it to get a crown that will not last; but we do it to get a crown that will last forever. Therefore I do not run like a man running aimlessly; I do not fight like a man beating the air. No, I beat my body and make it my slave so that after I have preached to others, I myself will not be disqualified for the prize" (1 Corinthians 9:24–27).

Paul compared the Christian life to the life of an athlete preparing for competition. They compete to win. They prepare for the contest through a regiment of strict training. They are focused. They concentrate on only one thing, winning the prize. Concentration is often the difference between winning and losing. Winning athletes are able to exert mind over body. Successful coaches remind their athletes that the mind gives up long before the body reaches its limits.

Ask any basketball player able to dunk a ball, "Which dunk is the hardest?" The answer is always the same, "The first one." But after they break the mental barrier, what took so long and seemed so difficult becomes routine. Mind-over-matter, bodily-discipline, self-control—call it whatever you like, it is an essential element of success.

In the same way Christians must overcome self-imposed limitations on their spiritual walk. The children of Israel had witnessed 10 miracles in Egypt, passed through walls of water on dry ground, drank water from rocks in the desert, and knew that God talked face to face with Moses. Yet, when they came to the edge of the land God had promised to give them, their faith failed. Why? Moses attributed it to bad thinking. "We seemed like grasshoppers in our own eyes, and we looked the same to them" (Numbers 13:33). They were beaten before they ever entered the battle. They had no faith in the Lord's promise, and certainly none in their own ability to dislodge the Canaanites and occupy the land which God had sworn to provide. They were literally their own worst enemy.

Paul, in an effort to make sure he was prepared for the challenge, worked hard at disciplining his body's natural tendencies which waged war against his spiritual nature. The stakes are much higher than a laurel wreath or a shiny brass trophy. Winning or losing the spiritual battle determines our eternity. Therefore, "I beat my body and make it my slave," Paul wrote, "so that I will not be disqualified for the prize," namely the upward calling of Christ Jesus on the day of His return.

We are a nation in love with sports and the spirit of competition that it brings. Our children's rooms are filled with trophies, ribbons, and pictures taken in the uniform of the season. One league gives way to the next as the pace quickens and the competition stiffens. As the athlete advances, tryouts and cuts reduce their number, until only the best are left to play before an ever-increasing audience of spectators. Along the way the competitors pick up various prizes, if they are fortunate, a college scholarship or a professional contract. Most walk away with less tangible rewards: a strong work ethic, an understanding of cooperation, and an appreciation for the value of adversity.

The Christian race is not for us to win, but it is one we can lose. While on the Isle of Patmos, John had a vision of the risen Jesus and learned firsthand of His victory. By means of His death and subsequent resurrection, Christ won the keys which assure our release from the chains of death and hell.[3] His victory is our victory, for the Lord intends to be only the first of many who will be saved by grace through faith in His accomplishment.[4] Paul wanted to make sure that Christ's victory would not be lost through careless living. Through spiritual exercise He used God's means of grace to maintain His spiritual strength. How? "A man reaps what he sows," Paul concluded. "The one who sows to please his sinful nature, from that nature will reap destruction; the one who sows to please the Spirit, from the Spirit will reap eternal life" (Galatians 6:7–8).

Faith in the Lord is the strength of every Christian. Paul wrote, "I can do everything through Him who gives me strength" (Philippians 4:13). The Christian leader who walks in that faith is noticeably different from those who talk the talk but fail to act. How different are they? Someone has described the difference in a simple comparison between winners and losers.

- Losers say, "It may be possible, but it's too difficult. Winners say, "It may be difficult, but it's possible."
- Losers see a problem in every solution. Winners see a solution to every problem.
- Losers say, "That's not my job." Winners say, "Let me help."

- Losers see the sand trap near the green. Winners see the green beyond the sand trap.
- Losers always have an excuse. Winners have a plan of attack.
- Losers become a part of the problem. Winners are a part of the answer.

Losers don't need to remain losers. Losers can turn their failure into an opportunity to rescue others. The only difference between the apostle Peter and the apostle Judas was how they responded to their failure. Both betrayed Jesus, in fact Peter denied His Lord three times while Judas denied Him only once. Peter went on to become a courageous leader in the early church, but Judas committed suicide. Judas failed to recognize and accept the forgiveness of the Lord. Peter repented of his past and received special encouragement from the Savior.[5] Restored losers make great leaders as Jesus predicted about Peter.[6] Even Michael Jordan learns from his mistakes, just ask his competition!

More Scriptural Insight

Samuel 17:41–50	What gave David the advantage against Goliath?
John 3:26–36	Why were John's disciples concerned and how did he handle it?
1 Corinthians 1:4–17	Should Christian churches be in competition?

A Leader's Prayer

Gracious Lord, I realize that my fight is not against flesh and blood, but against the world forces of darkness, against the spiritual forces of wickedness in heavenly places. Remind me of my great need to maintain the Christian faith through the regular use of Your Word so that I will be equipped and confident in the day of testing. Just as Paul knew that he could slip and fall, don't let me become over confident.

Although I have been used by You to bring others to faith, I am not immune to the attacks and deceitful cunning of the devil. He delights in my frustration and would rejoice in my downfall. As I continue in the race, keep me from an unhealthy spirit of competition against fellow servants or against other ministries being used by You to reach the lost and strengthen the saved. They too are running the race and it is my prayer that they would also be blessed by You to accomplish great things for the Kingdom. When I stumble, provide a Christian friend to pick me up. When I fall, restore me and renew me so that I might finish the race and receive the crown of glory which You have prepared for all the faithful. This I pray in the name of Jesus, the victorious King. Amen.

Notes

1. The editors of Sports Illustrated, *The 1993 Sports Almanac and Record Book,* (New York: Time Incorporated, by Bishop Books, 1993), 6.

2. Jack McCallum, *They're History!,* Sports Illustrated, (vol. 78, no. 25, June 28, 1995), 15–21. The article is reprinted courtesy of SPORTS ILLUSTRATED from the June 28, 1995 issue. Copyright © 1995, Time, Inc. All rights reserved.

3. See Revelation 1:18

4. See 1 Corinthians 15:20–24.

5. cf. John 21:15–19.

6. cf. Luke 22:31–32.

CHAPTER THIRTY-FIVE

DWIGHT DAVID EISENHOWER
Learning from the Past

Those who cannot remember the past are condemned to repeat it." Those words by the American poet George Santayana are posted as a warning at the Nazi extermination camp of Auschwitz. The Scriptures concur for Solomon wrote, "What has been will be again, what has been done will be done again; there is nothing new under the sun. Is there anything of which one can say, 'Look! This is something new'? It was here already, long ago; it was here before our time. There is no remembrance of men of old, and even those who are yet to come will not be remembered by those who follow" (Ecclesiastes 1:9–11).

Dwight David Eisenhower was a student of history and determined not to repeat the mistakes of the past. The fate of almost 1,000,000 men rested in his hands. The Allied invasion of Europe was scheduled for June 5, 1944, and he was the supreme commander of operation Overlord. The forecast was dismal, with winds up to 45 miles-per-hour, producing swells in the English channel that would swamp any landing craft's attempt to deliver troops and equipment to the beaches of France. But any further delay would mean postponement until June 19, when tidal conditions would again be high enough to permit the coastal strike. Eisenhower's chief meteorologist predicted a slight break in the weather on June 6, but the Atlantic was hard to predict.

Churchill was not so sure. With Dunkerque looming large in the back of his mind, he was hesitant. "When I think of the beaches of Normandy choked with the flower of American and British youth, and when, in my mind's eye, I see the tides running red with their blood, I have my doubts ... I have my doubts."[1] Although Churchill maintained public optimism, his private skepticism was little comfort for the supreme commander of the Allied invasion. Knowing the element of surprise would be lost by two-week's wait, he consulted with each of his commanders and gave the order, "Okay, we'll go."[2]

What appeared foolhardy to some was in truth a well-organized plan established upon documented odds. Eisenhower had learned all about calculated risk and percentages from a childhood mentor named Bob Davis. Davis was a family friend and an expert poker player. He taught young Dwight to play a scientific game based on mathematical probability. Eisenhower had learned well, so well in fact that he found army personnel easy pickins'. After an embarrassing incident, in which a subordinate had lost his family savings, Eisenhower found a way to restore his money and then quit the game. "I decided that I had to quit playing poker," he wrote in his autobiography. "Most of us lived on our salaries, and most losers were bound to be spending not only their own money but their family's. From then on I did not play with anybody in the Army."[3]

The advantage he refused to exercise with cards, he now employed as a military strategist. He knew that the Germans were expecting the assault to come hundreds of miles up the coast, following the shortest and most predictable path to Germany. A great deal of effort had been spent reinforcing that notion, massing nonessential troops, equipment, inflatable tanks and dummy artillery along the Dover coast to give this impression. To strengthen the bluff, the American 1st army, which would lead the attack across the southern channel, was renamed the twelfth, and phony radio dispatches confirmed the Nazi expectations. The weather, while bad, was also advantageous. The German high command and the troops were completely surprised by an attack under less than ideal conditions. (Field Marshal Rommel was actually home in Germany celebrating a birthday with his wife.) Eisenhower also knew Allied planes had almost completely destroyed the enemy rail lines and bridges leading into France, isolating the German front line from reinforcement and resupply. Two paratroop divisions would be dropped behind the enemy lines to attack the heavily entrenched beachheads from behind. It was a gamble, but a well-calculated one. To be sure, D-Day losses were significant, but also substantially less than had been anticipated.

Churchill had wished Ike well saying, "If by Christmas you have succeeded in liberating our beloved Paris, if she can by that time take her accustomed place as a center of western European culture and beauty, then I will proclaim that this operation is the most grandly conceived and best conducted (campaign) known to the history of warfare." The general was surprised. "Mr. Prime Minister," Eisenhower replied, "we expect to be on the borders of Germany by Christmas, pounding away at her defenses. When that occurs, if Hitler has the slightest judgment or wisdom left, he will surrender unconditionally to avoid complete destruction of Germany."[4]

Eisenhower was right. On August 25, the German garrison

in Paris surrendered and by September the allies were crowding the borders of Germany itself. After meeting stiff resistance from elite German troops, the Allies finally turned the tide, crossing the Rhine in March of 1945. On May 7, German Field Marshal Jodl signed the formal surrender in Eisenhower's headquarters at Reims.

Sometimes we don't realize how God is preparing us for later events in life. When we assume He is inattentive, He is teaching important lessons for our later benefit. Eisenhower loved to reflect on such things. He recalled one such lesson taught by a farmyard goose just before his fifth birthday. Visiting his uncle's farm, Dwight was repeatedly chased from the yard by an old gander. His uncle cut the handle off an old broom and after some instruction pointed him back toward the yard. When the goose again challenged his courage, young Ike let out a yell and charged the unsuspecting animal. Startled, the goose wheeled and ran, but not before being whacked across the tail feathers. "I learned," Ike recalled, "never to negotiate with an adversary except from a position of strength!"[5]

Ike later reflected on the many circumstances that had prepared him to command the invasion. A cross country truck convoy from Washington to San Francisco seemed frivolous before the war, but the experience proved to be important training for a mechanized army often in need of quick field repair. A chance assignment with General Patton established an important friendship and gave both men a peacetime opportunity to rethink strategies for using tanks in combat. Ike took full advantage of every opportunity to learn, especially from more experienced soldiers. "Always try to associate yourself closely with those who know more than you, who do better than you, who see more clearly than you. Don't be afraid to reach upward. The friendship might pay off at some unforeseen time, but that is only an accidental by-product. The important thing is that such associations will make you a better person."[6]

Leaders do well to make mental notes as they pass through life's experiences. During his years in Panama, Dwight was required to choose a horse from a corral already picked over by the officers who had preceded his arrival. Ike picked out a strong black gelding that had the legs and body of a fine horse but the short neck and large head of a mule. It was the best he could do. The animal proved exceptionally bright and was soon the best trained mount in the camp. Eisenhower took note. "In my experience with Blackie—and earlier with allegedly incompetent recruits at Camp Colt—is rooted my enduring conviction that far too often we write off a backward child as hopeless, a clumsy animal as worthless, a worn-out field as beyond restoration. This we do largely out of our own lack of willingness to prove that the animal can respond to training, that a field can regain its fertility, that a difficult boy can become a fine man."[7]

I am of the conviction that Christian leaders in particular should pray for the ability to remember. I recall, for instance, sitting in a small room converted for use as a church conference center. The table was so big and the room so narrow, you couldn't pass behind someone sitting in a chair. Once you were in place, you were in place for the night! The meeting that night was to consider how we would fund a $5 million expansion of our facilities to accommodate our growing church. We were encountering standing-room-only crowds at three back-to-back services every Sunday morning. Our entire annual budget wasn't even a million dollars! How we ever expected to fund a $5 million project was anybody's guess. Most of the members thought we were more than a little crazy, and we knew they were right. It didn't make good logical sense.

A neighboring congregation had just been "bought-out" by a shopping center. Someone told us they had received $3 million plus the gift of a new site on one of the busiest intersections in the county. I wouldn't say we coveted their good fortune, but the word *envy* comes to mind. About that time Al spoke up. "I'm happy for Lord of Life (the neighboring congregation)," Al said, "but I wouldn't trade spots with them even if we could. This challenge will make us all work harder, take greater faith, and require serious financial commitment on behalf of the whole church. In the long run we will be better off!" I was still thinking about what Al said when he offered to close the meeting with prayer. "Father," he said, "I want to thank You for the challenge before us, and for the opportunity we have to be part of something truly miraculous. Lord, help us to remember this night, and later, when things become easier and You grant success, let us never forget the depth of our concern and the absolute necessity of Your blessing. In Jesus' name. Amen."

That prayer haunted me for the next several years. Our congregation moved ahead with the construction and completed a sanctuary four times as large as the old one. Just this past week the treasurer reported to the lay council that the congregation was $8,500 "in the black" at midyear. Our cash projections had predicted a $60,000 deficit at midpoint with high hopes of recovery during the strong giving months of November and December.

As I sat in one of the spacious new classrooms listening to that remarkable report, my mind traveled back to Al's words and his prayer seven years earlier. Half of the members of the lay council, including the treasurer and chairman, were not even members when Al made his comments and offered his prayer. I still pray not to forget that night. I never want to forget what God did when we had great need, but no hope except in His blessing. All we had was a plan, a prayer, and absolute trust in the power of God who had made heaven and earth. God's strength was made perfect in our weakness.[8] No one present in that stuffy room seven years ago would dare stand up today and say, "Look what we have done!" Everyone knows firsthand the truth of Solomon's words, "Unless the LORD builds the house, its builders labor in vain. Unless the LORD watches over the city, the watchmen stand guard in vain. In vain you rise early and stay up late, toiling for food to eat—for He grants sleep to those He loves" (Psalm 127:1–2).

It is important for Christian leaders to have good memories. In the Old Testament the Lord established the Passover celebration so that the nation of Israel would never forget the miracle God performed in delivering them from the hand of Pharaoh. In the New Testament Jesus instituted the Lord's Supper so that we might never forget the cross and all that He did to deliver us from the hand of Satan. When Israel crossed the Jordan into the Promised Land, Joshua had 12 stones taken from the river, one for each tribe, and erected a monument of remembrance to recall how the Lord stopped the waters and allowed them to cross on dry ground.

As a pastor I am often called on to comfort and advise people in crisis. It has become common for me to urge our families to remember all the pain, heartache, and impossibility of their circumstance so that later, when they are delivered by the hand of God, they will always remember His ability to save.

We don't remember for memory's sake. Eisenhower resented the way history was studied at West Point. He once said, "I had little or no interest left in military history. My aversion was a result of its treatment at West Point as an out-and-out memory course. In the case of the Battle of Gettysburg, for instance, each student was instructed to memorize the name of every brigadier in the opposing armies and to know exactly where his unit was stationed at every hour during the three-day battle. Little attempt was made to explain the meaning of the battle, or why it came about."[9]

Memory's only value is in the lessons best by observation of the past. This is the only reason the Scripture recalls the exploits of the faithful. After listing the great heroes of faith, Hebrews 11 concludes, "Therefore, since we are surrounded by such a great cloud of witnesses, let us throw off everything that hinders and the sin that so easily entangles, and let us run with perseverance the race marked out for us" (Hebrews 12:1). Memory is the legacy of the righteous and the advantage of the faithful who recall the blessings of the Lord.

More Scriptural Insight

Psalm 103	List the blessings the psalmist wants to remember.
1 Corinthians 10:1–13	How does Paul use the past to serve the present?
John 13:1–7	Why did Jesus choose this means of teaching His disciples?

A Leader's Prayer

Gracious Lord, in the course of my life many unexplainable things happen which, at the time, seem totally unrelated to my life as a Christian leader. Help me to acknowledge that my times are in Your hands. I know that You are a creative God and in many and various ways You provide for my instruction. Especially help me during those times of difficulty to appreciate the necessity of hardship and the value of instruction that comes from personal experience. Lord, I desire to remember Your blessings. Keep me from the temptation to forget the difficulty or undervalue Your part in my rescue. Instead, keep me mindful of my despair and the hopelessness of my situation when I called out for Your intervention. Enable me to learn from my past so I do not repeat my errors. Strengthen the words of my testimony so that my experience will be a constant witness to Your greatness and the depth of Your compassion in Jesus Christ, my Lord. Amen.

Notes

1. Dwight D. Eisenhower, *At Ease: Stories I Tell to My Friends,* (New York: Doubleday & Co. Inc., 1967), 213.

2. Edward Ziegler, *Ike, the Man Behind the Soldier,* (Pleasantville, NY: Reader's Digest, date unknown), 136–40.

3. Dwight D. Eisenhower, 173.

4. Ibid., 214.

5. Ibid., 105.

6. Ibid., 183.

7. Ibid., 180.

8. See 2 Corinthians 12:9.

9. Dwight D. Eisenhower, 177.

CHAPTER THIRTY-SIX

HENRY FORD
Simplicity

There is power in simplicity. Robert Fulghum struck a responsive chord with Americans when he declared, "All I ever really needed to know I learned in kindergarten."

> Most of what I really need to know about how to live and what to do and how to be, I learned in kindergarten. Wisdom was not at the top of the graduate mountain, but there in the sandbox at nursery school.
>
> These are the things I learned: Share everything. Play fair. Don't hit people. Put things back where you found them. Clean up your own mess. Don't take things that aren't yours. Say you're sorry when you hurt somebody. Wash your hands before you eat. Flush. Warm cookies and cold milk are good for you. Live a balanced life. Learn some and think some and draw and paint and sing and dance and play and work every day some.
>
> Take a nap every afternoon. When you go out into the world, watch for traffic, hold hands and stick together. Be aware of wonder. Remember the little seed in the plastic cup. The roots go down and the plant goes up and nobody really knows how or why, but we are all like that.[1]

Henry Ford would have agreed with Mr. Fulghum. Things are best in their most simple form. Although one of the most successful men in America, he attributed his success to the simple things his mother taught him as a young boy.

> She taught me that disagreeable jobs call for courage and patience and self-discipline, and she taught me also that "I don't want to" gets a fellow nowhere. My mother used to say, when I grumbled about it, "Life will give you many unpleasant tasks ... Your duty will be hard and disagreeable and painful to you at times, but you must do it. You may have pity on others, but you must not pity yourself" ... I tried to live my life as my mother would have wished.[2]

In truth, the genius of Henry Ford was not innovation, but rather improvement, and improvement to Henry Ford was spelled s-i-m-p-l-i-f-y. Henry was born July 30, 1863, into a simple farm family. His folks, William and Mary, were hard-working immigrants from Ireland. They settled in Michigan where heavily forested land was still relatively cheap, and opportunities abounded for an industrious man like William. While clearing the land and establishing his own farm, he also worked as a carpenter, erecting buildings for the expanding American railway system. By the time Henry was born, his father was considered one of the more prosperous men in the region.

Henry's mother died in childbirth when he was only 12. Her death devastated Henry and brought a premature end to his childhood. The farm had lost its appeal and Henry, like many other farm boys of that time, ventured into Detroit looking for his future. He worked for a number of years in various machine shops before returning home to Dearborn. Using newly acquired skills, Henry was able to earn a good living running a steam engine which he transported from farm to farm across Michigan. He soon established a solid reputation for his mechanical ability and was hired by Westinghouse to service its machines throughout the area. Henry, by virtue of circumstance, entered the machine age on the ground floor. The noise and whirl of machines which intimidated many were Henry's claim to fame. He had found his niche.

Henry got into the automobile business partly due to mechanical fascination and partly due to his competitive nature. In the early days of the industry, financial prizes were awarded to winners of various mechanical races. Henry won his first race, not by speed, but by building the only machine able to finish the race. Financial backers who realized the huge future of the automobile industry urged Henry into production. Early in the era, an automobile was a status symbol owned only by the affluent. Henry's goal was to make a simple, reliable car within the financial reach of all Americans.

He worked around the clock with his engineers to produce an entirely new concept.

- A new more durable engine would be cast in one solid block, not four separate cylinders bolted together.
- A new steel alloy would be forged, making the car lighter but its frame even stronger than before.
- A better suspension would make it possible to drive on the worst roads.
- Toothed gears, which were so easily stripped, would be replaced by a new transmission system using circulating bands.
- A new sparking system would make cumbersome and inefficient batteries obsolete.
- And, perhaps most importantly, interchangeable parts would be manufactured to tighter specifications for easy repair and replacement.

In 1908, the Model T was born and Henry's promise fulfilled. By the end of World War I almost half of the cars on earth were Model T's. "No work with interest is ever hard," he said later. Indeed, Henry Ford felt that a man intent on success ought to keep his mind occupied day and night. "If he intends to remain always a manual laborer, then he should forget about his work when the whistle blows, but if he intends to go forward and do anything, the whistle is only a signal to start thinking."[3]

Unable to keep pace with demand and driven by a desire to make the Model T even less expensive, Henry experimented with ways to improve manufacturing. At first the automobile was moved from station to station where mechanics poured over its production at various stages. While this was an improvement over one team assembling a machine from start to finish, it was still too inefficient. What if the assembly section was designed to work like some of the production sections of the company? A 250 foot-long rope running the length of the factory was attached to a chassis with a team of six men moving with it from workstation to workstation until completion. The assembly time fell from twelve-and-a-half man hours to six! What if each person had only one job to do and the work came to them rather than they moving along with the work? A new experiment was tried. The assembly time fell dramatically, from six man hours to only one-and-a-half! "Within months, Highland Park was a buzzing network of belts, assembly lines, and subassemblies: a dashboard assembly line, a front-axle assembly line, a body-and-top assembly line. The entire place was whirled up into a vast intricate and never-ending mechanical ballet."[4]

As Henry Ford discovered, there is beauty and power in simplicity. This should come as no surprise to Christian leaders. Anyone who has ever stood before an audience will tell you that the simplest outlines produce the most effective messages. The truths of the Bible are not so complicated that you need a Ph.D. to explain or comprehend them. In a prayer He offered to His father, Jesus suggests that God's truth is best understood and appreciated by those of simple, even childlike faith. "I praise You, Father, Lord of heaven and earth," He prayed, "because You have hidden these things from the wise and learned, and revealed them to little children. Yes, Father, for this was Your good pleasure" (Matthew 11:25–26).

Some of the most powerful hymns of the church were written with children in mind:

- Jesus Loves Me, This I Know
- I Am Jesus' Little Lamb
- Away in a Manger
- Jesus Loves the Little Children
- I Am Trusting You, Lord Jesus
- Onward, Christian Soldiers
- There Is a Green Hill Far Away
- What a Friend We Have in Jesus

Visit any seminary campus in America and see for yourself the transformation that occurs to students after they have completed their internship. Before leaving academia they are consumed with topics which bear strange sounding Latin names such as: *filioque* (a reference to the Holy Spirit proceeding from both the Father and Son), *ex opere operato* (the work itself affects the result), or *genus maiestaticum* (the way Christ's divine attributes are communicated to His human nature). After a year of internship among God's people, students return for their last year more relaxed and yet more focused. They have come to realize that while theologians and seminary professors discuss the fine points of the communication of divine attributes to the human nature of Christ, they will probably never be asked to explain such a thing to the flock. *That is not to say that a good shepherd doesn't need to be highly educated and able to discern error and truth ... he does.* But it compares to a doctor setting a broken bone for her patient. It is important that she understands exactly how the bone, marrow, ligaments, and tendons are joined and how the physical process of mending takes place. But it is not likely that she will be asked to explain it to her patient. All they want to know is, "Will it heal properly? Will I regain full movement in my arm, leg, wrist, or finger? How long will I need to wear this cast?"

Jesus had a lot to say about simplicity. When the disciples were forbidding mothers from bothering Jesus with their little children, He admonished them.[5] The Syrophonecian woman could not be dissuaded by expressions of Jewish prejudice but pleaded, "Even the dogs under the table eat the children's crumbs." Jesus publicly acknowledged the greatness of her simple faith.[6] When describing the Christian faith to the Romans, Paul stressed its simplicity. "Do not say in your heart," he wrote, " 'Who will ascend into heavens.' " (that is, to bring Christ down), "or, 'Who will descend into the deep' " (that is, to bring Christ up from the dead). But what does it say? "The word is near you; it is in your mouth and in your heart," that is, the word of faith we are proclaiming: That if you confess with your mouth, 'Jesus is Lord,' and believe in your heart that God raised Him from the dead, you will be saved (Romans 10:6–9). The good news of salvation is a simple message intended for everyone. As Paul told the young man Timothy, "This is good and pleases God our Savior, who wants all men to be saved and to come to the knowledge of the truth" (1 Timothy 2:3–4).

His biographer has written of Henry Ford, "Throughout his career, the Dearborn boy who had left the one-room school house before he was fifteen was touchy on the subject of high-

er education. It was much overrated in his opinion—job seek-
ers who touted their university qualifications to Henry Ford
invariably received short shrift—and John Wandersee proved
the point. Cars for the people, by the people. The former factor-
floor sweeper went away for three months' training, and on
his return, he set up and ran a set of metallurgical laboratories
for Ford which remained, for many years, the foremost in
America."[7] Ford had a better idea: "Keep it simple."

More Scriptural Insight

2 Kings 5:1–14	How did people demonstrate simple trust or lack thereof?
Luke 10:1–20	How would you describe Jesus' strategy for evangelism?
Matthew 6:25–34	What is the key to a contented life?

A Leader's Prayer

Dear Father in heaven, I am guilty of making life more difficult than You ever intended it to be. Help me realize the
value of putting into practice the advice of Your Word. When I
am tempted to solve my own problems through worry, extra
effort, or a concerted attempt to out-maneuver my adversary,
remind me that my times are in Your hand. Let me again hear
the voice of the psalmist who wrote, "Cease striving and
know that I am God; I will be exalted among the nations, I will
be exalted in the earth." Indeed, the Lord of hosts is with us;
the God of Jacob is our stronghold. So here they are Lord, all
my worries, my problems, my hurts, and frustrations. Help
me to ask only what You would have me do, not "What would
be the smart, sure-fire, cannot-fail-solution to my problem?"
Reaffirm for me the value of simple things—the value of the
fruit of the spirit in my life: love, joy, peace, patience, kindness, goodness, faithfulness, gentleness, and self-control. I
commend my life to You. Help me to remember that I cannot

add even one day to my life through worry. Keep me in this faith unto life everlasting, through Jesus Christ. Amen.

Notes

1. Jack Canfield and Mark Hansen, *Chicken Soup for the Soul,* (Deerfield Beach, FL: Health Communications, Inc., 1993), 130.

2. Robert Lacey, *Ford—The Men and the Machine,* (New York: Ballantine Books, 1986), 12. Used by permission.

3. Ibid., 26.

4. Ibid., 116.

5. See Matthew 19:13–14.

6. See Matthew 15:28.

7. Robert Lacey, 96.

CHAPTER THIRTY-SEVEN

MARTIN LUTHER KING, JR.
Turn the Other Cheek

We shall overcome, we shall overcome,
We shall overcome ... some day ay ay ay;
Deep in my heart, I do believe,
We shall overcome someday.

We'll walk hand in hand, we'll walk hand in hand;
We'll walk hand in hand ... some day ay ay ay;
Deep in my heart, I do believe
We'll walk hand in hand someday.

I was a young boy of only 11 when Dr. Martin Luther King, Jr. made his famous "I Have a Dream" speech on August 28, 1963, but the images of that march on Washington are as vivid as any in my childhood.

Those were years of tremendous emotion in our country. Boycotts, marches, sit-ins, and freedom-rides for equality resulted in mass arrests, bombings, police brutality, riots, and inevitably, murder. Three months after those 250,000 marchers filled the streets of Washington, a sniper's bullet

275

would end the life of our nation's president as he rode in a motorcade through the streets of Dallas. In his honor, the Civil Rights Bill was quickly passed and on July 2, 1964—188 years after American patriots had approved Thomas Jefferson's *Declaration of Independence.*

America would no longer wait for "someday" to come. Conviction gave birth to action that could no longer be deterred, denied, or delayed. This thirst for freedom could not be slaked by promises of a better future. Like any great movement, the cause of black equality required leadership, leadership which arose from the black Christian community. That leadership would soon rediscover that a cause of such magnitude is rarely accomplished without sacrifice.

Because of his stand for civil rights, Dr. King's house was bombed, he was stabbed in New York, knocked to the ground by a rock in Chicago, and finally, assassinated as he stood on a balcony in Memphis. Kennedy and King were not the only martyrs. Medgar Evers was murdered in front of his family in Jackson, Mississippi, and four black children died when a bomb exploded in their Alabama Sunday school room. James Reeb, a white pastor who had flown from Boston to march for voting rights in Selma, Alabama, was beaten to death. Countless blacks and white sympathizers suffered losses of the most extreme kind. College students were beaten, abused, and even shot for demonstrating their belief in right.

"Violence begets violence" is a time-tested truth. Had it not been for King's strong stand against violence, our nation would have endured its second great civil war. How sincere was the intention of King toward nonviolence? Very—as can be seen in the pledge all protesters were required to sign before joining in demonstrations for desegregation in Birmingham, Alabama.

1. Meditate daily on the teachings and life of Jesus.

2. Remember always the nonviolent movement in Birmingham seeks justice and reconciliation—not victory.
3. Walk and talk in the manner of love; for God is love.
4. Pray daily to be used by God in order that all men might be free.
5. Sacrifice personal wishes that all men might be free.
6. Observe with both friend and foe the ordinary rules of courtesy.
7. Seek to perform regular service for others and for the world.
8. Refrain from the violence of fist, tongue and heart.
9. Strive to be in good spiritual and bodily health.
10. Follow the directions of the movement and of the captain on a demonstration.[1]

King made it clear that his dream was not only for the freedom and civil rights of black America. The establishment of justice is always to the benefit of oppressor as well as the oppressed. In his wisdom Solomon wrote, "If you falter in times of trouble, how small is your strength! Rescue those being led away to death; hold back those staggering toward slaughter. If you say, 'But we knew nothing about this,' does not He who weighs the heart perceive it? Does not He who guards your life know it? Will He not repay each person according to what He has done?" (Proverbs 24:10–12).

On January 1, 1863, Abraham Lincoln officially issued the Emancipation Proclamation abolishing slavery throughout the embattled South. On August 28, 1963, 100 years later, Dr. Martin Luther King, Jr. laid public claim to those rights in front of a quarter of a million citizens gathered at the massive Lincoln Memorial in Washington.

"I have a dream," he said. "It is a dream deeply rooted in the American Dream. ...

"When we allow freedom to ring—when we let it ring from every city and every hamlet, from every state and every city, we will be able to speed up that day when all of God's children, black men and white men, Jews and Gentiles, Protestants and Catholics, will be able to join hands and sing in the words of the old Negro spiritual, 'Free at last, Free at last, Great God Almighty, We are free at last!' "[2]

The power of returning good for evil is rooted in the Gospel of Jesus Christ. In the Sermon on the Mount, Jesus said,

You have heard it said, "Eye for eye, and tooth for tooth." But I tell you, Do not resist an evil person. If someone strikes you on the right cheek, turn to him the other also. And if someone wants to sue you and take your tunic, let him have your cloak as well. If someone forces you to go one mile, go with him two miles. Give to the one who asks you, and do not turn away from the one who wants to borrow from you. You have heard it said, "Love your neighbor and hate your enemy." But I tell you: Love your enemies and pray for those who persecute you, that you may be sons of your Father in heaven. He causes His sun to rise on the evil and the good, and sends rain on the righteous and the unrighteous. If you love those who love you, what reward will you get? Are not even the tax collectors doing that? And if you greet only your brothers, what are you doing more than others? Do not even pagans do that? (Matthew 5:38–47)

As Dr. King correctly understood, the value of such behavior is not only for the benefit of those on the receiving end of kindness. Conversely, bitterness has a way of extracting a heavy penalty and everyone who practices it will eventually suffer the consequence. It may not come from the target of our animosity, but it will always come.

A hill near my home is covered with trees of various sizes and types. Large sycamores grow at the bottom, near the dry creek bed. Oaks, maples, hickories, and cedars grow interspersed together. One particularly large oak is especially obvious. During a recent storm it was blown over and now rests at a 45 degree angle against equally large trees. There was nothing wrong with the fallen oak. Its trunk and limbs, though large, show no signs of sickness or internal rot. It was growing in soft, sloping ground which apparently could no longer support its great weight. A month of heavy rain and a stiff wind caused its roots to relinquish their grasp or snap under the strain. When it fell, its force snapped two mature and unyielding hickory trees nearby. A heart weighed-down with bitterness and resentment is equally vulnerable.

Under ideal conditions we may keep our bitterness well hid and under control. Our support system of family, friends, and faith is secure enough to handle the occasional storms and strains. But as our bitterness grows (and unresolved resentments always grow), the weight of the burden will eventually overtax the strength of our support. The inevitable outcome is our own downfall and the potential destruction of those nearby.

If we refuse bitterness and, according to the instruction of the Lord, return love for hatred, what will we do with all those natural emotions and the anger that accompanies them? Dr. King had advice worthy of consideration. In his sermon, *Three Dimensions of a Complete Life,* Dr. King outlined a balanced attitude based on John's Revelation, "as wide and high as it is long" (21:16). If the church is the new Jerusalem coming down out of heaven like a bride adorned for her husband, then the church (and Christians who make up the church) will demonstrate balance, like the Holy City described in this verse. He equated the length of the walled city with the purpose or drive for which Christians exist. The breadth of the walls were the measure of Christian love we have for our fellowman, and the wall's height was compared with the Christian church's relationship to God. In describing the last point he wrote, "Where will you find Him? Where else except in Jesus Christ, the Lord of our lives? He is the language of eternity translated in the words of time. By committing ourselves absolutely to Christ and His way, we will participate in that marvelous act of faith that will bring us to the true knowledge of God."[3] Christians with purpose, love for their fellowman, and a strong tie to Christ won't have time for bitterness. In fact, they will know no bitterness. The conditions are mutually exclusive.

Martin's wife, Coretta, wrote about the practical implications of turning the other cheek and the exhilaration that they experienced from God's way of handling hatred. "Day and night our phone would ring, and someone would pour out a string of obscene epithets. ... Frequently the calls ended with a threat to kill us if we didn't get out of town. But in spite of all the danger, the chaos of our private lives, I felt inspired, almost elated."[4]

Christian leaders who practice this kind of leadership will experience godly success whether they succeed or not. For example, it wasn't necessary for Dr. King to realize his dream; he experienced it from a distance, just like the people of the Old Testament who were not privileged to see the birth of the long-awaited Messiah (cf. Hebrews 11:13). On that fateful day in April 1968, King traveled to Memphis with his eyes wide open. He knew of the death threats and boldly referred to them in his last speech, the night before his assassination:

> "I don't know what will happen to me now," he said. We've got some difficult days ahead. But it doesn't matter to me now. Because I've been to the mountaintop. I won't mind. Like anybody else, I would like to live a long life. Longevity has its place. But I'm not concerned about that now. I just want to do God's will. And He's allowed me to

go up to the mountain. And I've looked over and I've seen the Promised Land. I may not get there with you, but I want you to know tonight that we, as a people, will get to the Promised Land. So I'm happy tonight. ... I'm not fearing any man. 'Mine eyes have see the glory of the coming of the Lord.' "[5]

Christian leaders have come to understand that it is not always the attainment of godly goals that determines success. The Bible says, "Men ought to regard us as servants of Christ and as those entrusted with the secret things of God. Now it is required that those who have been given a trust must prove faithful" (1 Corinthians 4:1–2). Not the outcome, but the walk itself is the measure of a servant in the sight of God.

More Scriptural Insight

1 Samuel 24	What are the lessons of this chapter?
2 Corinthians 4:7–12	What is Paul's main point? Subpoints?
Matthew 26:47–56	What do Jesus' words to Peter mean to us?

A Leader's Prayer

I am only human, Lord, and some people are especially good at exploiting my weakness. Keep me, by the power of Your Spirit, from conceding to my natural tendencies to return evil for evil and hurt for hurt. Help me to see the destructiveness of such an attitude in my own life and in the life of the church. Grant me greater appreciation for the power of kindness and the power of mercy. Give me the heart of David to resist opportunities for revenge. I know that revenge is Your work and will be accomplished by You in time and eternity. Inspire me by Your Spirit to follow the admonition to feed my enemy when he is hungry, and when he is thirsty to give him something cool to drink. Help me to understand that evil is never overcome by the proliferation of evil, but is overcome by good. Grant that I would not place too great an importance on the accomplishment of my goals, but concentrate more completely on the value of faithfulness in life itself. Help me to know that true success comes from Your hand as I walk the path You have laid before me. Grant it all for Jesus' sake. Amen.

Notes

1. Coretta Scott King, *My Life with Martin Luther King, Jr.*, (New York: Holt, Rinehart, and Winston, Inc., 1969), 318. Used by permission.

2. Ira Peck, *The Life and Words of Martin Luther King, Jr.*, (New York: Scholastic Inc., 1968), 67–69.

3. Ibid., 229.

4. Coretta Scott King, 279.

5. Ibid., 354.

CHAPTER THIRTY-EIGHT

DWIGHT LYMAN MOODY
Willing to Learn

S omeday you will read in the papers that Moody is dead,"
he had said in New York on a hot Sunday in August 1899.
"Don't you believe a word of it. At that moment I shall be
more alive than I am now. ... I was born of the flesh in 1837,
I was born of the Spirit in 1855. 'That which is born of the
flesh may die. That which is born of the Spirit shall live forever.' It would not be eternity merely, but eternity with Christ.
The thin veil would drop. On the evening of December 21,
lying on his bed at Northfield, Massachusetts, Moody wrote in
pencil in his usual bold hand, barely palsied by weakness: 'To
see His star is good, but to see His face is better.' "[1] The next
day, D. L. Moody passed from life to life eternal.

D. L. Moody's life is one of America's great stories of God's
strength made perfect in weakness. He was raised a Unitarian
in Northfield where his father died bankrupt when Dwight
was only four years old. Creditors took virtually everything
the family owned and, as if to make matters worse, within a

month after his father's death, his mother gave birth to twins. Dwight was now the fifth son in a single-parent family of nine with six brothers and two sisters. Dwight's uncles helped his mother keep the farm until such time as the children were old enough to contribute. His education was erratic at best. His spelling and grammar were so bad none would ever accuse him of intellectual snobbery! A critical professor once wrote of him,

> It is perfectly astounding to me that a man with so little training should have come to understand the public so well. He cannot read the Greek New Testament; indeed he has difficulty with parts of it in the English version, but he excels any man I have ever heard in making his hearers see the point of a text of Scripture.[2]

The life of this obscure New England farm boy would be a living verification of God's claim, "My power is perfected in weakness" (2 Corinthians 12:9). Wrapped in such an unseeming package, the message itself, not the man, was clearly the thing which brought thousands to listen and millions to renew their faith in the God of this unlikely evangelist.

How did it happen that a man of such limitations became America's equivalent to the renown Charles Spurgeon of England? Certainly by the grace of God, but also because D. L. Moody was never so impressed with himself that he was not willing to listen to others. This trait is rare in the world, but almost universal among truly great men and women.

Although it is not often my privilege to move in circles of greatness, I have observed that truly great Christians are more approachable than their less mature brothers and sisters of faith. Perhaps it flows from their own personal security, more likely from their Christlike nature. Commoners, children, lepers, and learned officials such as Jarius, Nicodemus, and even

Pontius Pilate were all intrigued and drawn to Christ. In response, each was received with respect and honor at the hands of the Lord. The more Christlike the Christians, the more approachable their nature.

Not only was Dr. Moody approachable, he was equally willing to learn from others. This trait epitomized the man even after he had developed a considerable reputation as a public speaker and man of God. He proved the Proverb true,

> Whoever corrects a mocker invites insult; whoever rebukes a wicked man incurs abuse. Do not rebuke a mocker or he will hate you; rebuke a wise man and he will love you. Instruct a wise man and he will be wiser still; teach a righteous man and he will add to his learning. The fear of the LORD is the beginning of wisdom, and knowledge of the Holy One is understanding. For through me your days will be many, and years will be added to your life. If you are wise, your wisdom will reward you; if you are a mocker, you alone will suffer. (Proverbs 9:7–12)

Few great leaders, Christian or otherwise, demonstrate such a sincere appreciation for the wisdom and experience of others. Much opportunity for improvement is lost, limited by the egos and pride of the potentially great—not so Moody. Although already an evangelist of some renown in America, Moody traveled to England to observe and learn from the famed Charles Haddon Spurgeon. Although only three years his senior, Moody unashamedly acknowledged, "Everything that I could get hold of in print that he ever said, I read."[3]

Arriving on a Sunday, he waited the entire week for his first opportunity to visit the Metropolitan Tabernacle where Dr. Spurgeon spoke. Although similar in his origins and the common style of Moody, Spurgeon's reputation was worldwide. Seating in the great hall was limited to 5,000 worshippers and tickets were required for admission. The street-wise

Moody bluffed his way into the gallery and anxiously anticipated the moment. He was not disappointed. He later wrote,
"As Spurgeon walked down to the platform, my eyes just
feasted upon him and my heart's desire for years was at last
accomplished." As is often the case when one observes simple
greatness, Moody was surprised by what he saw. "His manner
is very simple." Moody's wife, Emma, echoed the thought,
"He is a very plain-looking man, but he had the undivided
attention of his audience ... and the singing ... so many voices mingled together in such harmony and good time seemed
perfectly grand." Moody's biographer summarized the experience by writing, "Moody longed to preach like that, to see
singing led like that."[4] Almost taken back by the simplicity of
it all, Moody later concluded, "I came to understand something I had never realized before. It was not Spurgeon who
was doing that work: It was God. And if God could use Spurgeon, why should he not use me?"[5]

His encounter with Spurgeon was significant, but there was
an even more important lesson Moody would learn from an
unlikely teacher. While in England, Moody crossed paths with
Harry Moorhouse, a converted pickpocket with a growing reputation for preaching. Moody was unimpressed by his boyish
appearance and ignored his offer to preach for him in Chicago.
As good as his word, Moorhouse made the difficult trip to
America and soon contacted Moody. Although still doubtful of
his ability, Moody granted permission for a trial sermon while
he kept a previous commitment in St. Louis. Upon his return
Moody asked Emma her opinion of the man. "They like him
very much," she replied. "He preaches a little different from
you. He preaches that God loves sinners." Moody became
defensive. "If he preached different from me, I would not like
him. My prejudice was up." The next day he would see for
himself. Moorhouse chose for his text John 3:16. Moody later

recalled, "He went from Genesis to Revelation giving proof that God loves the sinner, and before he got through, two or three of my sermons were spoiled."[6]

Instead of becoming defensive for his own reputation and possessive of his own pulpit, Moody dissolved in tears. It was February 8, 1868, a turning point in the ministry and message of D. L. Moody. Before this date Moody had railed against sinner and sin. From this day forward he preached the love of Christ for sinners under the bondage of sin. Moody not only announced Moorhouse would preach every evening the rest of the week, he also willingly submitted himself to the instruction of his guest. Moorhouse taught him how to read and study the Bible, even commenting on the biblical ignorance of his host! "He made Moody see it is God's Word, not our comment upon it, that saves souls." His trusted friend and brother-in-law later wrote, "D. L. Moody had great power before, but nothing like what he had after dear Harry Moorhouse came into our lives and changed the character of the teaching and preaching in the chapel."[7]

What good is greatness if its only purpose is to glorify the one so recognized? In one of the most significant theophanies of the Old Testament, the Lord told Abraham, "I will make you into a great nation and I will bless you; I will make your name great, and you will be a blessing. I will bless those who bless you and whoever curses you I will curse; *and all the peoples on earth will be blessed through you*" (Genesis 12:2–3, emphasis added). When God raises up one of His children, it is always for the benefit of their brothers and sisters. Although He loves us, significant or not, our significance must remain a means to accomplish His ends, and not an end in itself. As the time-worn poem reminds us, no one is indispensable.

Sometime, when you're feeling important,
Sometime, when your ego's in bloom
Sometime, when you take it for granted
You're the best qualified in the room;
Sometime, when you feel that your going
Would leave an unfillable hole.
Just follow this simple instruction
And see how it humbles the soul.

Take a bucket and fill it with water;
Put your hand in it, up to the wrist;
Pull it out; and the hole that's remaining
Is a measure of how you'll be missed.
You may splash all you please, when you enter,
You can stir up the water galore,
But stop and you'll find in a minute
That it looks quite the same as before.

The moral in this quaint example
Is do just the best that you can,
Be proud of yourself, but remember—
There is NO indispensable man!

God is not limited by our availability. The sandals of Moses were filled by the feet of Joshua, the mantle of Elijah passed to Elisha, and the insight of David was surpassed by the wisdom of Solomon. The exercise of Christian leadership is more like a relay than a sprint. We each have our leg to run and are dependent upon the help of others. Those who win the race understand their part in the whole. The outstanding ability of any one runner is not significant apart from the combined effort of the team.

I like the way the Living Bible paraphrases Paul's analogy of our physical bodies to the body of Christ which is made up of varied and diverse people. "And some of the parts that seem weakest and least important are really the most necessary. Yes, we are especially glad to have some parts that seem rather odd! And we carefully protect from the eyes of others those parts that should not be seen, while of course the parts that may be seen do not require this special care. So God has put the body together in such a way that extra honor and care are given to those parts that might otherwise seem less important" (1 Corinthians 12:22–24, The Living Bible). The visibility of a D. L. Moody does not make him more significant than a less renown Harry Moorhouse, and he would be the last to claim preeminence.

More Scriptural Insight

2 Samuel 12:1–15	Why was Nathan so significant to the success of David?
1 Timothy 1:12–17	How did Paul's past play a role in his success?
Luke 10:17–24	Why did Jesus redirect the thinking of His disciples?

A Leader's Prayer

Lord, it is with fondness I recall the birth of my firstborn child. I remember the overwhelming sense of responsibility that flooded my heart. How could I, a child myself in so many ways, ever be considered worthy of molding and shaping another life? You have taught me that life is a continuous learning process. Although on that day I was given great responsibility, it was not necessary that I have all the answers. You surrounded me with the wise counsel of friends and more experienced people. I will never be so wise that I have no need to learn. Remove any barrier in me that would cause me to overlook or disrespect the Harry Moorhouses of my life. Keep my heart open to learn from any and everyone that has greater insight into any aspect of Your will. Give to

Your leaders the heart of D. L. Moody, who was willing not only to learn from others, but gladly shared his prominence with others who could further the cause of the Gospel and help your children grow in deeper faith. Let everything I do be done for the glory of Your name and not my own. Bless these intentions with a heart willing to honor only You as Lord of lords and the only true God, Savior of all. Amen.

Notes

1. J. C. Pollock, *Moody: A Biographical Portrait of the Pacesetter in Modern Evangelism,* (New York: The Macmillan Company, 1963), 316.

2. Ibid., 194.

3. Ibid., 64.

4. Ibid., 66.

5. Ibid., 99.

6. Ibid., 73.

7. Ibid., 72–74.

CHAPTER THIRTY-NINE

FLORENCE NIGHTINGALE
Sacrificial Service

The Crimean War preceded the American Civil War by a decade, and although half a million soldiers fell by sword and shell, they would be largely forgotten if not for the immortal words of Alfred, Lord Tennyson and the sacrificial, historic work of Florence Nightingale. Tennyson's words described the heroic charge of the English Light Brigade in the battle for Sevastopol:

'Forward the Light Brigade!'
Was there a man dismay'd?
Not tho' the soldier knew
    Some one had blunder'd.
Theirs not to make reply,
Theirs not to reason why,
Theirs but to do and die.
Into the valley of Death
    Rode the six hundred.
Cannon to right of them,
Cannon to left of them,

Cannon in front of them,
  Volley'd and thunder'd;
Storm'd at with shot and shell,
Boldly they rode and well,
Into the jaws of Death,
  Rode the six hundred.

The Crimean War has gone down in history as one of the worst managed, badly led, ill supplied, and inhumane wars of all time. The commanders of the English and French alliance were either too old or too inexperienced to effectively command their troops on distant Turkish soil against an entrenched Russian army. The czar was intent on defending the ocean front property he had seized at the fall of the Ottoman empire. Throwing Russians off Turkish soil meant displacing their fortifications. From his lofty observation point, an English lord had given the order to charge the outer gun emplacements of Sevastopol. In the relay of his command the message became confused. Instead of attacking only the outer artillery positions, a calvary unit of more than 600 men rode straight into the teeth of the main battery; only 195 returned.

Flash'd all their sabres bare,
Flash'd as they turn'd in air
Sabring the gunners there
Charging an army, while
  All the world wonder'd.
Plunged in the battery-smoke
Right thro' the line they broke;
Cossack and Russian
Reel'd from the sabre-stroke
  Shatter'd and sunder'd.
Then they rode back, but not,
  Not the six hundred.[1]

Tennyson's words of bravery could be equally applied to the bravery of the nursing corps led in that Crimean campaign by Florence Nightingale. At great risk to their own lives they left the comforts of England and began a service heretofore unknown in British warfare. "Theirs not to make reply, theirs not to reason why, theirs but to do and die ..."

Nightingale and her charges sacrificially battled a greater threat to the soldier than the entrenched Cossack. With no thought for her own safety or degree of sacrifice, Nightingale fought the enemies of cholera, typhus, dysentery, filth, vermin, inept facilities, insufficient supplies, and the prejudice of commanders unwilling to confess their losses or to work cooperatively with any woman in a military campaign. Before the era of modern nursing, those killed outright on the battlefield were envied by those who died the slow and painful death of a mortal wound.

What makes the life and work of Florence Nightingale so significant was the wealth and privilege of her birth. She was under no obligation or expectation to help in time of need. In fact, she had to overcome tremendous family and social pressure to dissuade her from working in a "profession" staffed by underpaid, underprivileged women of questionable moral character. Florence remained unfulfilled and resentful of prevailing attitudes toward both her sex and her station until she was able to break through the barrier of class and gender into a life of total dedicated service.

The sincerity of her convictions is seen in a letter describing her experience at Kaiserwerth, a German school of nursing established by Pastor Fliedner near Berlin. After the privilege of scrubbing the floors for Pastor Fliedner, she wrote to her bewildered mother, "The world here fills my life with interest. We have ten minutes for each of our meals, of which we have four. We get up at five; breakfast a quarter before six. The patients dine at eleven; the sisters at twelve. We drink tea, that is, a drink made of ground rye, between two and three, and sup at seven. Several evenings in the week we collect in the great hall for a Bible lesson. ... This is life! Now I know what it is to love life."[2]

Her words echo the Lord's description of the Christian life to His own disciples, "Whoever finds his life will lose it, and whoever loses his life for My sake will find it" (Matthew 10:39). A life without purpose is a life without meaning, and a life without meaning knows nothing of the abundance and satisfaction that God intends for His children.

After Moses had enjoyed a childhood of privilege in the courts of Pharaoh, a subtle discontent began to grow deep inside. Lesser men have silenced such thoughts through greater indulgence. But Moses was intended for a life greater than that experienced through wealth and privilege. Through the inspired insight of Hebrews we know of the struggle and wisdom of Moses.

> "By faith, Moses, when he had grown up, refused to be known as the son of Pharaoh's daughter. He chose to be mistreated along with the people of God rather than enjoy the pleasures of sin for a short time. He regarded disgrace for the sake of Christ as of greater value than the treasures of Egypt, because he was looking ahead to his reward. By faith he left Egypt, not fearing the king's anger; he persevered because he saw Him who is invisible." (Hebrews 11:24–27)

In retrospect, few would doubt the wisdom of Moses' decision. Under his leadership, the children of Israel left Egypt laden with the spoils of a war which God had fought single-handedly for them. Pharaoh's army, on the other hand, was drowned in the Red Sea and his son died by at the hand of the Lord. Yes, Moses exercised great wisdom. But lest we forget, at the time Moses made his decision the predicted outcome looked anything but wise! His stand went against all conventional wisdom. Insulting Pharaoh's daughter in preference of slaves! The Bible says Moses acted "because he was looking forward to his reward." He considered the ultimate approval of God to be of greater personal value than short-term pleasure. The Lord did not disappoint Moses.

The quality of leadership described as "sacrificial service" is rare among even successful leaders. Personal sacrifice? Yes. Most would concede that sacrifice is to be expected of a leader. "No pain, no gain" is one of the 10 commandments in the book of personal achievement. But such sacrifice is almost always motivated by the eventual personal payoff, not by a selfless desire to serve others.

Jesus told His disciples, "Whoever loses his life for My sake will find it" (Matthew 10:39). In a sense, you could say that both Jesus and Moses advocated present sacrifice in expectation of eventual personal reward, but that reward is viewed only through faith and expected to be received in the life to come. Jesus called it, "Storing up treasures in heaven."[3]

Florence Nightingale rejected almost every attempt the world made to grant her honor, title, and wealth. A hero before going to the Crimean campaign, she was more highly esteemed than the queen by its conclusion. But rather than accept her nation's accolades for faithful duty, Florence literally snuck back into the country on a French schooner under an assumed name. To the chagrin of politicians and her admiring public, Florence eschewed all public recognition. She consistently declined photography requests, and when asked permission to allow a statue to be crafted for Queen Victoria's Diamond Jubilee celebration in 1897, she initially refused saying, "I won't be made a sign at an exhibition." Later, having conceded the request, she stated, "I hope it gets smashed!"[4] Not only was it not smashed, her grateful public showered the likeness with wreaths of flowers as their sincere gesture of love and affection.

Although she suffered from the physical consequences of her sacrificial service, the Lord granted Miss Nightingale a long life of 90 years. Although a grateful nation wanted her enshrined at Westminster Abbey with all due pomp and circumstance, she was laid to rest next to her parents in the churchyard near Embley. Her instructions for the funeral were clear, "Keep it simple." At her direction the only hymn played at the memorial service was appropriately "The Son of God Goes Forth to War." Its words are militaristic in their tone, but clearly Christ-honoring in their call to sacrificial service.

1. The Son of God goes forth to war
    A kingly crown to gain.
    His blood-red banner streams afar;
    Who follows in His train?
    Who best can drink His cup of woe
    Triumphant over pain,
    Who patient bears his cross below—
    He follows in His train.
2. A noble army, man and boys,
    The matron and the maid,
    Around the Savior's throne rejoice,
    In robes of white arrayed.
    They climbed the steep ascent of heav'n
    Through peril, toil, and pain.
    O God, to us may grace be giv'n
    To follow in their train!

More Scriptural Insight

1 Samuel 30:21–25	What was so significant about David's decision?
1 Thessalonians 4:9–12	For what two reasons are Christians asked to work?
Matthew 6:1–4	What difference does motive make in providing godly service?

A Leader's Prayer

Gracious Father, almighty God, receive my life as a living sacrifice in Your service. Keep me from the temptation of helping others for the benefit of personal recognition. Help me model a humble and willing heart to all who observe my example. Keep me from considering any act of Christian service as beneath my office. Strongly support and establish those ministries that are committed to servicing the less fortunate and hurting. Provide resources for their work and leadership for their causes. Turn Christian congregations away from self-service towards missions of mercy and outreach on behalf of the Gospel. Surround Christian leaders with faithful and prayerful partners in ministry. Give them peaceful rest and an internal sense of their work's importance. Keep our eyes on the eternal rewards of heaven that await all those who follow the example of Jesus Christ, Your Son, our Lord. Amen.

Notes

1. Alfred, Lord Tennyson, *The Poems and Plays of Tennyson*, "The Charge of the Light Brigade" (selected verses).

2. Jeanette C. Nolan, *Florence Nightingale*, (New York: Simon & Schuster, Inc., 1946), 70.

3. See Matthew 6:20.

4. Jeanette C. Nolan, 208.

CHAPTER FORTY

BENJAMIN FRANKLIN
Observant

I've noticed a subtle change in the lay leadership of our congregation in recent years. We have always been led by godly men, but the size of the congregation, the computerization of our office, and the size of the budget now require cutting edge business expertise. Not that I could help—financial management and leadership training were not a part of the seminary curriculum. The Lord provided, and as the Lord provided, I was gradually surrounded by laymen who attended church meetings carrying lap-top computers and calendars in eight-ring binders.

Even I knew the value of a calendar and had been carrying one for a good many years, but these binders were not just calendars—they were *Franklin Planners!* After months of good-natured chiding, I was persuaded to take the plunge. The Franklin "traveling office" is based on an organizational system first conceived by Benjamin Franklin in the 1720s. Franklin's original design was intended to monitor his daily activities (each hour had an entry line), and perhaps more importantly, to establish goals, monitor virtues, and record daily observations. The introductory pages to modern Franklin Planners still quote from Ben Franklin's autobiography:

> I entered upon the execution of this plan for self-examination and continued it, with occasional intermission, but I always carried my little book with me ...[1]

> It may be well my posterity should be informed that to this little artifice, with the blessing of God, their ancestor ow'd the constant felicity of his life, down to his 79th year, in which this is written ... I hope, therefore, that some of my descendants may follow the example and reap the benefit.[2]

Franklin's system fit his character perfectly. From his earliest recollections until his death in Philadelphia, Pennsylvania, April 17, 1790, Benjamin Franklin was a keen observer of people and events. But Franklin had little use for knowledge without purpose, as attested by experiments which led to the development of the lightning rod, the Franklin Stove, and his famous bifocal. He was not content to simply observe life's lessons for personal edification. In 1732, Franklin began to publish his observations under the pseudonym, Richard Saunders. Poor Richard's Almanac was published each year for 25 years and became a profitable venture, selling nearly ten thousand copies annually. Franklin's original intent was to provide a simple guide to historic dates and simultaneously educate the common man "who bought scarcely any other books."[3]

His observations included advice on human nature:

- Men and melons are hard to know.
- The worst wheel of the cart makes the most noise.
- Seven wealthy towns contend for Homer dead—Thro' which the living Homer beg'd his bread.
- Write injuries in dust, benefits in marble.
- He is not well bred, that cannot bear ill-breeding in others.
- 'Tis great confidence in a friend to tell him your faults,

greater to tell him his.

Observations on business ethics:

- He that pursues two hares at once, does not catch one and lets the other go.
- He that cannot obey, cannot command.
- He's the best physician that knows the worthlessness of the most medicine.
- Industry need not wish.
- He that riseth late, must trot all day, and shall scarce overtake his business at night.
- Dost thou love life? Then do not squander time; for that's the stuff life is made of.

And especially observations on virtue and character:

- He that lieth down with dogs, shall rise up with fleas.
- Innocence is its own defense.
- Three may keep a secret, if two of them are dead.
- An old young man will be a young old man.
- Sin is not hurtful because it is forbidden, but it is forbidden because it is hurtful.
- You may give a man an office, but you cannot give him discretion.[4]

Although Franklin embraced deism as a young man, he later concluded, "I began to suspect that this doctrine, tho' it might be true, was not very useful."[5] As an old man, it was Franklin, who urged that a chaplain open every session of the Constitutional Convention of 1787, and although initially rebuffed, again addressed the matter to Washington, who was seated as president of the proceedings:

> The small progress we have made, after four or five weeks close attendance and continual reasoning with each other ... methinks a melancholy proof of the imperfection of the human understanding. ... In this situation of this Assembly, groping as it were in the dark to find

political truth, and scarce able to distinguish it when presented to us, how has it happened, Sir, that we have not hitherto once thought of humbly applying to the Father of lights to illumine our understandings?[6]

After reminding the entire assembly of how they had prayed in the very same room at the beginning of the war with England, he continued,

Our prayers, Sir, were heard, and they were graciously answered. All of us who were engaged in the struggle must have observed frequent instances of a Superintending providence in our favor. To that kind Providence we owe this happy opportunity of consulting in peace on the means of establishing our future national felicity. And have we now forgotten that powerful friend? ... I have lived, Sir, a long time, and the longer I live, the more convincing proofs I see of this truth—that God governs the affairs of men.[7]

Franklin had spoken from conviction based on past observation. It is important that leaders be observant and, on the basis of those observations, conduct the business of today informed by the lessons of yesterday. It is not uncommon to see leaders sitting on the edge of an assembly, or even standing at the back of a room where things are being decided. The outcome of the decision is not their only interest. They are also intrigued by *the way things are decided* and the opinions expressed. The dynamic of the situation can be as significant as the decision itself, especially if it will fall to them to implement the decision.

Why a thing is done and the motive behind it are of great importance in the kingdom of God. Mark tells of an incident in the life of Jesus, who intentionally sat down to watch the people make gifts to the temple treasury, a practice few pastors would be bold enough to imitate!

Jesus sat down opposite the place where the offerings were put and watched the crowd putting their money into the temple treasury. Many rich people threw in large amounts. But a poor widow came and put in two very small copper coins, worth only a fraction of a penny. Calling His disciples to Him, Jesus said, "I tell you the truth, this poor widow has put more into the treasury than all the others. They all gave out of their wealth; but she, out of her poverty, put in everything—all she had to live on." (Mark 12:41–44)

The observant nature of Jesus is consistent with the revealed nature of His Father in the Old Testament. When Samuel was sent to the house of Jesse to choose a king to replace the disobedient Saul, his eyes fell on Eliab, and on the basis of outward appearance, assumed he was the one the Lord had chosen. "But the Lord said to Samuel, 'Do not consider his appearance or his height, for I have rejected him. The Lord does not look at the things man looks at. Man looks at the outward appearance, but the Lord looks at the heart' " (1 Samuel 16:7). In an even more obvious reference, the prophet Hanani told Asa, king of Judah, "The eyes of the Lord range throughout the earth to strengthen those whose hearts are fully committed to Him" (2 Chronicles 16:9). Omniscience is an attribute of God. To be observant is therefore a godly characteristic, providing of course that the eye of the observer is as gracious, patient, and loving as the heart of God.

Mark's account of Jesus watching the offering is mirrored by an incident in the life of Ben Franklin, who had come to hear his good friend, the Rev. George Whitefield, speak of the establishment of an orphans home in Georgia. Franklin had urged Whitefield to establish the home in Philadelphia where he felt better care and education could be provided.

This I advis'd; but he was resolute in his first project, rejected my counsel, and I therefore refus'd to contribute.

I happened soon after to attend one of his sermons, in the course of which I perceived he intended to finish with a collection, and I silently resolved he should get nothing from me. I had in my pocket a handful of copper money, three or four silver dollars, and five pistoles in gold. As he proceeded I began to soften, and concluded to give the coppers. Another stroke of his oratory made me asham'd of that, and determin'd me to give the silver; and he finish'd so admirably, that I empty'd my pocket wholly into the collector's dish, gold and all.[8]

Franklin continued to act on his observations until the end. On February 12, 1790, he signed a memorial to Congress as president of the Pennsylvania Society for Promoting the Abolition of Slavery. A few weeks later, April 17, 1790, he succumbed to illness. His epitaph (written by Franklin at the age of 23 in 1728) reveals his confidence that even this was not the end.

The Body
Of
Benjamin Franklin
Printer
(Like the cover of an old book, its contents torn out
And stript of its lettering and gilding)
Lies here, food for worms.
But the work shall not be lost.
For it will (as he believes) appear once more
In a new and more elegant edition
Revised and corrected
by
The Author.[9]

More Scriptural Insight

Proverbs 22:1–5	What distinguishes the wise from the foolish?
Philippians 3:15–21	Why does Paul offer his life as an example?
Matthew 11:1–6	Notice how Jesus directs John's disciples to their own observations.

A Leader's Prayer

Gracious Father, every day I am surrounded by the works of Your hands and the activity of Your grace. Open my eyes to be more observant of Your blessings and the opportunities You provide for my instruction. Help me to become slower to speak and quicker to listen. Grant a greater appreciation for the wisdom of Your Word that I might make it my teacher and avoid the painful lessons of trial and error. Let the examples of others serve as an encouragement to me. Help me to realize that You constantly observe the hearts of Your people and strongly support those who are faithful to You. My heart is willing, but my flesh is weak. Forgive the many times I have compromised Your will and selfishly pursued my own goals and plans. I thank You, Lord, for the many opportunities I have in adversity and blessing. Keep me always focused on the purpose of my life that I might in all times and ways bring glory to Your name. This I pray in the name of Jesus, my Lord. Amen.

Notes

1. Benjamin Franklin, *Life and Letters*, (New York: American Book—Stratford Press, Inc., no date, no copyright), 55.

2. Ibid., 59.

3. Ibid., 63.

4. Ibid., 346–74.

5. Ibid., 37.

6. Catherine Drinker Bowen, *Miracle at Philadelphia—The Story of the Constitutional Convention May to September 1787*, (Boston: An Atlantic Monthly Press Book, 1966), 125.

7. Ibid., 126.

8. Benjamin Franklin, 70.

9. Ibid., 345.

CHAPTER FORTY-ONE

HELEN ADAMS KELLER
Optimism

A wise father once told his hesitant son, "It is the greatest of all mistakes to do nothing because you can only do a little. Do what you can." The limitations we impose upon ourselves are greater barriers to achievement than any handicap, obstacle, or opposition we might encounter.

Do what you can. It may seem insignificant—do what you can. Others can do in a few moments what it would take you hours to accomplish—do what you can. The size of the problem is so great that your effort would make little difference—do what you can. You are only one voice speaking for a cause which few support—do what you can. It will take a great deal more to accomplish the task than the resources available—do what you can. No one is willing to help—do what you can. It has never been done before—do what you can. Even if we succeed, there are no guarantees it will last—do what you can. Why should I help people who won't even help themselves—do what you can. Better people than me have tried and failed—do what you can. There are others that have more time, more money, and more talent—do what you can.

The Optimist International has a creed in which its members promise

- To be so strong that nothing can disturb your peace of mind.
- To talk health, happiness, and prosperity to every person you meet.
- To make all your friends feel that there is something in them.
- To look at the sunny side of everything and make your optimism come true.
- To think only of the best, to work only for the best, and to expect only the best.
- To be just as enthusiastic about the success of others as you are about your own.
- To forget the mistakes of the past and press on to the greater achievements of the future.
- To wear a cheerful countenance at all times and give every living creature you meet a smile.
- To give so much time to the improvement of yourself that you have no time to criticize others.
- To be too large for worry, too noble for anger, too strong for fear, and too happy to permit the presence of trouble.

It is a good creed and a wonderful way to live. Although it credits no divine origin and acknowledges no faith in God, the spirit of optimism is reflective of His design. The apostle closed his letter to the Christians at Philippi by urging, "Whatever is true, whatever is noble, whatever is right, whatever is pure, whatever is lovely, whatever is admirable—if anything is excellent or praiseworthy—think about such things (Phillipians 4:8). It's good advice for anyone, and for those whose optimism is grounded in the mercies and omnipotence of God, it is power.

March 3 would be a good day every year for the optimists of the world to unite in celebration of their common spirit. It was on that day in 1887, when a new light dawned on the darkened world of a young girl growing up in Tuscumbia, a little town in northern Alabama. The seven-year-old's name was Helen and the lady who arrived that day to turn on the light was Anne Mansfield Sullivan. Describing the moment, Helen later wrote,

> Have you ever been at sea in a dense fog, when it seemed as if a tangible white darkness shut you in, and the great ship, tense and anxious, groped her way toward the shore with plummet and sounding line, and you waited with beating heart for something to happen? I was like that ship before my education began, only I was without compass or sounding line, and had no way of knowing how near the harbor was. "Light! Give me light!" was the wordless cry of my soul, and the light of love shone on me in that very hour.[1]

Who would have known this meeting would unlock the hidden talents of America's foremost spokesman for the interests and challenges of the physically impaired? Although much credit must be given to her novice teacher, Helen possessed a spirit of unequaled zeal and optimism which enabled her to climb the steep sides of what she called her "valley of twofold solitude." Three months after her arrival, Miss Sullivan wrote, "I know that Helen has remarkable powers, and I believe that I shall be able to develop and mould them. She is no ordinary child and people's interest in her education will be no ordinary interest ..."[2]

Helen Keller was born with all her senses intact. She was only 19 months old when a severe illness deprived her of both sight and hearing. Through Helen's triumph we are permitted to see the power of the human spirit when it is resolved and focused on accomplishment. Through dogged determination she mastered the ability to communicate by spelling words through hand gestures and by touching the lips of those addressing her. She was fluent in three types of braille—English, American, and New York Point. With the assistance of these "languages," she went on to master French, Latin, German, and Greek. After attending various special schools for the deaf and learning to speak, Helen tackled the seeing world, attending the Cambridge School for Young Ladies, and then graduating with honors from Radcliffe College in 1904. She loved poetry and memorized volumes of her favorite authors. She counted among her friends some of the most famous people of her day, including Alexander Graham Bell, Oliver Wendell Holmes, John Whittier, and Mark Twain.

Helen was able to overcome because she saw hardships as opportunity for growth, always thanking God for the privilege of learning something new. "For, after all," she concluded, "everyone who wishes to gain true knowledge must climb the Hill Difficulty alone, and since there is no royal road to the summit, I must zigzag it in my own way. I slip back many times, I fall, I stand still, I run against the edge of hidden obstacles, I lose my temper and find it again and keep it better, I trudge on, I gain little, I feel encouraged, I get more eager and climb higher and begin to see the widening horizon. Every struggle is a victory. One more effort and I reach the luminous cloud, the blue depths of the sky, the uplands of my desire."³

Helen was greatly influenced by what she read, including the Bible, which she read from cover to cover several times. Her reflections mirrored Paul when she wrote, "Is it not true, then, that my life with all its limitations touches at many points the life of the world Beautiful? Everything has its wonders, even darkness and silence, and I learn, whatever state I may be in, therein to be content."⁴

Optimism in the face of adversity is all too rare, making those who possess it valued as leaders. To David the solution to Goliath seemed pretty basic. He said to Saul, "Let no one lose heart on account of this Philistine; your servant will go and fight him." Thinking very logically, Saul replied, "You are not able to go out against this Philistine and fight him; you are only a boy, and he has been a fighting man from his youth (1 Samuel 17:32–33).

There is no Scripture I know of more optimistic than David's reply to Goliath's taunt as he approached the giant on the field of battle. "You come against me with sword and spear and javelin, but I come against you in the name of the LORD God Almighty, the God of the armies of Israel, whom you have defied. This day the LORD will hand you over to me, and I'll strike you down and cut off your head ... and the whole world will know that there is a God in Israel" (1 Samuel 17:45–46).

David had good reason to be optimistic. The Lord had proven His faithfulness in the past. As a shepherd he had successfully defended his father's flock against the attacks of wild animals. He told Saul, "The LORD who delivered me from the paw of the lion and the paw of the bear will deliver me from the hand of this Philistine" (1 Samuel 17:37).

Christian leaders should draw on their own personal history when facing new challenges. The Lord who delivered you out of past difficulties is able to overcome the presenting problem and grant the victory. There were three existing conditions that contributed to David's confidence. 1) He took no credit for the past victories. 2) His confidence was in God's power not his own strength. 3) He was fighting against those who opposed the Lord.

Christians living in the shadow of the cross have the same basis for optimism. The apostle wrote, "What, then, shall we say in response to this? If God is for us, who can be against us? He who did not spare His own Son, but gave Him up for us all—how will He not also, along with Him, graciously give us all things?" (Romans 8:31–32). The Lord's love is without question. On the cross He showed the depth of His total commitment to us. Not only did He accomplish our redemption, He ascended into heaven and, as Paul explains, "—is at the right hand of God and is also interceding for us" (Romans 8:34).

As the little poem reminds us, facts are the basis for faith which is the basis for confident feeling.

Three men were walking on a wall,
Feeling, Faith and Fact.
When Feeling took an awful fall,
Then Faith was taken back.
So close to Faith was Feeling,
That he stumbled and fell too.
But Fact remained and pulled Faith back,
And Faith brought Feeling too. (Author Unknown)

If faith rested on feelings, we would fall in and out of faith every time things went well or badly. Because faith rests on fact we are secure, for nothing we do can undo what God has already done for us in the factual death, resurrection, and ascension of Jesus, our Savior.

We never walk alone. Helen Keller could not have accomplished so much had it not been for her dearest friend and teacher, Anne Sullivan Macy. The closing sentences of Helen's autobiography tell the tale. "Thus it is that my friends have made the story of my life. In a thousand ways they have turned my limitations into beautiful privileges, and enabled me to walk serene and happy in the shadow cast by my deprivation."[5] Likewise the Christian leader David spoke of the Lord, "The LORD who delivered me ... will deliver me ... and the whole earth will know that there is a God in Israel. All those gathered here will know that it is not by sword or spear that the Lord saves; for the battle is the Lord's, and He will give all of you into our hands" (1 Samuel 17:37, 46–47).

More Scriptural Insight

Esther 4:12–17   Describe Esther's attitude at the time of her greatest risk.
Hebrews 4:14–16   What is the basis of confidence in this passage?
Luke 5:4–11   Describe the "feeling, faith, and facts" of the account.

A Leader's Prayer

Lord, make me an optimist of the best kind. Let my optimism flow freely from faith that rests upon the objective fact of Your great victory on my behalf. Grant me also a sound memory of Your past interventions that I may draw on those experiences and be bold in Your service. Thank You for the rescue of David from lion, bear, and giant. Thank You even more for the heart of David, who gave all honor to You and You alone. Gracious Lord, You know the obstacles that stand in the way of my leadership. The greatest of these are internal and seem insurmountable. Control my thinking and strengthen my faith in Your provision. Let me never be too big to be small. Help me maintain a constant dependence on You, now and also after You grant the victory. When I face the challenges of leadership, I seem so small and they seem so great. Help me to understand that there is no child of Yours who is insignificant and incapable when You grant Your blessing. You have brought me to this moment, strengthen, uphold, and keep me faithful in the exercise of my given duties. This I pray in the name of Jesus, the Lord and Giver of every good and perfect gift. Amen.

Notes

1. Helen Keller, *The Story of My Life,* (Mahwah, NJ: Watermill Press, 1980), 21.

2. Nell Henney, *Anne Sullivan Macy: the Story behind Helen Keller* (New York: Doubleday, Doran & Co., Inc., 1933), p 52.

3. Helen Keller, 106.

4. Ibid., 141.

5. Ibid., 152.

CHAPTER FORTY-TWO

HIN-MAH-TOO-YAH-LAH-KEKHT
Peace Loving

Born in a cave near Joseph Creek in the Oregon mountains, he was called Chief Joseph by the white settlers, but to his people he was known as Hin-mah-too-yah-lah-kekht—"Thunder Rolling Up the Mountains." It is a good name for a man born in the high Wallowa Valley of Oregon about 1840. It was a beautiful valley, cherished as sacred by his Nez Perce tribe of Native Americans. As Tuekakas, his father and tribal chief lay dying, he made a pact with his son,

> My son, ... you are now the chief of these people. They look to you to guide them. Always remember that your father never sold his country. You must stop your ears whenever you are asked to sign a treaty selling your home. A few years more, and white men will be all around you. They have their eyes on this land. My son, never forget my dying words. This country holds your father's body. Never sell the bones of your father and your mother.[1]

Chief Joseph never did sell the Wallowa Valley. In 1873 he

315

skillfully negotiated a treaty with the United States, giving up the Nez Perce claim to thousands of acres of hunting grounds for permanent rights to the valley of his father's bones. But President Grant soon found himself petitioned to rescind his grant, moving the Indian tribes to less valued land, and farther away from frightened white settlers. On June 10, 1875, President Grant conceded to those requests and retracted his executive order of 1873.

When told to relocate, Chief Joseph and other Nez Perce chiefs would not consent to the new order and refused to sign the documents. For almost two years nothing changed, but then came the battle of the Little Big Horn. The Sioux's annihilation of General George Custer and his company of 200 men caused widespread panic in the West, and United States policy towards the Native American tribes became less tolerant. Fears were running high. In 1877, the noncompliant Nez Perce were given 30 days to relocate or be forcibly removed. When one of their chiefs openly challenged General Howard's authority at a public meeting, he was immediately jailed for disobedience. Twelve days before the deadline, 600 Nez Perce Indians gathered in their beloved valley before relocating to the new reservation. A young brave, whose father had been killed by a white settler, broke ranks, and against the counsel of his elders, killed four whites known to have mistreated members of the tribe. Joseph, a peace loving man, later said, "I would have given my own life if I could have undone the killing of white men by my people. ... My friends among white men have blamed me for the war. I am not to blame. When my young men began the killing, my heart was hurt. Although I did not justify them, I remembered all the insults I had endured, and my blood was on fire. Still I would have taken my people to buffalo country without fighting, if possible."[2]

Even after the killings, Joseph attempted to restore peace

and end the violence, but the damage could not be undone. The Nez Perce Indians were at war. Joseph made a valiant effort to escape to Canada with his tribe of men, women, and children. Of the 600 people, many were elderly or very young, only 200 were able-bodied warriors. Chief Joseph's 1,000-mile retreat across swollen rivers and through the steep mountain passes is legendary. Pursued by General Howard and his troops, the Nez Perce fought off three attacks and skillfully eluded the man they called, "General Day after Tomorrow." One historian has written,

> Chief Joseph's retreat was begun in August 1877. With 200 warriors, but burdened with 350 women, children, and aged, he moved up Clearwater, across the mountains, through Yellowstone Park, up the Bighorn and across the Missouri. Howard covered 1,321 miles in seventy five days of pursuit. Both General Miles and General Gibbon were sent to stop Joseph, while Colonel Sturgis and the Crows were on his flank. Howard was outmaneuvered, the Crows were defeated, Miles was eluded after a brief encounter, and Gibbon was left flat-footed. ... The retreat of Chief Joseph and the Nez Perce was the most remarkable military exploit in the long history of the wars between the reds and whites ... when that group managed to keep ahead of a superior and well equipped white force, and to elude other detachments sent to stop it, the exploit comes close to the miraculous.[3]

Thinking he had reached safety, Chief Joseph made the mistake of stopping to tend to his wounded and elderly. Still 30 miles from the protection of the Canadian border, the Nez Perce were surprised and overtaken in an early morning attack. Rather than face certain annihilation, Chief Joseph surrendered with words that reveal a heart of compassion for his people.

I am tired of fighting. Our chiefs are killed. Looking Glass is dead. It is the young men who say "yes" and "no." He who led the young men is dead. It is cold and we have no blankets. The little children are freezing to death. My people, some of them, have run away to the hills and have no blankets, no food. No one knows where they are—perhaps freezing to death. I want to have time to look for my children and see how many of them I can find. Maybe I shall find them among the dead. Hear me, my chiefs. I am tired. My heart is sick and sad. From where the sun now stands I will fight no more forever.[4]

Joseph was transferred under arrest to Fort Leavenworth, Kansas, and later to the Oklahoma territories. He never gave up the hope of reclaiming the Wallowa Valley and made trips to Washington to talk directly to President McKinley and later to President Roosevelt. On September 21, 1904, with his dream still unrealized, Joseph died in his tepee on the Colville Indian Reservation in Washington State. Although furnished with a farm and a comfortable home, Chief Joseph and many of his closest followers had refused the white man's housing, preferring to maintain their nation's customs.

In his biography, Chester A. Fee wrote, "Joseph ranks with Lee, Jackson, and Grant as one of the best generals this country has produced. ... Had Joseph led thousands and had he been born ... in a place less remote from the main currents of history, his name would resound in our ears like thunder."[5] To the end, he was admired by both his friends and enemies as a man of integrity and peace.

To be peace loving is not only an admirable quality, it is listed prominently among Paul's requirements for those who aspire to spiritual authority. "Now the overseer must be above reproach, ... temperate, self-controlled, respectable, ... not violent but gentle, not quarrelsome ..." (1 Timothy 3:2ff.). The ability to establish and maintain peace is so important it is the most mentioned trait in Paul's list of leadership qualities. And for good reason, when passions run high, as they often do in matters of faith, a spiritual shepherd must soothe the situation, not contribute to the natural inclination towards aggression.

In two of his pastoral letters, Paul's concluding admonition is for pastors to avoid argumentation. To Timothy he counsels, "Turn away from godless chatter and the opposing ideas of what is falsely called knowledge, which some have professed and in so doing have wandered from the faith" (1 Timothy 6:20–21). His advice to Titus is even more pointed. "Avoid foolish controversies and genealogies and arguments and quarrels about the law, because these are unprofitable and useless. Warn a divisive person once, and then warn him a second time. After that, have nothing to do with him. You may be sure that such a man is warped and sinful; he is self-condemned" (Titus 3:9–11).

There are only three kinds of people to look out for when it comes to keeping the peace: those that don't like you, those that do, and the orneries.

Those that don't like you will pretty much oppose anything and everything you attempt to accomplish. It doesn't really matter why they don't like you. You may remind them of a teacher who kept them from being valedictorian, or you may look like their boss. Perhaps your sermons have been "plowing close to the corn" and they feel you wait to see what they're going to do before you write your Sunday morning message. It doesn't matter "why" they don't like you, but it does matter that you love them anyway. They are not the enemy and by fighting with them you only lower yourself to their standards. Someone once said, "Never fight with a skunk. You aren't equipped to fight on his level and will always lose."

Those that do like you may be just as troublesome. They will fight you "for your own good." Maybe they've seen others try and fail and they want to spare you the heartache. I've found that no matter what the issue, there will always be people on your team that you wish would switch jerseys. They are not the enemy. They wish you well and are only obstructing your efforts out of misguided concern for your well-being. They usually want you to slow down, not take things so seriously, and realize that it's not that important. Peter once obstructed Jesus in this manner after the Lord began to reveal openly the suffering and death He was about to encounter in Jerusalem. The Bible says Peter took Jesus aside and rebuked Him saying, "This shall never happen to You!" Jesus quickly told him, "Get behind Me, Satan! You are a stumbling block to Me; you do not have in mind the things of God, but the things of men" (Matthew 16:22–23).

The last group of detractors I call the orneries. They are always ready to fight. You can never take the orneries personally, because you are rarely their only interest. They oppose almost anyone trying to accomplish something or lead in any capacity. You will notice their name at the bottom of letters to the editor, on the page describing the public debate at city hall, and on the first line of petitions circulated in the neighborhood. These are hurting people. I sometimes wonder if they haven't been raised in a cage and poked with sticks. Like a mistreated animal, they snap at anyone who gets within reach. They are not the enemy. Although you may be tempted out of self-preservation, "giving as good as you get," is not the answer. Paul was thinking of people like these when he wrote, "Do not repay anyone evil for evil. Be careful to do what is right in the eyes of everybody. If it is possible, as far as it depends on you, live at peace with everyone. Do not take revenge, my friends, but leave room for God's wrath, for it is written: 'It is mine to avenge; I will repay,' says the Lord" (Romans 12:17–19).

Not only is revenge futile, the Lord recommends a more

powerful response. "If your enemy is hungry, feed him; if he is thirsty, give him something to drink. In doing this, you will heap burning coals on his head. Don't be overcome by evil, but overcome evil with good" (Romans 12:20–21). This is the legacy of Hin-mah-too-yah-lah-kekht. At the dedication of a dam named in his honor, Erskine Wood said, "There was no hatred in his soul in spite of the wrongs our race had done him. He was a man of true magnanimity."[6]

More Scriptural Insight

Genesis 50:15–21	What made Joseph so kind and why could they not believe it?
James 3:13–18	According to this definition, did Chief Joseph possess true wisdom?
Matthew 26:47–56	Explain Jesus' response to Peter's violent defense.

A Leader's Prayer

Lord, so often force seems quicker than negotiation and I am tempted to wield the club. I know it was not Your way, but I am not as patient, kind, or able to forgive. Grant me greater wisdom so that I can see the value of peace and make it my goal. Often, like David hiding in the cave near Saul, others around me are willing to spare me the trouble and exercise power on my behalf. It is tempting to have them help in this way, especially when my cause seems so right. Let my example be evident to all and enable me to redirect such misguided people to the path of peace. Grant me the ability to see past the actions of those who oppose me so that I can understand their hurts and fears. Enable me thus to address the true concerns and not be drawn into a battle that will solve nothing. As I grow in faith, instill in me the spirit of Jesus, who prayed for His executioners from the cross. I commend my enemies to You, Lord, and ask that You deal with their plots and schemes on my behalf. As for me, show me the path of peace and give me the greater courage needed to pursue its course, in Jesus' name. Amen.

Notes

1. Lois Warburton, *The Importance of Chief Joseph,* (San Diego: Lucent Books, 1992), 35–36.
2. Ibid., 49.
3. Robert Riegel, *America Moves West,* (New York: Henry Holt & Company Publishers, 1930), 486.
4. Ibid., 486–87.
5. Lois Warburton, 92.
6. Ibid., 98.

CHAPTER FORTY-THREE

ANNE MANSFIELD SULLIVAN
Teacher

The sign in the school zone read, "Drive Carefully—Acute Shortage of Teachers." There are millions of people who work with children in the field of education, but only a small percentage of them deserve the title of "teacher."

A good teacher is as rare as a cool summer day in Tuscumbia, Alabama, the birthplace of Helen Keller. Her teacher, Anne Mansfield Sullivan, was inexperienced and suffered from handicaps of her own. She was only 21 years old when she arrived at the Keller home, just 14 years older than her soon-to-become-famous pupil. But it wasn't knowledge of facts and figures that Miss Sullivan came to teach, she came to awaken a spirit of adventure and to create an unquenchable thirst for knowledge in the heart of a child. About these things, Miss Anne Sullivan knew a great deal.

"Teacher" is what Helen Keller called Miss Sullivan, never anything else. In her autobiography Helen recalls the exact day of Anne's arrival—March 3, 1887—"The most important day I remember in all my life."[1] In describing the importance of that event, Helen used a prophetic parallel, "Thus I came up out of Egypt and stood before Sinai, and a power divine touched my spirit and gave it sight, so that I beheld many wonders. And from the sacred mountain I heard a voice which said, 'Knowledge is love and light and vision.' "[2]

Those who assume the difficulty of Anne's task lay in the handicaps of the child would be only half right. It is always the inner spirit of the child, not the outward limitations, that enable or inhibit instruction, and Helen had a considerable inner spirit. The seven-year-old deaf/blind child was notorious for her stubborn and strong-willed nature. Never mind that she had lost her sight and hearing at the age of 19 months, she ran the house. Any assumption that the lack of sight and sound would create a naturally timid and withdrawn child would be a great miscalculation. Helen was mischievous as the incident of the key verifies.

> I locked my mother up in the pantry, where she was obligated to remain three hours, as the servants were in a detached part of the house. She kept pounding on the door, while I sat outside on the porch steps and laughed with glee as I felt the jar of the pounding. This most naughty prank of mine convinced my parents that I must be taught as soon as possible. After my teacher, Miss Sullivan, came to me, I sought an early opportunity to lock her in her room. I went upstairs with something which my mother made me understand I was to give to Miss Sullivan; but no sooner had I given it to her than I slammed the door, locked it, and hid the key under the wardrobe in the hall. I could not be induced to tell where the key was. My father was obliged to get a ladder and take Miss Sullivan out through the window—much to my delight. Months after I produced the key.[3]

Undeterred, Miss Sullivan rose to the challenge and demanded the opportunity to isolate Helen from her usual surroundings and permissive relationships. Helen's father was a man of some means, able to provide a nice home, a nearby annex, and even a cottage for family retreats. With great reluctance, Miss Sullivan received permission to remove Helen to the annex where the proverb could be fulfilled, "As iron sharpens iron, so one man sharpens another" (Proverbs 27:17). Two strong wills were on collision course and both would be forever changed by the impact.

As Miss Sullivan recalls, the experiment began badly. Helen was homesick and would have nothing to do with her teacher. Helen's father snuck peeks through the windows. Blinded by his pity for Helen, and dismayed by the shambles she had made of the annex, he all but fired the inexperienced teacher before the breakthrough at the well. As any teacher can tell, before knowledge comes discipline. Not discipline which breaks the heart and spirit of a child, but discipline that enables the child to focus its spirit and heart on the lesson at hand. After two weeks in the annex, Miss Sullivan wrote, "My heart is singing for joy. The little savage has learned her first lesson in obedience, and finds the yoke easy. It remains my pleasant task to direct and mould the intelligence that is beginning to stir in the child-soul."[4]

Helen compared that moment to the blooming of Aaron's rod, a sign of God's special favor. "It would have been difficult to find a happier child than I was as I lay in my crib at the close of that eventful day and lived over the joys it had brought me, and for the first time longed for a new day to come."[5]

Helen, of course, went on to achieve personal greatness as America's chief advocate for the needs of the physically challenged. Many have desired to recognize and honor Helen's humble teacher but she steadfastly refused, claiming Helen's life was the only biography she desired. When Temple University desired to confer Helen and Anne with the degree of Doctor of Humane Letters in 1931, Helen accepted but Miss Sullivan declined. "In the Temple auditorium, after the other speakers had showered praise upon Helen, Dr. A. Edward Newton asked all in the audience who felt the degree should be conferred upon Mrs. Macy (Anne had married in 1905), by force if necessary, to rise. Only one person remained seated, and that was Anne Sullivan Macy."[6] A year later she consented and the degree was awarded.

A teacher's greatest reward is the expressed appreciation of their pupils. No greater accolade could be given to Miss Sullivan than this reference by her grateful Helen,

> Any teacher can take a child to the classroom, but not every teacher can make him learn. ... My teacher is so near to me that I scarcely think of myself apart from her. How much of my delight in all beautiful things is innate, and how much is due to her influence, I can never tell. I feel that her being is inseparable from my own, and that the footsteps of my life are in hers. All the best of me belongs to her—there is not a talent, or an aspiration of a joy in me that has not been awakened by her loving touch.[7]

To be admired as a teacher is an honor conferred only to a select group of leaders. Not every leader discussed in this volume would qualify. Some lead through independence and bold self-assertion. Others lead through courage, skill, or daring. They are rightfully acknowledged as leaders who have inspired, discovered, or boldly opened new horizons for the benefit of others—but such accomplishments don't make them teachers.

A leader/teacher is able to multiply himself/herself so that others are equipped to accomplish the thing that they have discovered to do well. It is God's intention that Christian leaders would also be teachers of others. The ability to teach is listed in the traits expected of those who aspire to the office of spiritual overseer.[8] When Paul described God's intention for the administration of the church he said, "It was He who gave some to be apostles, some to be prophets, some to be evangelists, and some to be pastors and teachers, to prepare God's people for works of service, so that the body of Christ may be built up until we all reach unity in the faith and in the knowledge of the Son of God and become mature, attaining to the whole measure of the fullness of Christ" (Ephesians 4:11–13).

Those in leadership positions are all established, according to the Bible, for the same purpose; namely to prepare God's people for works of service and to build up the body of Christ. Apart from the body of Christ, our leadership positions have no purpose. They exist to teach, encourage, and enable all God's people to achieve greater maturity and render Christian service. In effect, the greatest among us exist as servants to the servants of the Lord. Like Anne Sullivan, the people we touch, not our degrees, are the true biography of our achievement in the kingdom of God.

An old proverb says, "When the oak is felled, the whole forest echoes with its fall, but a hundred acorns are sown in silence by an unnoticed breeze." I like that proverb. It is profound. We pay more attention to the end of things than we ever do to their beginnings. Even now, while the whole world is focused on the mighty and the powerful of the world, off in some obscure corner of the kingdom a seed is being planted, another being nurtured, and yet a third breaking forth into its first expression of greatness. At the fall and rise of the mighty the world takes notice, but somewhere, perhaps under your care, maybe in your own home, there is "an acorn" taking root. Who knows what mighty oak may grow up in the sphere of your influence?

How easy it is to lose our perspective and become impressed with our own accomplishments, or court the attention of people of renown. The Bible says the Lord is no respecter of persons. He is not impressed by our awards, by the size of our house, the newness of our cars, and the plushness of our office. He is more interested in the quality of our heart. As Christian leaders we need to take our eyes off our own careers, or the accomplishments of others, and look through the eyes of Christ. The Bible says, "God so loved the world that He gave His one and only Son, that whoever [great or small] believes in Him shall not perish but have eternal life" (John 3:16).

This spirit is still best seen in the lives of humble and dedicated teachers. I like the story of the kindergarten teacher who had just finished putting on the last pair of boots before sending her class out to meet their waiting parents on a snowy day in the North—30 pairs in all. The last little girl said, "You know what, Teacher? These are not my boots."

With hardly a sigh, the teacher smiled and removed the boots in anticipation of a swap with some less observant student among her class. When she held the boots up and asked the class whose boots she was holding, the same little girl raised her hand. "I thought you said these weren't your boots," the teacher said, somewhat confused. "Oh, they aren't. They belong to my sister, but she said I could wear them today." The teacher smiled knowingly and quietly put the boots back on the feet of her pupil.

So many qualities combine to make a truly great teacher. It takes patience, kindness, humility, self-sacrifice, self-control, the ability to forgive, personal conviction about right and wrong, compassion, trust, and perseverance—the same qualities described by Paul in Romans 13 as godly love.

My teacher friends love to remind me that Jesus was often

called Rabbi. They prefer to think of Him more as a teacher than a preacher. Although it pains me to admit it, I'm inclined to agree. The Lord's use of parables, and His style of proclamation is more didactic than exhortatory. At the conclusion to His most famous sermon, Matthew describes the results by saying, "The crowds were amazed at His teaching, because He taught as one who had authority, and not as their teachers of the law" (Matthew 7:28–29).

I am much more willing to listen to someone who instructs me in the Christian life than the image of a preacher exhorting me with his rhetoric. I prefer the title of teacher myself, knowing it implies an attitude of continual learning by the instructor for the benefit of his pupils. It was a wise person who said, "Every adult needs a child to teach; it's the way adults learn." May it ever be so.

More Scriptural Insight

Deuteronomy 6:4–15	What obligation is owed to future generations?
Acts 18:24–28	What were the most admirable qualities of Apollos?
Matthew 28:16–20	How important is teaching to the Great Commission?

A Leader's Prayer

Rabbi, Lord and Savior of us all, teach me so that I might teach others. I have seen in Your Word how important it is that Christian leaders be able to teach. Lord, I want to teach only Your truth, not my ideas or personal preferences. Help me first to see more clearly Your will on the issues I must address. Secondly, give me a heart for my students. Help me to gain patience and to understand the issues from their perspective so that I may teach with sensitivity and insight. Keep me from becoming autocratic. When I need to accomplish a lot of things in a short period of time, I am tempted to dictate and command my way through the issues. In my heart I know that it may take more time to teach and equip others, but it is always the most profitable long-term strategy. Keep me from any selfish attempt to maintain false importance by keeping knowledge from those whom I can help. I am honored and humbled to be considered worthy of Your service. Bless my service of teaching so that more might be saved and come to the knowledge of the truth in Jesus Christ. Amen.

Notes

1. Helen Keller, *The Story of My Life,* (Mahwah, NJ: Watermill Press, 1980), 20.

2. Ibid., 19.

3. Ibid., 13.

4. Nella Braddy, *The Other Half of Helen Keller,* The Reader's Digest 20th Anniversary Anthology, (A condensation of the book, "Anne Sullivan Macy: The Story behind Helen Keller, Pleasantville: the Reader's Digest Association, 1941), 54.

5. Helen Keller, 24.

6. Nella Braddy, 56.

7. Helen Keller, 40.

8. Cf. 1 Timothy 3:2; Titus 1:2.

CHAPTER FORTY-FOUR

ALEXANDER GRAHAM BELL
Solitude

The pastor stands before the altar poised for action. The bride is arrayed in a beautiful white gown with her handsome groom at her side. Their attendants nervously fidget, not sure if they are positioned correctly and wondering what to do when the couple moves to light the unity candle. The time for declaring solemn intentions is at hand. The pastor reverently asks, "Will you freely and gladly take —insert name here— to be your lawful wife; to live together after God's counsel concerning Christian marriage? Will you love her, comfort her, honor and keep her in sickness and in health, stand by her in trial, share her joy in times of rejoicing, and forsaking all others, keep yourself only for her so long as you both shall live?" I am still waiting for a sharp-witted groom to answer: "I'll take better, richer, healthy, with times of rejoicing!"

At that moment no one can predict with any certainty how the couple's life will unfold. It is a moment of prayer and best wishes on the part of those who want only good things for the young couple. Despite their best wishes, a life of "better, richer, and healthy with times of rejoicing," without their counterparts—"worse, poorer, and sickness with seasons of trial"—may not produce the intended results. All good can be no good. We call those climates where the sun always shines and the rain never falls—deserts.

How many successful leaders "crash and burn" because they were able to handle failure better than success? The Lord knows the value of balance, especially during times of rejoicing. Consider His counsel to the children of Israel as they anticipated entering the Promised Land.

> Do not be terrified by them, for the LORD your God, who is among you, is a great and awesome God. The LORD your God will drive out those nations before you, little by little. You will not be allowed to eliminate them all at once, or the wild animals will multiply around you. But the LORD your God will deliver them over to you, throwing them into great confusion until they are destroyed. (Deuteronomy 7:21–23)

Too much, too soon can destroy a nation (or a Christian leader) as quickly as adversity and strong opposition. Just like a game of tug-of-war can be lost to overwhelming strength or the quick release of slack, the leader must be alert for sudden gain as well as gradual loss. The wise leader will carefully consider the proverb of Solomon, "The crucible for silver and the furnace for gold, but man is tested by the praise he receives" (Proverbs 27:21). The leader who successfully navigates the treacherous shoals must be vigilant not to run aground under favorable winds and smooth sailing.

Perhaps the best guide for managing success is the example of our Savior, Jesus, who during those early and popular years of His ministry, sought solitude for quiet prayer and meditation.

> News about Him spread quickly over the whole region of

Galilee. ... That evening after sunset the people brought to Jesus all the sick and demon-possessed. The whole town gathered at the door. ...Very early in the morning, while it was still dark, Jesus got up, left the house and went off to a solitary place, where He prayed. Simon and his companions went to look for Him and when they found Him, they exclaimed: "Everyone is looking for You!" Jesus replied, "Let us go somewhere else—to the nearby villages—so I can preach there also. That is why I have come." (Mark 1:28:32-33, 35-38)

There are always at least three different perspectives in the Gospel accounts of Jesus' life. First, Jesus is focused on His own game plan, solely intent on doing the will of His Father. Secondly, the disciples—who believe in the kingdom of the here-and-now—are continuously confused by the Lord's unpredictable behavior. And finally of course, there are the common people and the religious leaders who are awed and confused by the miracles and teachings of Jesus.

Peter and his companions were amazed by the attitude of Jesus. They assumed that crowds and public recognition were the goal of every rabbi. Why would Jesus avoid the very thing most teachers worked so hard to obtain? In words that seem close to rebuke, Peter asked what in the world Jesus was doing seeking solitude! Not unlike John the Bapitzer's disciples who once warned him of Jesus' growing popularity as if it were a threat to his own. They assumed popularity and recognition were the payoff for work well done. Jesus shows no desire to court the adulation of the people, and even redirects the disciples' subtle rebuke with a simple statement, "Let us go somewhere else—to the nearby villages—so I can preach there also. That is why I have come." His mission was the salvation of the world by way of the cross, not popularity.

Truly great leaders understand Jesus' repeated need for solitude. And like Christ, the greatest leaders combine times of reflection with healthy levels of prayer and meditation. From early in life, until his dying day Alexander Graham Bell cherished moments of solitude.

Alexander Graham Bell's invention of the telephone revolutionized almost every aspect of life; and with the advancement of cell phones, computer modems, and fax machines, the world is still reeling more than a century later. He was only 29 years old that momentous day of March 10, 1876, when his famous words, "Mr. Watson, come here; I want you!" broke the barriers to long distance voice transmission. His fame came early and because of the immediate and lasting popularity of his invention, it never waned. To dramatize the impact of Bell's life, at the exact time of his burial all telephone service in the United States was halted for one minute.[1] Such an interruption in service today would carry multi-million dollar consequences.

Telephones were not Dr. Bell's only interest. Before all else, even the development of the telephone, Bell worked tirelessly for the education of the deaf and considered it his most rewarding accomplishment. He also advanced the theory of hydrofoil boats and set a water speed record of over 70 miles per hour that stood for 10 years. He served as president of the National Geographic Society, experimented with aviation, measured the ocean's depths by bouncing echoes off the ocean floor, and experimented with the distillation of salt water to fresh. His biographer has written,

> Bell never gave up striving, not even as he grew older. He believed that no one ages, "who continues to observe, to remember what he observes, and to seek answers for the unceasing hows and whys about things." His rule of Three was, "Observe! Remember! Compare!" Only eight months before he died, Bell declared; "I cannot hope to work out half the problems in which I am interested."[2]

How did Bell keep early success from ruining his 75 years of productive life? Alexander made an effort to distance himself from the adulation of his admirers and continued to honor the value of solitude. He called his wife, Mabel, his "link to the living world," and try as she might, it became increasingly difficult to convince Dr. Bell to experience greater social interaction. Ironically, long before the days of aluminum siding and telemarketing, Bell lamented the loss of privacy brought about through his own invention. When a visitor to his Washington home asked to use the telephone, Bell replied: "There is a telephone in the house but the pesky thing is as far from here as I could possibly get it."[3]

Throughout most of his life, Bell preferred working late into the night and sleeping till midday. By this means he avoided distractions and interruptions caused by a more normal schedule. Bell would not tolerate any intrusion into his thinking time and, to the aggravation of his family, would even disconnect the chimes for the hall clock. "To take night from me is to rob me of life," he once admitted.[4] A picture in his Boston laboratory tells the tale. His dear wife, Mabel, had promised to paint her famous husband's portrait in response to his personal request. When the portrait was finally unveiled, it was discovered Mabel had painted a portrait of a great white owl.[5]

If disruption of solitude was a problem for Bell, it has reached epic proportions today. We can't move the phone to the farthest corner of the building when it's tucked into our pocket and our international paging service is able to interrupt dinner at a campfire in the boundary waters of northern Minnesota. Had Alexander Graham Bell allowed such routine interruptions and not sequestered himself from his admiring public, his continued productivity would have been severely limited. Like Jesus, Bell needed to limit the accessibility of admiring crowds, because his mission was not notoriety.

Leadership is about knowing your unique purpose and pursing your unique goals. Someone defined a *goal* as "a preferred future condition." In order to accomplish the changes which will result in those future conditions, a leader must have the time and solitude necessary to think, plan, strategize, and organize necessary activities. How ironic that Bell's solitude resulted in the end of loneliness for those isolated by distance and impaired hearing. One evening during a walk with Helen Keller at his side, the great inventor placed her hand on a telephone pole near the road. Helen could feel the currents of conversation which pulsated up and down the line. "I had never put my hand on a pole before," Helen later wrote. "Does it hum like that all the time?"

" 'Yes,' he told me, 'all the time. That even-singing never stops; for it is singing the story of life, and life never stops. Those copper wires up there are carrying the news of births and death, war and finance, failure and success, from station to station, around the world. Listen! I fancy I hear laughter, tears, life's vows broken and mended.' "[6]

In solitude we gain the objectivity needed to observe the way things are, and can begin to picture the way things ought to be. In solitude we are able sit in judgment of present restraints and formulate solutions that make life better for the people we serve. It should come as no surprise that the psalm which inspired Luther's great reformation hymn, "A Mighty Fortress Is Our God," contains the thought, "Be still, and know that I am God" (Psalm 46:10). Rarely is anything great accomplished without quiet reflection.

More Scriptural Insight

1 Kings 19:1–13	Explain how God cared for Elijah in the wilderness.
Matthew 14:13–23	What lessons about solitude are taught in this example?
Galatians 1:11–20	Why did Paul isolate himself from the rest of the apostles for three years immediately after his conversion?

A Leader's Prayer

Lord, I treasure our quiet times together. They are not long enough, nor do they occur frequently enough for my good. I admit that often (like Peter) my spirit is willing but my flesh is weak. When I find the time, I am often so exhausted from the hectic press of life, that I have little energy for our private communion. Restore my appreciation for solitude and enable me to find time to be alone with You in prayer and meditation. Keep me physically strong so that my thinking is clear and my working time is spent more efficiently. Drive away any guilt which the devil may use to keep me from quiet meditation. I thank You for the example of my Savior, who constantly took time to retreat from the demands of people to pray and sit with You in peace. Enter those moments when I seek Your face and desperately need Your reassurance. Strengthen me, renew my soul, and grant fresh insight into the challenges of my calling. Like David, "I lift up my eyes to the hills—where does my help come from? My help comes from the LORD, the Maker of heaven and earth" (Psalm 121:1–2). I will continue to look for You in the counsel of Your Word, and I will expect Your response in the often unexpected sound of a gentle wind. Accept my praise and bless my life through the Lord of lords, Jesus the Christ. Amen.

Notes

1. Judith St. George, *Dear Dr. Bell ... Your Friend, Helen Keller,* (New York: Scholastic Incorporated,

1992), 86.

   2. Ibid., 78.
   3. Ibid., 52.
   4. Ibid., 15.
   5. Ibid., 17.
   6. Ibid., 67, 68.

CHAPTER FORTY-FIVE

GEORGE WASHINGTON CARVER
Wonder

Carver's George Washington (so called as a slave owned by Moses and Susan Carver) started life so far down that the bottom looked like up. The consequences of his childhood were so difficult mere survival would have qualified the boy for honorable mention in the list of great achievers.

He was born in January in the early 1860s on a farm near Diamond Grove, Missouri. The Carvers were German immigrants, not fond of slavery but it seemed the best way to secure help and companionship for Susan who was unable to have children. George was the second of two sons born to the Carver's Mary and a black slave from a neighboring farm. When he was only a few months old, both he and his mother were kidnapped and taken to Arkansas by bushwhackers who often stole and resold livestock from the isolated farms of the Ozarks. Mr. Carver pursued the thieves with no success, but upon his return offered a sizable reward for the mother and her child. Within days, the nearly dead baby George was returned for the reward, but his mother Mary was never heard of again. The boy's father was permitted regular visits but tragically died in a farm accident a few years later.

Few believed Susan Carver would succeed in saving the sick baby. He had developed a severe cough and was barely breathing. Although George survived, his health was never strong and the residual scars of his early illness gave his voice an awkward quality which many found difficult to understand. Undaunted by obstacles, Carver's natural fascination with the whys and wherefores of life started him on a lifelong quest for knowledge. At the age of 10 he left the security of the Carver farm to attend a Negro school being taught in a nearby community, not knowing where he would stay or how he would live; he just knew he had to go. Thus began a journey that would take him from town to town and state to state until at last he was able to study and teach at the highest levels.

What great gift did this hapless black child possess that would bring him to greatness and earn the respect of his entire nation? George Washington Carver never lost his fascination with the mysteries of life.

This devotion to wonder was both a blessing and a curse. His love for pure research nearly drove Tuskegee's founder, Booker T. Washington, crazy. He had hired Carver to head his department of agriculture. The natural expectation of Washington was for a teacher who could lead, inspire, and teach Tuskegee's students and the department's faculty. While George enjoyed the challenge of imparting knowledge, he loved research more and could not easily be constrained to spend precious time guiding others at elementary levels. Washington wisely conceded to Carver's passion, creating a department of agricultural research over which Carver would have complete control. "This new position was supposed to relieve him of all teaching, but students begged for classes with him and would not be refused. For many more years he continued to teach a limited number. Loving young people and seeing their possibilities, he was able to inspire as well as instruct them."[1]

His fascination with the complexities of nature was contagious.

> More and more he was asked to speak to all kinds of groups in the South, where he was warmly welcomed, in the Midwest and along the eastern coast. Illustrating with exhibits, he lectured on such topics as "The Earth Is Full of Riches." He won his hearers, even when at first they were hostile. ... One summer when he was on the staff of a Youth Conference, his whole group formed the habit of getting up before five, in order to share his early morning walks. Increasing numbers of boys followed him, for he made their world shine with fresh beauty and wonder. Everything he saw, heard, smelled, was of use and interest.

> "He could pick up a common weed that I hadn't even noticed," recalls Jack Boyd, a leader in that conference. "He'd pull it apart, saying, 'Now if you ever give yourself a cut when you're shaving, just put on some of this juice. It's antiseptic.' "[2]

The inspiration he provided often awakened a thirst in his students for even greater knowledge—the mark of a true leader. "Many applied to study under him. If they were white, it was impossible, since Alabama law made it illegal for whites and Negroes to study together. But they could write to him and did, and he answered, busy though he was. From one Youth Conference seven boys wrote him nine hundred and four letters."[3]

Of course it was not just curiosity that attracted people to Carver. His discoveries of nature's mysteries also proved useful. He taught Southern farmers, black and white alike, to rotate their crops instead of planting only cotton year after year. When his advice made peanuts so plentiful that the bottom fell out of the market, he went to work to discover new uses for this otherwise novelty plant. He developed more than 300 synthetic products from peanuts including: milk, butter, cheese, coffee, flour, breakfast food, ink, dyes, soap, wood stains, and insulating board.

To demonstrate the peanut's versatility he had his class serve Dr. Washington and other staff members a five-course meal made entirely of peanuts. "The menu was soup, mock chicken, peanuts creamed as a vegetable, bread, ice cream, cookies, coffee and candy. The only item that did not contain peanuts was the salad, of pepper grass, sheep sorrel and chicory."[4]

His research led to so many discoveries that entire industries were changed forever. Although offered thousands of dollars for his discoveries, Carver refused to profit financially from his laboratory work. He turned down Henry Ford's offer of a six figure salary. Another offered $175,000, which he also declined.

He discovered the secrets of the lowly soy bean and the sweet potato, and helped the armed forces discover how best to dehydrate food. His wartime help also reduced the nation's dependence on foreign rubber by creating it synthetically. An artist of some ability, he showed poor farmers how to make paints from the colorful Alabama clay. Before it was popular to conserve natural resources, he urged the reduction of logging and the production of paper and "wood" products from okra and other pulp producing plants. He was more amused than honored by the many awards bestowed on him in his later years. Although urged to give up his thread-bare suits and his favorite apron made of flour sacks for an appearance more fitting his station, he stubbornly held to his old ways. Gifts of suits and finery offered by admirers for special occasions were quietly stored away in boxes. "If they want to see me, all right.

If they want to see my clothes, I'll take them upstairs and show them a trunkfull!" he would say with a twinkle.[5] He died at Tuskegee Institute on January 5, 1943, at an undetermined but old age. He succumbed after falling down an outdoor staircase, evidently intending to allude his alert keepers for one last stroll through God's wonderful creation. His monument bears the inscription

GEORGE WASHINGTON CARVER

DIED IN TUSKEGEE, ALABAMA

January 5, 1943

A life that stood out as a gospel of self-sacrificing service. He could have added fortune to fame but caring for neither he found happiness and honor in being helpful to the world. The center of his world was the South where he was born in slavery some 79 years ago and where he did his work as a creative scientist.[6]

Dr. Carver was a strong Christian from his early life until the day of his death. Although childhood illness left him with a strange, high-pitched voice, it served him well when singing praises to his Creator and Savior. He loved music and was an accomplished pianist and organist, often called on to contribute his talents in worship.

His love of nature showed a close affinity with the Lord, who used countless illustrations from the earth to teach eternal truths. A Bible acquired in childhood was one of his most prized possessions. Imagine the wonder of Dr. Carver as he read,

Therefore I tell you, do not worry about your life, what you will eat or drink; or about your body, what you will wear. Is not life more important than food, and the body more important than clothes? Look at the birds of the air; they do not sow or reap or store away in barns, and yet your heavenly Father feeds them. Are you not much

> more valuable than they? Who of you by worrying can add a single hour to his life?
>
> And why do you worry about clothes? See how the lilies of the field grow. They do not labor or spin. Yet I tell you that not even Solomon in all his splendor was dressed like one of these. If that is how God clothes the grass of the field, which is here today and tomorrow is thrown into the fire, will he not much more clothe you, O you of little faith? (Matthew 6:25–30)

Something has been lost by a generation that picks its crops by the look of their pictures on the grocery store labels. The wonder of creation is too often missed by children who believe babies come from hospitals and puppies from kennels. Perhaps it's more important now than ever that people be exposed to leaders of Carver's sensitivities and insight. We swat bugs and spray weeds with little or no thought of their hidden and often miraculous qualities. Parents have not done their job until they have helped their children plant a garden, looked for mushrooms among the spring wildflowers, and chased fireflies across the yard at dusk. Limited access is no excuse. It did not stop Carver from establishing a world-class lab out of canning jars and tin scraps at Tuskegee. As Dr. Carver was fond of saying, "You can always make what you want out of what you have."

I am ever grateful for a wife who loves to plant and surround my world with the beauty of God's creation. Our country home had barely been completed when she insisted on the construction of flower beds. Not just one, but several, on every corner of the home and along the drive. I chided her that next she would want topsoil, and then flowers! She did. Now, when I leave the house at the break of dawn, the fragrance of nature's beauty greets me and the butterflies and hummingbirds startle at the banging of the screen door.

To be observant is to be grateful and to be grateful is to live above the aggravations of daily life. I often pray for an "attitude of gratitude" and for the ability to see my blessings more clearly. If people could daily notice the wonders of creation around them, we would rarely have cause for despondent thoughts. I have come to love the singing of the old stewardship hymn "This Is My Father's World," especially the second stanza:

This is my Father's world, the birds their carols raise,
The morning light, the lily white, declare their Maker's
praise.
This is my Father's world, He shines in all that's fair;
In the rustling grass I hear Him pass, He speaks to me
everywhere.

As the apostle reminds us, "In the past, He let all nations go their own way. Yet He has not left Himself without testimony: He has shown kindness by giving you rain from heaven and crops in their seasons; He provides you with plenty of food and fills your hearts with joy" (Acts 14:16–17). All creation bears testimony to the power and love of God. He has not left us without all the encouragement needed to meet life's demands. The rejuvenation of daily energy may be dependent on our ability to maintain a perspective of wonder.

More Scriptural Insight

Genesis 8:20–22	What promise does the Lord make regarding nature?
Romans 1:18–25	Why are unbelievers without any excuse?
Luke 12:4–9	Explain the Lord's reference to sparrows and human hair.

A Leader's Prayer

"O Lord my God, when I in awesome wonder Consider all the works Thy hands hath made, I see the stars, I hear the mighty thunder, Thy pow'r throughout the universe displayed; Then sings my soul, my Savior God, to Thee, How great Thou art! How great Thou art!" Help me remember that all Your greatness would be a fearful thing if it were not for Your compassion and grace displayed in Christ Jesus, my Lord. As I read His parables and am instructed in the faith through His illustrations, help me to see Your wisdom displayed in all You have made. Slow me down long enough to see the ladybug's spots and marvel at the limitless maneuvers of the hummingbird. Enable me to see the genius and love shown through creation so that I might hold the Creator of all things in greater honor. The next time I feel overwhelmed by life's demands, remind me of the one whose mere words silenced the wind and the waves. Grant me peace in my storms, for I look to You for that which the world cannot give. Amen.

Notes

1. Florence Means, *Carver's George,* (Boston: Houghton Mifflin Company, 1952), 109. Copyright © 1952, renewed 1980 by Florence Crannell Means. Reprinted by permission of Houghton Mifflin Company. All rights reserved.

2. Ibid., 134.

3. Ibid., 135.

4. Ibid., 119.

5. Ibid., 156.

6. Ibid., 172.

7. Copyright © 1953. S. K. Hines. Assigned to Manna Music, Inc., 35255 Brooten Road, Pacific City, OR 97135. Renewed 1981. All Rights Reserved. Used by Permission.

CHAPTER FORTY-SIX

GERONIMO
Intensity

*"I may only be one person,
but I can be a person who makes a difference."*
Vandra Francine Grace, age 10
Bowling Green, Kentucky

Vandra's simple but powerful statement is scrawled across a wall of quotes near a popular display in Disney's Epcot Center. I was impressed by her powerful resolve. Ten years old or not, Vandra's words deserved to be alongside the more elegant quotations of renown poets and world leaders.

"Total Commitment" has been described by more than one biographer as the most common trait of successful leaders. As a study of this kind proves, success comes to all kinds of people but they have this in common—they are not easily dissuaded. They, like Vandra, have resolved to make a difference and they are willing to pay the price.

Geronimo was such a man. He won battle after battle, and although he eventually surrendered, he was never captured.

Had he received replacements in numbers equal to his enemy, North America would now include another nation—the Apache nation. In the end, General Nelson Miles was given 5,000 soldiers, 500 Indian scouts, and the job of arresting or killing Geronimo and his band of 18 warriors. The mathematics of sheer attrition made further resistance futile. Tired and concerned for the well-being of his tribe, the Apache chieftain sought surrender terms from his nemesis, General Miles. In his official journal, Miles wrote, "He was one of the brightest, most resolute, determined looking men that I have ever encountered … every movement indicated power and determination."[1] Even in surrender, Geronimo impressed his adversary.

Like every great leader, Geronimo didn't inherit the respect of his people; he had to earn it. The wealth of an Apache was measured by the number of horses he owned, and Apache boys were taught to ride at a very young age. Not only were they taught to ride, the best Apache warriors were able to ride their mounts at full gallop without reins or saddle, using their knees for balance and guidance. Such ability allowed complete use of both hands to thrust a spear or shoot their arrows with great accuracy. No other tribe surpassed them in horsemanship, and no warrior outrode Geronimo. By the age of 12 he killed his first buffalo, and as a novice brave, he defeated in hand-to-hand combat the soldier sent to stampede the warriors' mounts. Geronimo's intensity impressed his elders and intimidated his enemies.

It was an Apache custom to give children descriptive names derived from observations in early childhood. It was not unusual to wait months, even years, to select just the right name.[2] Geronimo's childhood name was Gokliya. In Apache it meant "one who yawns," perhaps a character trait the great warrior exhibited as a baby. He would soon earn a different name, one that would strike fear into the hearts of all Apache enemies.

Apache warriors earned new names in battle, often taking the name by which his enemy identified him in combat. Geronimo's chief was called Mangas Coloradas, which in Spanish means "red sleeves." He earned his warrior name when a Mexican soldier shouted it in warning to his friends. Hand-to-hand combat had left Mangas' arms bloody to the shoulder. The story was retold at the victory feast, and out of respect for his bravery, his name was changed. Likewise, the unknown Gokliya would be given a warrior's name which would become known worldwide. He would soon be called Geronimo.

How Gokliya got his warrior name is evidence of his intense spirit. A large party of Apache women, children, and warriors had journeyed south to trade skins, beads, and furs with a friendly Mexican village. By this means they would acquire sugar, salt, axes, knives, and bright bolts of cloth. While the warriors were trading in the village, a band of Mexican soldiers attacked the unsuspecting Apache camp, killing more than 100 women, children, and old men. Unknown to the Apache nation, the Mexican government had established bounties for the scalps of any Indian, $100 for a man, $50 for a woman, and $25 for a child.[3] When the warriors returned and found their families massacred, their bows burnt, and their ponies stolen, they were overcome with grief and rage. With their weapons destroyed there was no recourse but to retreat. The fear of further attack was so great they took no time to bury their dead, fleeing on foot by cover of night.

Once safe, the warriors burned their family tepees in respect for the dead and made plans for revenge. Gokliya's wife and three children had been among those mutilated. He was so shaken by the loss, he began a self-imposed silence after the massacre. But his silence would soon be ended. Out of respect of his emerging leadership skills, the honor and critical task of recruiting braves from neighboring tribes was given to Gokliya. He rode from tribe to tribe across Arizona, and by the force of his conviction recruited an unprecedented number of Apache warriors for battle. Counted among the war party was the great chief Cochise, perhaps the most respected Apache chieftain of his time.

Gokliya was chosen by the counsel of chiefs to lead their combined forces in battle. The Mexican garrison, expecting a reprisal, awaited the approach of the Apache war party. For more than a day the battle raged with neither side gaining the advantage. The turning point came the afternoon of the second day. As witnesses remembered it, three Apache warriors were wounded and trapped, their spears broken and their arrows spent. Gokliya witnessed four Mexican soldiers charge the unarmed Indians with fixed bayonets and raised swords. He responded instinctively, grabbing a spear from the battlefield, he dispatched the first soldier, caught his sword in midair, and used it to attack the other three. The second quickly fell and the remaining two wheeled about in retreat. Gokliya flung himself on a horse and gave hot pursuit towards the enemy line. As the soldiers neared the safety of their troops Gokliya caught and killed the third, pressing on towards the fourth. The Mexican troops watched in stunned disbelief, and for encouragement began yelling the fleeing soldier's name, "Geronimo! Geronimo!" (Spanish for Jerome.) The Apache warriors, rallied by Gokliya's courage, joined in the charge and in a mocking cry of Geronimo's name. The entire Mexican regiment broke and ran in total defeat. That night during the victory feast, Gokliya's name was formally changed. From that day forward, he was called Geronimo in remembrance of his courageous and fearless attack in the defense of his fellow warriors.[4] No Apache was more feared in battle, nor more elusive than Geronimo.

Geronimo believed in the maxim, "He who hesitates is lost." In the face of an overwhelming challenge, leaders step forward and by their action inspire the hesitant. The challenge can come in many forms, as an impossible task or in the form of outspoken criticism. By virtue of experience and observation the truth of the proverb is seen, "If you falter in times of trouble, how small is your strength! Rescue those being led away to death; hold back those staggering toward slaughter. If you say, 'But we knew nothing about this,' does not He who weighs the heart perceive it? Does not He who guards your life know it? Will He not repay each person according to what he has done?" (Proverbs 24:10–12).

Two years ago our family built a house 10 miles west of our church in the rolling hills of south central Missouri. For years we had been promising our boys they could have a dog, and Carol decided it was time to make good on the pledge. So off we went to the animal shelter where every kind of dog was displayed for adoption. We settled on a forlorn black puppy with swirls of chocolate through her coat.

Carol finally had the daughter she had always wanted and quickly christened her Sarah, a name she loved but felt was inappropriate for both Joshua and Jacob when they were born years before. To say that Sarah was a timid puppy would be an understatement. She showed every sign of complete submission according to dog etiquette. At the mere mention of her name she would lower her head, drop her hind quarters, and leave a puddle!

Carol and I enjoy walking down our gravel lane to the blacktop and from there to the highway. It's a pleasant walk through a beautiful part of God's creation. It is not unusual to see foxes, racoons, squirrels, wild turkeys, and white tail deer as we walk the lane along a wooded tract near the entrance to our development. It is also common to see Danny, a German shepherd owned by neighbors who live between us and the blacktop. The first time Danny noticed our puppy, Sarah, prancing happily on her leash near his home, he thought it important to announce his reign over the region. At full charge, with hair raised and fangs bared, Danny covered the distance between us in a blur. Sarah wrapped her leash around my legs trying to get in my pocket while I turned to face the challenge.

Having been raised in the country and carried a newspaper route since the age of nine, I have learned a few things about aggressive dogs. It is the same lesson the United States has learned repeatedly in world affairs—you never negotiate with a terrorist. The best defense is a good offense. In an absolute show of strength I faced Danny, called his name with authority, and with my walking stick upraised, took a step toward the reigning king. Danny flinched. His charge was broken as his own insecurities kept him at a 10-foot distance. He was no longer sure he could win the fight.

Last night we went walking again. Sarah is now a two-year-old, 50-pound dog who still prances happily on her braided red leash whenever we walk down the lane. Danny is twice her size and never hesitates to mount his charge, but now he comes through the cover of low hanging evergreens, Sarah no longer cowers. She pulls hard against her leash, returning bark for bark and snarl for snarl, eager for the chance to engage. Both Danny and Sarah have learned the lesson of intimidation and courage in the face of challenge. He who hesitates is lost.

Christian leaders will often be tested by the Dannys of this world. From both within the body and without, others will charge our position, barking, and snarling to proclaim their self-appointed authority. The Christian leader must be prepared to face such hostility with all the conviction of his heart. The qualifications for leadership in the body call us to be, "not violent but gentle, not quarrelsome" (1 Timothy 3:3), and we must honor that standard. It would however be a mistake to equate these qualifications with timidity and passivity. While we must not court a fight, neither can we waver in the face of hostility.

Jesus urged Christians to avoid the trap of fighting as the world fights when He told Peter, "All who draw the sword will die by the sword" (Matthew 26:52). Those who wield the sword of the world will die by the sword of the world. We are not of the world. We fight spiritual battles with spiritual weapons, always ready and willing to wield and die by the sword of the Lord, which is the Word of God.

On the night He warned Peter about inappropriate aggression, Jesus also prayed on behalf of those He would be leaving in a such a hostile environment. "My prayer is not that You take them out of the world but that You protect them from the evil one. They are not of the world, even as I am not of it. Sanctify them by the truth; Your word is truth" (John 17:15–16).

Steeped in God's truth, we are well-equipped to stand our ground and confront the enemies of the Gospel. Timidity? Paul, who was beheaded for his conviction, told the impressionable Timothy,

> I remind you to fan into flame the gift of God, which is in you through the laying on of my hands. For God did not give us a spirit of timidity, but a spirit of power, of love and of self-discipline. So do not be ashamed to testify about our Lord, or ashamed of me his prisoner. But join with me in suffering for the gospel, by the power of God, who has saved us and called us to a holy life. (2 Timothy 1:6–9)

Passivity? In closing what is sometimes called his "Last

Will and Testament," Paul concluded;

> In the presence of God and of Christ Jesus, who will judge
> the living and the dead, and in view of His appearing and
> His kingdom, I give you this charge: Preach the Word; be
> prepared in season and out of season; correct, rebuke and
> encourage—with great patience and careful instruction.
> For the time will come when men will not put up with
> sound doctrine. Instead, to suit their own desires, they
> will gather around them a great number of teachers to say
> what their itching ears want to hear. They will turn their
> ears away from the truth and turn aside to myths. But
> you, keep your head in all situations, endure hardship, do
> the work of an evangelist, discharge all the duties of your
> ministry. (2 Timothy 4:1–5)

The name Geronimo is synonymous with courage in action.
Skydivers prepared to jump cannot hesitate when their
moment arrives. Overcoming one of man's greatest fears, they
call the name of an Apache warrior, and step into the heavens.

More Scriptural Advice

Proverbs 27:17   Explain this passage in light of this study.
Acts 16:36–40   What purpose did Paul's action serve?
Luke 4:24–30   How would you describe the spirit of Jesus in this account?

A Leader's Prayer

Lord, I do not wish to be argumentative or develop a spirit
of contention, but neither do I want to ever hesitate in the face
of spiritual opposition. As Geronimo so boldly defended his
own in the face of superior numbers, give me the same spirit.
But let my defense be established in such a manner that You
would be honored and not embarrassed. The enemy knows
how to push all my buttons and build unholy anger within my
heart. Quench his flaming arrows without quenching the fire
of Your Spirit. There is a fine line between righteous anger and

the anger which James warns, "does not bring about the righteous life that God desires" (James 1:20). Help me distinguish between the two and live as a faithful witness of the Prince of Peace. If I hesitate, push me. If I fall, pick me up. If I am over-zealous, surround me with honest counsel and rescue me from myself. This I pray in expectation of Your blessing through Jesus Christ, my Lord. Amen.

Notes

1. Zachary Kent, *The Story of Geronimo*, (Chicago: Children's Press, 1989), 27.

2. Charles Morrow Wilson, *Geronimo, the Story of an American Indian*, (Minneapolis: Dillon Press, Inc., 1973), 19.

3. Edgar Wyatt, *Geronimo, the Last Apache War Chief*, (New York: McGraw Hill Book Company, 1952), 96.

4. Ibid., 109.

CHAPTER FORTY-SEVEN

SAMUEL CLEMENS
Circumstance and Temperament

Many leaders have looked back over a lifetime of achievement and wondered why they were privileged to succeed. Psychologists have documented the phenomenon as a common occurrence. It causes many to discredit their achievement, and creates guilt in others. Victims experience an overwhelming sense of unworthiness, as if the recognition of their success were undeserved. Much like survivors of catastrophes, they are troubled by the question, "Why me and not someone else?" To be sure, they have worked hard, paid their dues, and overcome enormous odds—but so have others. Perhaps there is another explanation—perhaps within the heart of all people there is an intuitive sense that God chooses some to succeed for reasons known only to Him.

Christian leaders know in their heart-of-hearts that they have feet of clay. They are the cracked pots of 2 Corinthians 4, used by God to accomplish His purpose for His glory. Make no mistake about it, the Lord could have easily used another vessel. Like the shepherd boy that God made a king, godly leaders are aware that success is God's business. Why He blesses some and not others remains a mystery. David wrote, "Who am I, O LORD God, and what is my family, that You have brought me this far?" (1 Chronicles 17:16).

Later, at the dedication of all the gifts which he collected to build the temple, the king expressed this same attitude more publicly.

> Yours, O LORD, is the greatness and power and the glory and the majesty and the splendor, for everything in heaven and earth is Yours. Yours, O LORD, is the kingdom; You are exalted as head over all. Wealth and honor come from You; You are the ruler of all things. In Your hands are strength and power to exalt and give strength to all. (1 Chronicles 29:11–12)

America's great storyteller, Mark Twain, echoed the notion that notoriety and success are determined more by external conditions than internal choices. A popular magazine once asked Twain to describe the turning point of his life. In response, Twain concluded that the outcome of life is actually determined by a series of conditions, not one incident. A man's chance at success, he explained, was determined largely by a strange combination of circumstance and temperament. He was amused by the theory that success was mostly the result of wise planning and hard work.

Twain had no doubt observed Solomon's paradox at work. "I have seen something else under the sun: The race is not to the swift or the battle to the strong, nor does food come to the wise or wealth to the brilliant or favor to the learned; but time and chance happen to them all" (Ecclesiastes 9:11).

As evidence of his hypothesis, Twain cites several historic decisions. Caesar was confronted with a circumstance at the Rubicon and given his temperament crossed the bridge into history. Twain described the moment:

Coming up with his troops on the banks of the Rubicon, he halted for a while, and, revolving in his mind the importance of the step he was on the point of taking, he turned to those about him and said, "We may still retreat; but if we pass this little bridge, nothing is left for us but to fight it out in arms.[1]

While Caesar was contemplating his decision, a stranger playing a flute nearby began to gather a crowd of amused listeners, among them some of Caesar's own trumpeters. The stranger snatched one of the trumpets, ran across the bridge, and sounded the advance in a piercing blast. Caesar took this strange occurrence as an omen, and as Twain explains, "So he crossed—and changed the future of the whole human race, for all time."[2] The world was changed by the circumstance of a moment interpreted by the temperament of a man.

Twain was equally fascinated by an answer his good friend General Ulysses S. Grant once gave to a question on strategy. "General, who planned the march through Georgia?" Grant replied without hesitation, "The enemy!"

"He meant," wrote Twain, "that the enemy by neglect or through force of circumstance leaves an opening for you, and you see your chance and take advantage of it."[3] Many a battle strategy has been determined by the circumstance of a moment and the temperament of a leader.

Circumstance is only half of Twain's equation for success. The final outcome of life is not determined by circumstance alone, but also by the temperament of the one who responds to the circumstance. He wondered how the world might have been different if Martin Luther and Joan of Arc had been in the Garden of Eden in the place of Adam and Eve!

I cannot help feeling disappointed in Adam and Eve. That is, in their temperaments. Not in them, poor helpless young creatures—afflicted with temperaments made out of butter; which butter was commanded to get into contact with fire and be melted. What I cannot help wishing is, that Adam and Eve had been postponed, and Martin Luther and Joan of Arc put in their place—the splendid pair equipped with temperaments not made of butter but of asbestos. By neither sugary persuasion nor by hell fire could Satan have beguiled them to eat of the apple. There would have been results! Indeed, yes. The apple would be intact today.[4]

Twain's personal temperament was self-described as one who does things and then reflects afterward. For evidence he recalled that while working as a printer in Iowa, he was captivated by a book on the wonders of the Amazon.

By temperament I was the kind of person that does things. Does them, and reflects afterward. So I started for the Amazon without reflecting and without asking any questions. That was more than fifty years ago. In all that time my temperament has not changed, by even a shade. I have been punished many and many a time, and bitterly, for doing things and reflecting afterward, but these tortures have been of no value to me: I still do the thing commanded by Circumstance and Temperament, and reflect afterward. Always violently. When I am reflecting, on those occasions, even deaf persons can hear me think.[5]

Christian leaders, by virtue of faith and their God-given responsibilities, should spend a great deal of time discerning the will of God. God's will, to be sure, is often kept secret until revealed by circumstance. Although it falls to Christian leaders to make plans and pursue them, an ability to adjust as circumstance warrants is also required. The apostle James was inspired to offer this advice:

Now listen, you who say, "Today or tomorrow we will go to this or that city, spend a year there, carry on business and make money." Why, you do not even know what will happen tomorrow. What is your life? You are a mist that appears for a little while and then vanishes. Instead, you ought to say, "If it is the Lord's will, we will live and do this or that." As it is, you boast and brag. All such boasting is evil. Anyone, then, who knows the good he ought to do and doesn't do it, sins. (James 4:13–17)

Most circumstances are out of our control, but not outside God's control. Only a fool would proclaim the absolute outcome of any venture since even the greatest leader lacks the divine attribute of omniscience. As did Caesar, Grant, and Twain, we must wait to see which doors open or close, and then react to the opportunities which the Lord lays before us.

Twain believed that inability to accurately predict the future should not justify failure to act. Twain acted on the circumstances of his life without hesitation. He understood the importance of seizing the moment to the best of his God-given ability. When we understand our uniqueness and act upon it, we fulfill the intention which God has created and redeemed us to accomplish. Everyone is gifted in some way for a purpose of significance. Peter wrote, "Each one should use whatever gift he has received to serve others, faithfully administering God's grace in its various forms" (1 Peter 4:10).

Our peculiar gift may not be significant in the eyes of the world. It may not result in notoriety. It may even be an ability or attitude which the world despises and mocks. It really doesn't matter what the world thinks or how the newspapers measure importance. On the last day, the world will not judge us, nor will the value of our life be measured by the notoriety we have achieved. We will stand before God who "will judge the world in righteousness and the peoples in His truth" (Psalm 96:13).

In his early life, the gifts of Twain seemed largely unappreciated. His tendency to act and then reflect often landed him in trouble. He was mischievous and an instigator of trouble from the time he could walk. Like other boys who grew up in Mississippi River towns, Twain spent a good deal of his life in, on, and near the water. It was both a fascinating and dangerous childhood. He said that he almost drowned nine times before he grew up. His mother was never too greatly concerned. She held to the theory, "A boy born to be hanged was safe in the water!"[6] Despite the prediction, Samuel Clemens died of natural causes at the full age of 74 years.

If greater appreciation for the role of circumstance keeps the successful leader humble, it should save others from despair. The Bible clearly teaches that God is not the source of evil, neither does He perpetuate it.[7] He does however discipline and strengthen His children through times of testing. He even describes such conditions as sometimes necessary.[8] Solomon understood this when he wrote, "When times are good, be happy; but when times are bad, consider: God has made the one as well as the other. Therefore, a man cannot discover anything about his future" (Ecclesiastes 7:14). We cannot predict what circumstance God will allow us to encounter, but we can trust that it will always be for our benefit, or for the greater benefit of the Kingdom. The sacrifice of His only Son on our behalf forever established the integrity of His motive. As the Bible says, "He who did not spare His own Son, but gave Him up for us all—how will He not also along with Him, graciously give us all things?" (Romans 8:32).

A wise person once said since we can't do anything about the past and have no control over the future, so we must learn to be content with the present. Acting on the present was something Twain was good at. He would say the combination of circumstance and his God-given temperament served him well. By taking full advantage of life's circumstance, the Lord through Twain served everyone well. In his humorous style Twain had always urged, "Let us endeavor so to live that when we come to die even the undertaker will be sorry."[9] He lived to accomplish his goal.

More Scriptural Insight

Job 31:13–15   Explain why Job felt an obligation to the less fortunate.

Luke 19:1–10   What role did circumstance and temperament play in the life of Zacchaeus?

John 21:4–14   Describe the temperament of Peter. Was it a hindrance or a benefit in his service to the Lord?

A Leader's Prayer

Keep me mindful, Lord, that it is You and You alone who has the power to make great or bring low. What good would success be if it were achieved apart from You? What would it profit me to gain the whole world and forfeit my soul? Grant that my success would be godly both in outcome and in effort. When I am tempted to sacrifice my integrity for the cause of gain, help me embrace the value of faithfulness. Keep me from being envious of those who succeed through compromise. Remind me that a war is seldom won or lost by one battle. When I fail, help me to learn the lessons of failure. When I succeed, grant that I would give all glory and honor to You, the provider of opportunity and source of my strength. Thank You, Lord, for the privilege of Christian service. Bless all those efforts done to Your glory by grace through Jesus Christ, our Lord. Amen.

Notes

1. Mark Twain, *The Turning Point of My Life,* from *Great Short Works of Mark Twain,* (New York: Harper and Row Publishers, 1967), 222. Used by permission.

2. Ibid., 223.

3. Ibid., 229.

4. Ibid., 230.

5. Ibid., 227.

6. May McNeer, *America's Mark Twain,* (Boston: Houghton Mifflin Co., 1962), 8.

7. "When tempted, no one should say, 'God is tempting me.' For God cannot be tempted by evil, nor does He tempt anyone; but each one is tempted when, by his own evil desire, he is dragged away and enticed" (James 1:13).

8. cf. 1 Peter 1:6.

9. May McNeer, 159.

CHAPTER FORTY-EIGHT

WALT DISNEY
Dream

When you wish upon a star,
makes no difference who you are;
Anything your heart desires will come to you.

If your heart is in your dream,
no request is too extreme,
When you wish upon a star as dreamers do.[1]

Jiminy Cricket sang those words in the Disney classic, *Pinocchio.* Jiminy, of course, was the ever-present adviser who rescued Pinocchio from self-destruction. "Dreams" he sang, "can make the future come true!" Walt Disney and Jiminy Cricket had a lot in common. Dreams also rescued the fourth son of Elias and Flora Disney from a life of mere existence, and the whole world with him.

Walter Elias Disney was a dreamer from the beginning. Dreamers are not inclined to study subjects just because their teachers or their parents say they're important. Walt marched to the beat of his own making, learning more from life and the experiences of others than any homework he was ever assigned. He read everything he could find by Mark Twain, loved the adventures of Tom Swift, and poured over the stories of Stevenson, Scott, and Dickens.[2]

But Walt's real love was drawing. Nevermind that his childish dream of becoming an artist frustrated his more conventional and hardworking father. How unusual was this dreamer? Even in the exercise of his passion Walt resisted conformity. "When his fourth grade teacher, Artena Olson, instructed the class to sketch a bowl of flowers on her desk, she strolled around the room and stopped at Walt's desk. He had drawn human faces on the flowers with arms where the leaves were supposed to be. The teacher chastised him for not following the assignment."[3]

How can dreamers be leaders if they march through life focused on a vision which only they can see? Gifted dreamers exercise leadership by inspiring others to join their quest. Their dream becomes a shared destiny pursued by those who believe in their vision. Disney, like Jiminy Cricket, had the ability to transform conventional thinking into dreams, and dreams into reality. Who else but a dreamer would

- Quit high school, and lie about his age for fear of missing World War I?
- Quit a job paying $100/month to take a job paying $50/month just so he could draw?
- Decline a prestigious offer as a newspaper cartoonist to pursue a more risky future filming commercials?
- Quit his job making commercials so he could start his own business making cartoons for theaters?
- Buy a first class, one-way ticket to California after going bankrupt?
- Believe there must be a way to put sound on film rather

than sequence separate recordings?

- Refuse money to make sequels in favor of trying something new?
- Draw 15,000 pictures to make a seven-minute film?
- Draw over 2 million pictures to make an 80-minute feature cartoon?
- Risk $1.5 million in the middle of the depression to make a feature length cartoon that insiders called "Disney's folly"?
- Hand paint animated film stock even though experts said it would fade and chip?
- Develop paints that wouldn't chip or fade after the experts were proved right?
- Begin a weekly TV show when everyone in movies believed TV was the greatest threat to their own survival?
- Invest millions in an amusement park venture against the advice of friends, family, and business advisors?

Dreamers do such nonsensical things! Dreamers, like Walt Disney, do them in ways that challenge the status quo, rock industry, and appeal to millions. How successful was Disney in accomplishing his dreams? The $1.5 million "Disney's Folly" (a.k.a. "Snow White and the Seven Dwarfs") grossed $8 million in its first release—remember, this was during the depression when adult movie tickets cost 25 cents and children's only a dime! When Disney produced Davy Crockett for TV, more than 10 million coonskin hats were sold in one year. The series was so successful there weren't enough raccoons to fill the requests. Hats were made out of everything from rabbit to mink. Not even the squirrels were safe!

Before Disney, cartoon music was used to cover the sound of the film feeding through the projector sprockets. Disney features produced songs that became chart busters year after year. To this day the world's finest singers, composers, and orchestras vie for the chance to produce the next Disney spectacular. Who hasn't heard these Disney classics?

- "Heigh-Ho" (*Snow White and the Seven Dwarfs*)
- "Some Day My Prince Will Come" (*Snow White and the Seven Dwarfs*)
- "Whistle While You Work" (*Snow White and the Seven Dwarfs*)
- "Who's Afraid of the Big Bad Wolf?" (*Three Little Pigs*)
- "When You Wish upon a Star" (*Pinocchio*)
- "Give a Little Whistle" (*Pinocchio*)
- "I'm Late" (*Alice in Wonderland*)
- "Zip-A-Dee-Doo-Dah" (*Song of the South*)
- "The Mickey Mouse March" (*Mickey Mouse Club*)
- "The Ballad of Davy Crockett" (*Davy Crockett, King of the Wild Frontier*)
- "Chim Chim Cher-ee" (*Mary Poppins*)
- "It's a Small World after All" (*New York World's Fair*)

Not to mention recent blockbuster soundtracks from *The Little Mermaid*, *The Lion King*, and *Pocahontas*!

Someone has said most people see things the way they are and ask why. Disney, and people like him, dream of the way things ought to be and ask why not. There is a little dreamer in every great leader. Those consumed by the moment forfeit their right to lead when they fail to dream about the future. It is impossible to inspire others to greatness without great thoughts of your own. Zig Ziglar urges leaders to ask what it is they would do if there were no limits, and then begin making plans to achieve those goals.

Christian leaders will find inspiration for incredible dreams by spending time alone with God in His word, the Bible. Moses was inspired to exercise great leadership after spending

40 days and 40 nights with the Lord on Mount Sinai. The man who was initially intimidated by God's expectations later inspired a nation of slaves to follow him into the desert. All he had to offer was God's promise of freedom and a new life in a land overflowing with milk and honey.

When the children of Israel arrived at the border of the Promised Land, they sent spies to see if the dream was real. The news was both good and bad. The dream was real. The land was truly overflowing with blessings, rich and plentiful, which the spies proved by bringing back large quantities of fruit suspended from poles carried upon their shoulders. They told Moses, "We went into the land to which you sent us, and it does flow with milk and honey! Here is its fruit" (Numbers 13:27).

But fruit was not all they saw. They also reported, "The people who live there are powerful, and the cities are fortified and very large. We even saw descendants of Anak there. The Amalekites live in the Negev; the Hittites, Jebusites and Amorites live in the hill country; and the Canaanites live near the sea and along the Jordan. ... We can't attack those people; they are stronger than we are" (Numbers 13:28–29, 31).

From among the 12 spies sent by Moses, only Caleb and Joshua believed the dream was within the grasp of God's people. The power of negativity is strong and the insecurities of God's people resonated to it. The children of Israel despaired and regretted their decision to follow the dream. They even began looking for someone to lead them back to Egypt and slavery. Joshua and Caleb were amazed at their unbelief and tore their clothes in anger. They reminded the people of God's power to accomplish all that He had promised.

> The land we passed through and explored is exceedingly good. If the LORD is pleased with us, He will lead us into

> that land, a land flowing with milk and honey, and will
> give it to us. Only do not rebel against the LORD. And do
> not be afraid of the people of the land, because we will
> swallow them up. Their protection is gone, but the LORD is
> with us. Do not be afraid of them. (Numbers 14:7–9)

The power of negative suggestion was so strong, not even Joshua and Caleb's optimism was enough to overcome the people's fears. The faithless spies said, "The land we explored devours those living in it. All the people we saw there are of great size. We saw the Nephilim there (the descendants of Anak come from the Nephilim). We seemed like grasshoppers in our own eyes, and we looked the same to them" (Numbers 13:23–33).

Notice how their thinking affected their attitudes which quickly affected their behavior? Because they "seemed like grasshoppers in their own eyes," their confidence waned, which in turn bolstered the confidence of their potential enemies. The power of suggestion can be more influential than the reality of any given situation. Walt Disney understood the power of the dream better than most. His official biographer commented:

> Certainly in the years following his death, Disney remained
> a presence to the world's millions. The classic films were
> being seen by greater audiences than ever before. Even the
> early Mickey Mouse cartoons were being rediscovered and
> cherished, and such features as Fantasia and Alice in Won-
> derland, commercial failures in their first releases, had
> been vindicated by a new generation. If Walt Disney had
> only made film entertainment, his place in American histo-
> ry would be assured. But he did more.[4]

It wasn't the things Disney accomplished that made him such a great leader. If he were still living, who knows what dreams would be taking shape? It was not what he did, but his way of thinking that made the world a different and better place—as dreamers do.

More Scriptural Insight

Deuteronomy 13:1–5   What does the Lord say about testing the dreams of dreamers?

Hebrews 11:13–16   What makes the faithful stand out from the crowd?

John 6:60–69   What happened when Jesus held steadfastly to His teaching?

A Leader's Prayer

Rekindle the innocence and optimism I had when I began my work, O Lord. The years and the people I lead have nearly robbed me of my dreams. Never let a pessimistic or defeatist attitude take root in my heart. With David I pray, "Create a clean heart in me, O God, and renew a steadfast spirit within me. Restore unto me the joy of Thy salvation and uphold me with a willing spirit" (Psalm 51:10–12, NASB). Help me to take heart from the small successes of life, without giving too much attention to the setbacks I encounter. I know that popularity isn't the mark of success, but remind me from time to time. Help me to see in Jesus the perfect model of leadership and the inspiration for my life. In Him I find my hope, my forgiveness, and my motivation to carry on. Keep me in childlike faith, willing to believe that by faith anything is possible. Quicken my thoughts to better understand Your will and to accomplish Your desires through the exercise of godly leadership. Thank You, Lord, for the privilege to serve You by serving others through Jesus Christ, my Savior. Amen.

Notes

1. Ned Washington, and Leigh Harline, *"When You Wish upon a Star,"* Copyright 1940 Bourne Co., USA.

2. Bob Thomas, *Walt Disney: An American Original,* (New York: The Walt Disney Company, 1976), 36.

3. Ibid., 36.

4. Ibid., 359.

CHAPTER FORTY-NINE

GEORGE WASHINGTON
Prayer

Whatever happened to prayer by and for the leaders of America?

Our greatest presidents did not hesitate to pray and fervently requested the prayers of our nation on their behalf. Artists preferred portraying their strength by recording those occasions when our leaders humbled themselves before their people and before their Lord in prayer. What school child a generation ago had not seen our presidents on bended knee—Washington at Valley Forge, Lincoln in his study, and Eisenhower as bombers flew toward the European coast on D-Day?

S. D. Gordon was right when he said,

> The greatest thing anyone can do for God and man is pray. It is not the only thing, but it is the chief thing. The great people of earth are the people who pray. I do not mean those who talk about prayer; nor those who say they believe in prayer; nor yet those who can explain about prayer; but I mean those people who take time to pray.[1]

Washington was certainly not the most articulate president

ever elected. Any leader who has experienced stage fright can take comfort in the example of Washington, who often found himself tongue-tied. "Officers who served under him in the war testified they had never seen him smile, that his countenance held something austere and his manners were uncommonly reserved. Certainly, Washington was not a ready talker."[2] The great writer and orator Thomas Jefferson observed that neither Washington nor Ben Franklin spoke often during the Constitutional Convention of 1787. (Franklin was the oldest in attendance and often ill during the proceedings.) Jefferson wrote, "I never heard either of them speak ten minutes at a time, nor to any but the main point which was to decide the question." In a positive fashion, he reasoned, "They laid their shoulders to the great points, knowing that the little ones would follow themselves."[3] Jefferson was being kind.

During the French and Indian War of 1754–63, Washington led the Virginia regiment against French strongholds in the Ohio River valley. Serving under the orders of the British General Edward Braddock, Washington joined the attack on Fort Duquesne which failed when the British general insisted on fighting the concealed enemy from exposed ranks in the middle of the road. Although Braddock fought bravely, he and more than half of his 1,400 men were wiped out. Washington, the only field officer to survive, assumed command and saved the troops from capture. During the battle Washington miraculously escaped personal injury although he had two horses shot from under him and four bullets passed through his coat. Having learned the lesson of concealment, in the fall of 1758 Washington succeeded in leading a renewed attack on Fort Duquesne, driving the French from their position and securing the valley for England. The lessons of warfare taught by the Indians and French would not be forgotten in the battle for American independence.

When the Virginia House of Burgesses gave Washington a hero's reception for the victory, he rose to respond but became so flustered and self-conscious he was unable to say anything. The speaker reportedly came to the rescue saying, "Sit down, Mr. Washington. Your modesty is equal to your valor, and that surpasses the power of any language I possess."[4]

He may have even been the poorest of orators, but story after story recalls his integrity, his honesty, and his simple but sincere prayer life. My favorite painting of the general depicts him kneeling in the snow with his cape swirled over his shoulders and down his back. Kneeling some distance from his troops, his head is bowed, his eyes are closed, and his hands are tightly clasped in prayer.

A popular story of that day recalls how a simple farmer came unexpectedly upon the general while bringing food for the army. There he saw the general on his knees, his cheeks wet with tears, praying to God.

The farmer reportedly returned home and said to his wife, "George Washington will succeed! George Washington will succeed! The Americans will secure their independence!"

"What makes you think so?" asked his wife. The farmer replied: "I have seen him pray out in the woods today, and the Lord will surely hear his prayer. He will. You may rest assured, He will."[5]

Whether the story is true or embellished we cannot tell. But it does reveal the kind of reputation the general had among the people and among his men.

As the Lord showed the apostle Paul, greatness in leadership is best seen in times of struggle not in the exercise of strength.[6] It is precisely at the darkest hour that a leader's character becomes transparent. Only then is the source of character revealed. Historians have preserved sufficient documentation to verify Washington's steadfast reliance on divine strength. Without a doubt Washington felt overwhelmed by the expectations of his calling, first as commander in chief, and later as the nation's first president. When asked to assume leadership of the military he responded,

> Tho' I am truly sensible of the high honor done me in the appointment, yet I feel great distress from a consciousness that my abilities and military experience may not be equal to this extensive and important trust: However, as the congress desires I will enter upon the momentous duty and exert every power I possess in their service for the support of the glorious cause.[7]

Similar words were recorded in his journal as he left his beloved Mount Vernon to accept the presidency in New York. (Washington was in the habit of keeping personal diaries, 40 of which have survived to the present.) An entry in his diary, dated April 16, 1789, says:

> About ten o'clock I bade adieu to Mount Vernon, to private life, and to domestic felicity; and with a mind oppressed with more anxious and painful sensations than I have words to express, set out for New York ... with the best disposition to render service to my country in obedience to its call, but with less hope of answering its expectations.[8]

Washington not only kept diaries, he was known to keep a regular devotional life as well. His private secretary Robert Lewis of Fredricksburg, Virginia, noted that during his entire service as president, Washington made it his practice to conduct personal devotions both in the morning and evening. His custom when at Mount Vernon was to arise at four o'clock for devotions in his study, eat breakfast, and spend the day touring his various farms. Fittingly, on the altar of the Washington Memorial Chapel at Valley Forge, visitors will find a prayer written by Washington as an enduring testimony to the faith of the first president:

> Almighty God: We make our earnest prayer that Thou wilt keep the United States in Thy holy protection: that Thou wilt incline the heads of the citizens to cultivate a spirit of subordination and obedience to government, and entertain a brother-affection and love for one another and for their fellow citizens of the United States at large.
>
> And finally that Thou wilt most graciously be pleased to dispose us all to do justice, to love mercy, and demean ourselves with that charity, humility, and perfect temper of mind which were the characteristics of the Divine Author of our blessed religion and with a humble imitation of whose example in these things we can ever hope to be a happy nation.
>
> Grant our supplication, we beseech Thee, through Jesus Christ our Lord, Amen.

Whatever happened to prayer by and for the leaders of America?

Our nation's leaders must endeavor to reclaim our spiritual birthright of prayer. As General Washington said in his first inaugural address, "The propitious smiles of heaven can never be expected on a nation that disregards the eternal rules of order and right which heaven itself has ordained."[9]

Prayer on behalf of leadership and by leadership is an expectation of the Lord. In his letter to the young pastor Timothy, Paul wrote, "I urge, then, first of all, that requests, prayers, intercession and thanksgiving be made for everyone—for kings and all those in authority, that we may live peaceful and quiet lives in all godliness and holiness. This is good, and pleases God our Savior, who wants all men to be saved and to come to a knowledge of the truth" (1 Timothy 2:1–4).

To those in leadership positions a similar expectation

exists. "Masters," the apostle wrote, "provide your slaves with what is right and fair, because you know that you also have a Master in heaven. Devote yourselves to prayer, being watchful and thankful. And pray for us, too, that God may open a door for our message, so that we may proclaim the mystery of Christ, for which I am in chains. Pray that I may proclaim it clearly, as I should. Be wise in the way you act toward outsiders; make the most of every opportunity. Let your conversation be always full of grace, seasoned with salt, so that you may know how to answer everyone" (Colossians 4:1–6).

Prayer is not empty talk. It is activity requested by God for the privilege of responding to the needs of His people. We would be foolish to ignore His invitation and face insurmountable odds without divine recourse. "Call upon Me in the day of trouble," He asks. "I will deliver you, and you will honor Me" (Psalm 50:15). Washington saw the Lord's deliverance in Boston, New York, Valley Forge, Trenton, Princeton, Yorktown, and many places in between. It would be impossible for a man of prayer to interpret the outcome of these "days of trouble" as mere coincidence, or good planning on his part. When you have wept before the Lord with only questions and no answers, and by His grace have been rescued, then you know prayer is more than a pious ritual—it is the fuse which God has provided to ignite the powder kegs of heaven.

As evidenced in the achievements of Washington, leaders need not be inhibited by their inability to articulate flowery prayers in public—or in private for that matter. The Lord Himself taught us,

> When you pray, do not be like the hypocrites, for they love to pray standing in the synagogues and on the street corners to be seen by men. I tell you the truth, they have received their reward in full. But when you pray, go into your room, close the door and pray to your Father, who is

unseen. Then your Father, who sees what is done in secret, will reward you. And when you pray, do not keep on babbling like pagans, for they think they will be heard because of their many words. Do not be like them, for your Father knows what you need before you ask Him. (Matthew 6:5–8)

The Lord's words should not be used to forbid public prayer. The Scriptures are filled with references such as Psalm 96. "How can I repay the LORD for all His goodness to me? I will lift up the cup of salvation and call on the name of the LORD. I will fulfill my vows to the LORD in the presence of all His people" (Psalm 116:12–14). He clearly wants us to know, however, that the power of prayer is in the answer of the Lord, not in the beauty of its composition. Powerful prayer flows from a heart of faith which trusts all that God has accomplished on our behalf through the Savior, Jesus Christ. As the Bible shows, "Without faith it is impossible to please God, because anyone who comes to Him must believe that He exists and that He rewards those who earnestly seek Him" (Hebrews 11:6).

A little poem an older pastor shared early in my ministry sums up the Lord's teaching and evidently Washington's appreciation for sincerity in prayer.

1. *'Tis not enough to bend the knee,*
   And words of prayer to say;
   The heart must with the lips agree;
   Or else we do not pray.

2. *For words, without the heart,*
   The Lord will never hear;
   Nor will He to those lips attend,
   Whose prayer is not sincere.

3. *The saints in prayer appear as one,*
In word, and deed, and mind;
While, with the Father and the Son,
Sweet fellowship they find.

More Scriptural Insight

2 Kings 20:1–11   What strikes you most about this account of the king's prayer?
1 Thessalonians 5:12–28   What lessons are taught about leadership and prayer?
Luke 11:1–13   Why was the Lord's Prayer given and what other lessons with it?

A Leader's Prayer

Heavenly Father, I come to You in prayer because You have asked me to and have promised to hear me. I am not especially good at praying, but I know that You show little interest in how a prayer is said. I know You care more about why a prayer is said, and under what conditions. Lord, my status is simple; I pray because I desperately need Your assistance in all I say and do. By the very nature of my station in life I am often in "hot water" way over my head. Without Your intervention, guidance, and provision I would soon make a mess of things. I am concerned not only for my own embarrassment but for the many who might suffer by my mistakes. Keep me close to You and hear my prayers when I offer them through faith in the great intercessor, Jesus Christ. I don't expect You to grant my every request, for then I would be God and You would be my servant. I ask only that the conditions for which I present my prayers be known to You and that You would bring about the outcome to Your glory and the benefit of those I serve; through Jesus Christ, my Lord. Amen.

Notes

1. Nancy Leigh DeMoss, (Editor) *The Rebirth of America,* (The Arthur S. DeMoss Foundation; pub-

lished in the United States, January 1986), 190.

2. Catherine Drinker Bowen, *Miracle at Philadelphia—The Story of the Constitutional Convention May to September 1787;* (Boston: Little, Brown, and Company; 1966), 28.

3. Ibid., 29.

4. Unknown, *George Washington—First President of the United States,* A tract by John Hancock Mutual Insurance Company; Boston, MA, 1956, 7.

5. Paul Lee Tan, *Encyclopedia of 7,700 Illustrations: Signs of the Times,* (Chicago: R. R. Donnelley and Sons, Inc., 1979), 1,037.

6. cf. 2 Corinthians 12:1–12.

7. Unknown, tract.

8. Unknown, *George Washington—First President of the United States,* 13.

9. Nancy Leigh DeMoss, 225.

CHAPTER FIFTY

FREDERICK DOUGLASS
Passion

When a distinguished Russian was informed that some American Negroes were radical and some conservative, he could not restrain his laughter. The idea of conservative Negroes was more than the Cossack's risibilities could endure. "What on earth," he exclaimed with astonishment, "have they to conserve?"[1]

Professor Kelly Miller
Howard University, 1903

Miller's turn of the century essay compared Frederick Douglass to Booker T. Washington. In many ways the two men were in nature and personality comparable, respectively, to Malcom X and Dr. Martin Luther King, Jr. The former being bold and blunt, and the latter more diplomatic and refined. Frederick Douglass would, according to Professor Miller's anecdote, be described as a radical.

My encyclopedia describes Douglass as "an American lecturer and journalist,"[2] and then politely relates the details of his life. It would be akin to describing General George Patton as "a high-ranking military officer who served overseas during World War II." Although technically true, the words don't begin to describe the spirit of the man, and Frederick Douglass was definitely a spirited man.

An escaped slave turned abolitionist, Douglass was a man of abiding passion whose words had the sound of thunder in them. Shortly after his flight north, Douglass was invited to speak at an anti-slavery meeting on the island of Nantucket. Neither Douglass nor the mostly Quaker audience was prepared for the moment. Years of personal suffering found expression in a passionate recalling of the abuse and heartache of slavery. An eyewitness account described the moment.

> His first phrases were the apologies of the novice, but then all that he had taught himself with *The Columbian Orator*;³ all that he had within him from the start poured forth. The Quaker quiet of the room was cut through with an electricity of excitement that everyone from twelve-year-old Phoebe Ann Coffin to her most somber, senior relative would never forget. With intense concentration, these New Englanders heard Frederick telling them about his life. It was the story of a runaway slave, yes, but it was his story. He was telling it, he was calling himself into being, and people—people he had never seen before, white people, important people—were listening. ... Frederick Douglass knew triumph so intense, so total, that he would spend his entire life seeking to sustain it. He had spoken, he had been heard.⁴

It was his first speech, but it would not be his last. He was hired to speak for the Abolitionists' cause and began touring the northern states fanning the anti-slavery fires. In response to overwhelming support, Douglass wrote the story of his life which was published in 1845. It was so widely read that it had the unfortunate consequence of making the runaway slave famous. He could no longer hide from the slave-catchers and was forced to flee to England until friends purchased his freedom two years later. Thus liberated, his passion for the freedom of his race only intensified. As the testimony of others verifies, Douglass was not afraid to speak forcefully and bluntly.

- "We do not overrate the African. He is a swarthy Ajax, and with ponderous mace, he springs into the midst of his white oppressors and crushes them at every blow. With an air of scorn he hurls his bolts on every hand. He feels his wrongs, and his heart is in every blow."

  —The Liberator (Boston) April 20, 1849

- "The cause of the oppressed could not have found a more eloquent defender than Mr. Douglass. Himself oppressed and denied the rights and privileges of a freeman, he felt what he said and said what he felt. The Negro's cause was his cause, and his cause was the Negro's cause. In defending his people he was defending himself. It was here that the brilliancy of his oratorical powers was most manifest."

  —William Scarborough, 1893

- "To Democracy in America, Douglass was a whip and a spur."

  —The Washington Post, August 27, 1887

And if these are not enough, the recorded speeches and essays of Frederick leave little doubt to his character or tone. He admired President Lincoln and met with him on several occasions. He later said of the president, "I was impressed with his entire freedom from popular prejudice against the colored race. He was the first great man that I talked with in the United States freely, who in no single instance reminded me of the difference between himself and myself, of the difference of color, and I thought that more remarkable because he came from a state where there were black laws."[5]

But even such treatment by Lincoln did not keep Douglass

from blunt honesty at the dedication of a statue in honor of the fallen president on April 14, 1876. It was the 11th anniversary of the assassination and those present at the dedication included President Grant, his cabinet, the Supreme Court justices, and no few congressmen and senators. The statue had been commissioned solely through contributions of Negroes and it depicted the president breaking the shackles of a slave. Among other things, Douglass said,

> Abraham Lincoln was not, in the fullest sense of the word, either our man or our model. In his associations, in his habits of thought, and in his prejudices, he was a white man. ... The race to which we belong were not the special objects of his consideration. ... His great mission was to accomplish two things: first, to save his country from dismemberment and ruin, and, second, to free his country from the great crime of slavery. ... Had he put the abolition of slavery before the salvation of the Union, he would have inevitably driven from him a powerful class of the American people and rendered resistance to rebellion impossible. ... No man who knew Lincoln could hate him—but because of his fidelity to union and liberty, he is doubly dear to us, and his memory will be precious forever.[6]

Douglass was not afraid to tell it like he saw it. Not only did he press for freedom, once freedom was granted, he boldly attacked racist attitudes that continued the oppression. In a speech he made at the age of 77, it is obvious that neither time nor opposition had quenched his spirit or his fire. Concerning the plight of the Negro after emancipation, Douglass lamented, "The difference between his past condition and his present condition is that in the past the old master class could say to him, 'You shall work for me or I will whip you to death'; in the present condition he can say to him, 'You shall work for me or I will starve you to death.' "[7]

Despite popular portrayals of limp-wristed, wishy-washy,

mealy-mouthed Christian leaders on the evening sitcoms, the biblical model of zeal is well established. In the Old Testament, when Balaam was unable to curse the children of Israel against the will of God, he advised the king of Moab to compromise the young men through sexual temptation leading to idolatry. His plot worked all too well and the young men of Israel were enticed by the foreign women and began to worship their gods. When Aaron's grandson Phinehas witnessed this evil with his own eyes, he took a spear in his hand, entered the tent of the offenders, and, consumed by zeal for the Lord and His clear command, thrust it through them both, thus stopping the plague of God.

The apostle Paul was zealous even before his conversion. In his letter to the church at Philippi, he reminded them of his life before coming to the knowledge of salvation.

> If anyone else thinks he has reasons to put confidence in the flesh, I have more: circumcised on the eighth day, of the people of Israel, of the tribe of Benjamin, a Hebrew of Hebrews; in regard to the law, a Pharisee; as for zeal, persecuting the church; as for legalistic righteousness, faultless. But whatever was to my profit I now consider loss for the sake of Christ. (Philippians 3:4–7)

Paul came to realize that his zeal was insufficient. His words might have been the inspiration for the old gospel hymn "Rock of Ages." The second stanza draws heavily on Paul's discovery.

> *Not the labors of my hands, Can fulfill Thy laws*
>   *demands;*
> *Could my zeal no respite know, Could my tears forever*
>   *flow,*
> *All for sin could not atone; Thou must save, and Thou*
>   *alone.*

Before his conversion, Paul tried in vain to earn his acceptance before God. Like catching the evening breeze in nets, it was an impossible quest. Now, having received the gift of salvation by grace through faith in Jesus, Paul's zealous character is transformed into something satisfying and useful. In response to God's love and assured of God's blessing he pursues his mission with abandon.

> Though I am free and belong to no man, I make myself a slave to everyone, to win as many as possible. To the Jews I became like a Jew, to win the Jews. To those under the law I became like one under the law (though I myself am not under the law), so as to win those under the law. To those not having the law I became like one not having the law (though I am not free from God's law but am under Christ's law), so as to win those not having the law. To the weak I became weak, to win the weak. I have become all things to all men so that by all possible means I might save some. (1 Corinthians 9:19–22)

So clear was God's claim on his life that Paul concluded, "Your body is a temple of the Holy Spirit, who is in you, whom you have received from God. You are not your own; you were bought at a price. Therefore honor God with your body" (1 Corinthians 6:19–20).

Zeal, submitted to the authority of the Lord, and lived in the absolute assurance of salvation which was achieved by Christ on our behalf, honors the Lord and can accomplish great things. A poetic epitaph for Frederick Douglass contemplates the tremendous power of managed zeal.

And he was no soft-tongued apologist;
*   He spoke straight-forward, fearlessly uncowed;*
The sunlight of his truth dispelled the mist,
*   And set in bold relief each dark-hued cloud;*
To sin and crime he gave their proper hue,
And hurled at evil what was evil's due!

Oh, Douglass, thou hast passed beyond the shore,
But still thy voice is ringing o'er the gale!
Thou'st taught thy race how high her hopes may soar,
And bade her seek the heights, nor faint, nor fail.
She will not fail, she heeds thy stirring cry,
She knows thy guardian spirit will be nigh,
And rising from beneath the chastening rod,
She stretches out her bleeding hands to God! [8]

More Scriptural Insight

1 Kings 19:9–18	What good was the zeal of Elijah?
2 Timothy 4:1–5	Describe the spirit of ministry expected by God.
John 2:13–17	What was the motive behind the actions of Jesus?

A Leader's Prayer

Almighty and most holy God, You alone are God and there is no other. Although my life is offered in such high service, I sometimes feel my work is insignificant and unimportant. Help me maintain a sense of the eternal, and an appreciation for the great value of work in Your Kingdom. Rekindle my zeal and instill in me a boldness that reflects the value of eternal things. Frederick Douglass recalled his memory of slavery and used it to motivate others to help rescue the oppressed. Lord, help me to fathom the depth of my loss without You. Let me never take for granted the value of my redemption and the restoration of our relationship accomplished by Jesus on the cross. As I recall the bondage of my sin, enable me to communicate the urgency of our work to those called to help. Grant that zeal for the lost might burn bright in Christian hearts before it is too late and even one more soul is beyond our reach, lost in the grasp of Satan. Oh, Lord, hear my prayer, through Jesus Christ, my mediator and intercessor. Amen.

Notes

1. Kelly Miller, Boston Transcript, The Colored American Magazine, Boston, MA, November 1903, 824–26. From the book *Frederick Douglass*, Edited by Benjamin Quarles, (Englewood Cliffs, NJ: Prentice Hall Inc., 1968), 133.

2. Encyclopedia Americana; *"Frederick Douglass,"* (New York: Americana Corporation, 1964), vol 9, 281.

3. *The Columbian Orator* was a book of stories, poems, and speeches that Douglass had bought for 50 cents when he was only 12 years old. He bribed and tricked white children his age to teach him how to read.

4. William S. McFeely, *Frederick Douglass,* (New York: Simon and Schuster, 1991), 88–89. Used by permission.

5. Russell Freedman, *Lincoln, a Photobiography,* (New York: Scholastic Inc., 1987), 104.

6. Frederick Douglass, Speech at Lincoln Park, Washington D.C., on the unveiling of the Freedman's Monument, April 14, 1876. From a collection of essays and speeches edited by Benjamin Quarles, Prentice Hall, Inc., Englewood Cliffs, NJ, 1968, 72–79.

7. Frederick Douglass, From a speech delivered to the American Missionary Association in Lowell, Massachusetts, late in 1894. From a collection of essays and speeches edited by Benjamin Quarles, Prentice Hall, Inc., Englewood Cliffs, NJ, 1968, 93.

8. Paul Dunbar, *Frederick Douglass—in Lyrics of Lowly Life,* (New York: Dodd and Mead Co., 1897). From a collection of essays and speeches edited by Benjamin Quarles, Prentice Hall, Inc., Englewood Cliffs, NJ, 1968, 130–31.